More OLD FRIENDS

More OLD FRIENDS

BARBARA D. LIVINGSTON

LEXINGTON, KENTUCKY

ECLIPSE PRESS

Library of Congress Control Number: 2007928391

ISBN 978-1-58150-171-1

Printed in China
First Edition: 2007

a division of
Blood-Horse Publications
PUBLISHERS SINCE 1916

Contents

Introduction

When *Old Friends* was published in 2002, its warm reception overwhelmed me. I received countless e-mails and hand-written letters, many of which included recollections — and even photos — of some of the ninety old friends.

One man sent a beautiful race photo of Horatius, and another sent a gorgeous black-and-white win photo of Freetex. A German gentleman, who once tended to Allegretta, sent priceless photos of a youthful Allegretta as well as members of her family.

It was tremendously heartwarming to realize that others felt as I did about these aged horses.

Yet, when asked why I feel that way, a concrete reason eludes me just as it did five years ago. Certainly, nostalgia plays a part. Memories of Sugar and Spice, at age three at Saratoga, evolved into a longtime love affair.

For others, however — horses I've never met, or even heard of, before photographing them — explaining why I love them is impossible.

But clearly, they're special — to me and to all those who lovingly tend to their own older Thoroughbreds. Three examples are forever etched in my mind.

On April 18, 2006, I received this e-mail in response to a *Blood-Horse* pictorial:

> We wanted to tell you how much we enjoyed the article, OLD FRIENDS, in … The Blood-Horse. Our farm has an old friend, too. Her name is KNIGHTLY SPRITELY, and she is 31 … Although she never won a race, she produced multiple stakes winners and has twice been voted broodmare of the year in Louisiana. Her daughters are now part of our broodmare band, and her son is one of the stallions that we stand at our farm. We are now training and racing her grandsons and granddaughters.
>
> KNIGHTLY SPRITELY was foaled in Canada, so she enjoys daily showers that we provide for her, on our hot Louisiana days. We cut out your photographs in OLD FRIENDS, and put them on KNIGHTLY's stall walls, so she could have friends her own age!
>
> Without KNIGHTLY SPRITELY, our farm of twenty-five years would have little claim to fame. She is our foundation broodmare. Thank you for recognizing the greatness of our OLD FRIENDS.
>
> Sincerely, DOUBLE DAM FARM, LLC Jo Ann Thompson & Dr. Delmar Caldwell

Knightly Spritely with foal

I set my mind on visiting Knightly Spritely, but a short time later another e-mail arrived. Knightly Spritely died June 20 and was buried on Double Dam Farm.

I was able to photograph King's Swan one last time at his farm some two hours from my home in upstate New York. He was one of my favorite *Old Friends'* subjects. King and Jean Lazio were a team both at the track and in retirement. She could not help but smile around him, and his eyes glowed with kingly contentment.

Yet King's ulna bone — and Jean's life — were

shattered November 30, 2005, when King was kicked by another horse. Jean considered euthanasia, but, she said, "He got that 'I'm gonna fight' look in his eyes.' " A veterinarian said that, over time, his bones might knit. An equine sling was located, and nine friends unraveled it. They attached it to a large beam, and wrapped it around King's body. He willingly accepted the constraints.

Jean visited him daily, exercising his muscles by having him reach around for treats, and she modified the sling when he was uncomfortable. At night, a baby monitor transmitted sounds — muffled noises of shifting leather, metal chains, shuffling straw — to the farm owner's house.

In February 2006, King was removed from his sling while the support chain was adjusted. Despite Jean's attempts to keep him standing, King lay down and aggravated his injury. Jean shipped him to the Mid-Atlantic Equine Center, where she learned how much King would suffer if they operated on him.

The fact that Jean's efforts were unsuccessful — King's Swan was euthanized February 7 as Jean stood by him — made her attempt no less heroic. This was not a stallion or racehorse worth millions, but Jean could do no less.

Nearly a year after his passing, she wrote: "I feel like a part of my identity died with him."

And then there was Cormorant. I knew that each time I visited him at Jerry Bilinski's Waldorf Farm, about an hour from my house, might be the last. After all, Cormorant was even older — by a year — than

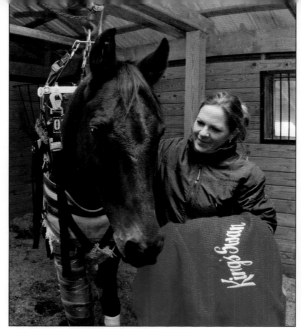

King's Swan and Jean Lazio

John Henry. While John Henry's birthdays are well-attended celebrations, Cormorant's passed quietly. Through it all, Jerry tended to his high-spirited, smoldering friend.

I last saw Cormorant, then thirty-three, in February 2007. Jerry brought him out for photos, as he kindly did each time I could make up a reason to visit. While Cormorant was rickety, his eyes still burned. Jerry stroked the bay's face, and his head dipped in what seemed an uncharacteristically affectionate gesture.

"He wouldn't have let me do this ten years ago," Jerry said, laughing. With that, Cormorant snapped to and tried to bite Jerry. Good boy, Cormorant.

He died three months later, on May 4, and was buried on Jerry's farm.

Several horses in this book died before it went to press — so many that when I asked trainer Tom Voss if Mickey Free could be included, he quipped, "Doesn't he have to be dead first?"

It seemed unfair not to include them as, after all, each still had a life's story. I wanted to include many others, too, but there simply weren't enough pages. To them, and their caregivers, I offer my apologies.

Again, why did Cormorant touch me so? What about him — and others — so stirs the heart?

I still can't put it into words, but it's a feeling shared by countless people, for countless horses, around the world. And so, here's to Knightly Spritely, King's Swan, Cormorant and all those others out there — both the famous and the unknown.

Here's to old friends.

Cormorant and Jerry Bilinski

Alidiva (IRE)

1987 DK. B/BR. M. BY CHIEF SINGER — ALLIGATRIX, BY ALLEGED

Although Taylor Made Farm is home to many outstanding broodmares — grade I winners or producers grace seemingly every paddock and barn — one truly stands alone: Alidiva.

When I visited the bay beauty in July 2005, it was immediately clear that her broodmare record wasn't the only extraordinary thing about her. She was absolutely gorgeous.

She was muscle on muscle, with a stallion-like crest. Her coat, heavily dappled, reflected the countless brown tones of an artist's palette, and her black points glowed. Her tail, sporting a straight European cut, nearly swept the ground. Her eyes seemed small on her thick face, but they possessed a dreamy, faraway look. Her large ears swiveled toward every sound.

She was relaxed and comfortable as I entered her paddock, but one of her mates, a younger filly, was not. She was quite excited about a visitor and seemed to say: "Hey! A playmate!" I got the feeling that Alidiva might be a little boring for her.

The youngster happily charged me, time and again, her head and tail on high. Each time she got too close, I scurried onto the fence in a less than professional manner. I'd chuckle. She'd chuckle.

She eventually wandered away on other flights of fancy, and I traipsed back into the field toward Alidiva, who watched the goings-on with a worldly countenance.

Bred in Ireland by W. Lazy T and C.H. Wacker III, Alidiva is a thick, handsome, and willing mare, described in *Timeform* as "close-coupled" when racing. She competed five times and won three races, including the Oak Tree Stakes at Goodwood in England. She won from six furlongs to a mile, and even as a broodmare, her stout physique fits that profile.

The blood coursing through Alidiva is indeed rich. Her sire, Chief Singer, was a group I winner and a second-highweight in England. From a limited number of foals — 308 over fourteen years — he sired thirteen stakes winners and three champions.

Alidiva's dam, Alligatrix, bred by Wacker in partnership with Shirley Taylor, produced two stakes winners in addition to Alidiva. Alligatrix's best racehorse, Croco Rouge, won two group Is and became a sire. Alligatrix's second dam, Shore, was a stakes-winning Round Table mare.

Even with that stellar breeding, no one could have expected Alidiva to produce a legacy of immortality in the span of three years.

Alidiva's first foal, Taipan, by Last Tycoon, was born in 1992, and he won nine races, including four group Is. He was named Italy's champion older horse in 1997 and earned a champion's crown in both Italy and Germany the next year. After graduating from a five-year racing career — in England, France, Germany, Ireland, Italy, and Hong Kong — he became a sire.

Alidiva's second foal was Ali-Royal, by Royal Academy. He won seven races, including the group I Sussex Stakes at Goodwood. At age four, he was England's champion older horse at seven to 9½ furlongs. He also became a stallion.

Next came Sleepytime, a handsome Royal Academy filly born in 1994 who was the highweighted three-year-old filly on the European Free Handicap for seven to nine furlongs.

Although the youngest of the trio, Sleepytime had the first group I win for Alidiva, the 1997 One Thousand Guineas. Soon after, Ali-Royal took the group I Sussex Stakes. Both raced for Charles Wacker's Greenbay Stables.

"It's incredible to produce two group I winners in a season, and it could be three," Wacker's racing manager, Tote Cherry-Downes, told *The Blood-Horse* after the Sussex. "I believe Taipan … is going to run next in a group I in Baden-Baden."

When Taipan then won Germany's group I Kurierpost-Europa-Preis, Alidiva had pulled off the ultimate hat trick: three group I winners in one season. It earned her 1997 Broodmare of the Year in both Italy and Ireland.

Seven years later, *The Blood-Horse* noted that only thirty-eight mares in history — in America and Europe combined — had produced foals that won two grade/group Is in the same year. Only Alidvia had produced three, and she remains the only mare to do so.

She has produced one other stakes winner so far. Oonagh MacCool, a Giant's Causeway filly born in 2002, captured two grade IIs. Another Alidiva daughter, Sometime, did not race but has produced two stakes winners. And Sleepytime, Alidiva's first group I winner, has produced a stakes winner as well.

In December 2004, Alidiva arrived from foreign shores to take up residence at beautiful Taylor Made near Nicholasville, Kentucky. Three of her daughters — Dear Girl, Oonagh MacCool, and Sleepytime — reside there as well, producing foals and carrying on the family line.

Alidiva, now twenty, foaled a chestnut Giant's Causeway filly — a full sister to Oonagh MacCool — on February 27, 2007. She is now in foal to Distorted Humor. Also, Sleepytime foaled a dark bay or brown Gone West filly on April 11, 2007.

Banquet Scene

1981 B. M. BY LYPHARD—SWEET MARJORIE (FR), BY SIR GAYLORD

In December 2005, an Internet plea came from Jana of the Czech Republic. Her posts, appearing on several racing-related forums, sought an elderly American mare.

Searching one mare … Banquet Scene

We are looking for any informations and pictures of her. She produced ten foals so far, and three of them were racing in Czech Republic …

1999 Quest for Fame filly named Pomada, gorgeous dark bay who was placed in classic; 2001 Southern Halo filly Banka, classy sprinter and very powerful horse; and finally 2000 Lear Fan filly Barborka. Expected to run the lowest category races, she managed to get to very solid level and reached 70 kg in classification, which was highly above the limit she had to have.

And especially because of the last filly we are searching Banquet Scene. Barborka was leased to Racing Club Finis, a group of people who owns only one horse. Naturally Barborka is their darling and "leader" of that group, Martin, asked me to help with searching of Banquet Scene …

I wrote a friend. Who bred Banquet Scene's most recent foal? His reply: "The most recent foal is an '04 filly by Bianconi, bred by Sive Doyle in Kentucky. The filly is already named, Mo Chroi."

I called Sive. Her voice was unusually youthful with a blithesome Irish accent. She was tickled that someone was inquiring about her old mare, whom she called Granny.

She snapped several photos of Banquet Scene and e-mailed them to the Czech racing club members. They were as overjoyed as if they had just located their own long-lost grandmother.

At that time Racing Club Finis consisted of nine members, most between ages twenty-two and thirty-two. They leased one horse at a time for racing

purposes, and Banquet Scene's daughter Barborka was only their second horse — and, therefore, their star.

Barborka's breeder, Václav Kozel, had hoped she would shine for him. The filly's older half sister, Pomada, had been highly successful, running second in the Czech One Thousand Guineas and eighth in the Czech Derby. Yet Barborka did not run well at two or three, and Kozel leased her to the racing club.

She rewarded its youthful members by winning two races. They cheered her every move and visited each weekend to take her picture and feed her apples. You'd have thought she was the greatest horse ever to set foot in the Czech Republic. Their enthusiasm was infectious, and Barborka was voted the "Most Popular Racehorse in Prague for 2005," according to the club's leader, Martin Cáp.

A journalist and photographer, Cáp said: "Our story shows how international horse racing is. An American filly by Lear Fan out of Banquet Scene got to the far Czech Republic. Barborka means 'Little Barbara' in Czech, and she was my darling horse for two years. Now she has returned to her first owner's stud, and we dream that her foals will be as good as she was."

Meanwhile, back in the United States, Barborka's dam, Banquet Scene, had settled into a quiet retirement.

Buckland Farm had bought her as a yearling in 1982 for $375,000. The lovely, dished-faced bay filly finished second in the grade III Miss Grillo Stakes, but her claim to fame came October 5, 1983, when she carried Jorge Velasquez to his five thousandth victory.

Banquet Scene remained with Buckland until its 1997 dispersal at the Keeneland November breeding stock sale. While she had produced a minor stakes winner, Charming Scene, she had not produced a standout foal. Kozel,

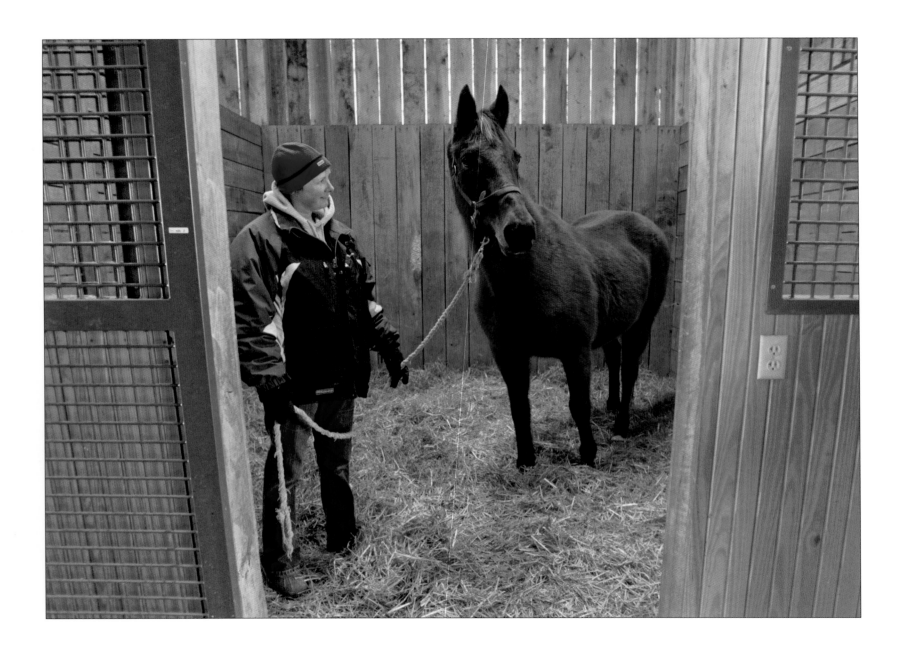

the Czech breeder, bought Banquet Scene, then sixteen, for $20,000 from the dispersal and boarded her in Kentucky. She produced three foals for him, including Barborka. Banquet Scene's third foal for Kozel was Banka in 2001. The mare came up barren when she was rebred that season.

What happened next is unclear, but, that autumn, Sive Doyle was working for Kentucky farm owner Walter B. Mills when a vet told her about an older mare who needed a home. It was Banquet Scene, and in October 2001 she entered Mills' broodmare band.

She provided Mills one foal, a 2003 Storm Creek colt — a winner — named Prince's Pleasure. Mills then dispersed his stock for health and financial reasons, and Sive took ownership of Banquet Scene. In 2004 Banquet Scene produced the Bianconi filly. Sive named her Mo Chroi, which is Irish for "My Love" or "My Heart."

"She was my first ever Thoroughbred foal," Sive said. "I didn't make any money on her, but the simple pleasure of raising her was worth more than a million dollars to me."

A native of Dublin, Sive came to America twelve years ago. She worked at the Kentucky Horse Park for 2½ years before returning home. Yet the lure of horses — and America — was strong.

Seven months later Sive came back to attend her brother's wedding. Somehow, she kept finding reasons to stay.

"You start accumulating things," she said. "Oh, I've got a dog, you say. I could never go home without my dog. I could never put my dog in quarantine. I guess I'm here till she dies. And then I got another dog. And then I got a pig, and … well, five or six horses now."

At thirty-five, only nine years older than Banquet Scene, Sive is a true horsewoman with rosy cheeks, joyful eyes, and an exuberant nature. She works for Neal Clarke, who owns Atlas Farm near Nicholasville, Kentucky. That's where Banquet Scene resides, gallivanting

with an ancient Belgian/Tennessee Walker cross named Bubba and a pensioned Thoroughbred mare named Little Fuzzy.

The farm provides the pensioners the same care it gives its active producers, and it shows. Banquet Scene looks grand. Her eyes are bright, and her movement is fluid. She appears much younger than her twenty-six years.

Of her occasionally grumpy Granny, Sive said: "She's good. She just doesn't want to be messed around with. She doesn't like to be caught if she thinks there's something bad coming. You can catch her fine if she hasn't eaten. But if she has eaten? Wait until tomorrow."

She laughed. Then she added, "She's had about thirteen foals, so she's done her part. You take responsibility for them. I'm going to have her until she dies."

Banquet Scene, right, with Little Fuzzy; opposite, Sive Doyle with Banquet Scene

Battle Creek Girl

1977–2004 B. M. BY HIS MAJESTY—FAR BEYOND, BY NIJINSKY II

Battle Creek Girl posed with grace that warm autumn afternoon at Lane's End Farm. Her coat was a deep reddish bay, her mane was trimmed, and her eyes were wistful. A slim blaze extended from high on her forehead, widening near her nostrils. Her finely tapered face was unusually feminine and refined.

Her two hind socks were mottled with black coronet markings, and a few small white spots flecked her hindquarters, as if she'd wandered too near a house painter. Her face and body belied her quarter-century existence.

In the manner of a cherished matriarch, she was a model of contentment and class. She was a model of much more, too — consistency and quality.

Since 1930, only two American Thoroughbred mares have produced more foals than Battle Creek Girl. She stands in a thirteen-way tie for third place with twenty. And of those mares, Battle Creek Girl has the most winners (fifteen) and her offspring the most earnings ($4,255,073). Of her fifteen winners, an incredible six were stakes winners. That number, too, ranks her among the best.

She has a lovely pedigree, being a half sister to Darby Dan Farm's wonderful Wings of Grace, who is the dam of Soaring Softly and Plenty of Grace. David Greathouse and John Greathouse Jr., of Glencrest Farm, bought then three-year-old Battle Creek Girl for $60,000 while she was racing. They sent her to their house stallion, Full Out.

As David told *The Blood-Horse*: "When we bought her, we really didn't know if we were buying her to breed or race. When she was in heat, we decided to breed her, and she caught on one cover."

Battle Creek Girl raced in foal for the Greathouses on both turf and dirt, before entering Glencrest's broodmare band. Overall, she won three of twenty races and earned $40,240.

Battle Creek Girl delivered her first foal at age four, and the filly, Full Retreat, became a winner. Yet it was her sixth foal, Tricky Creek, by the Glencrest stallion Clever Trick, who earned her rave reviews. He annexed four graded stakes and won $873,288.

The next year's model, Wavering Girl, by Glencrest's Wavering Monarch, became Canada's 1989 champion two-year-old filly. She won four stakes and earned $314,084.

By the time Speed Dialer took her first breath in 1989, Battle Creek Girl was a proven commodity. Will Farish, owner of Lane's End Farm, bought Speed Dialer as a yearling, and she won a grade II stakes and two other stakes and earned $384,656. In 1991 Farish bought Battle Creek Girl as well.

For Farish and his partner, E.J. Hudson, Battle Creek Girl's dance card included the top stallions Danzig, Kingmambo, and A.P. Indy. She produced three more stakes winners at Lane's End: Everhope, who won the Edgewood Stakes; Parade Ground, a four-time graded stakes winner who earned $794,995; and Parade Leader, a grade II winner who made $712,507. Parade Ground entered stud at Lane's End, and Parade Leader was sold to South Africa for stud duties.

Battle Creek Girl's final foal — number twenty — was a 2003 Dixie Union filly named Union Creek.

On August 25, 2004, Battle Creek Girl died of old age and was buried at Lane's End. She was twenty-seven.

Among the stakes winners her daughters have produced so far are the grade I winner Military (out of Wavering Girl) and the grade III winner Star of Valor (out of Matriarch). All told, six of her daughters have thus far produced stakes winners, yet none have approached their mama's produce record.

There's no shame in that. Few mares in history have.

Bedouin

1981–2006 RO. G. BY AL HATTAB — LADY IN RED, BY PRINCE JOHN

Caterman (NZ)

1976–2004 B. G. BY ADIOS (GB) — PROUD ANN (NZ), BY PROUD LOOK (IRE)

When John Henry retired in the mid-1980s, Grace Belcuore wondered what happened to all the other, less-famous geldings. Certainly, John Henry's future was secure. But to ensure that other retiring geldings also had homes, Belcuore, a former teacher, founded the California Equine Retirement Foundation in 1986.

Her first arrivals were geldings, sent by owners and trainers who often paid for their keep. Belcuore and her staff solicited donations to help with the others. As CERF evolved, it began retraining and placing horses, including performance horses, and offering an educational program for potential industry employees. In two decades CERF has cared for and placed hundreds of horses.

Many remain at the Winchester, California, ranch. (Current residents are featured on CERF's Web site, www.cerfhorses.org.) Of the seventy-odd horses there when I visited in 2004, I focused on two special geldings: Caterman and Bedouin.

Caterman, a New Zealand-bred who won four stakes and earned $673,735, was a familiar name to me. Bedouin, a beautiful Al Hattab gelding, was not. Yet he was intriguing because he not only had run in the 1984 Kentucky Derby but also was CERF's official mascot.

The ranch was unusually vast and remote. I'd never seen a place like it — with roomy pens for so many horses and a story behind each inhabitant. They usually grazed in a large paddock, Belcuore said, but this day they were confined because of recent rains.

Belcuore took me from horse to horse, and the pensioners — the eldest was thirty-one-year-old Bigtime Baby — often strolled up to greet us. There were bays, chestnuts, grays, dark bays; geldings, mares, and a pony. Many enclosures had plaques identifying the horses and their sponsors.

Caterman, then twenty-eight, was a bay gelding with an unremarkable look and a kind disposition. He had been boarded at Jenny Craig's ranch, but when his owner, Tom Cavanagh, passed away, the ranch asked whether Belcuore would take the old stakes winner. She obliged, and Caterman arrived at CERF in 2002, sponsored by the Cavanagh estate. At the time, Caterman had the highest earnings of any CERF horse.

"He can be a little feisty for his old age," Belcuore said. "He demands respect. Horses respect him in the field — they know he's somebody."

Caterman was clearly infirm, with one front leg unable to straighten due to an old knee injury. Yet he had no trouble rolling and jogging, and he seemed in good spirits. Belcuore said that on occasion he still galloped.

Caterman

His defining moment, however, came in defeat. He finished first in the 1981 Hollywood Gold Cup but was disqualified to second. However, he beat John Henry, who finished fourth.

Eight months after my visit, in September 2004, Caterman passed away. In CERF tradition, his body was cremated, and he was buried on the ranch. A rose bush and marker adorn his grave. His marker reads, in part:

Caterman — A True Thoroughbred With A Heart Bigger Than Life That Outran The Legendary John Henry.

His best buddy was Plenty Zloty, a fourteen-year-old gelding. Caterman had picked his friends well. Plenty Zloty set a world record for 5½ furlongs (1:01.10) in 1995 at Turf Paradise.

"You can't separate them, but he's the boss of the two," Belcuore said of Caterman. "With him and Zloty, one comes to drink water, and the other comes along."

After starting his career in New Zealand, Caterman came to race in the United States. Based in California, he won the grade III Golden Gate Handicap and the San Jacinto, Citation, and Cabrillo handicaps. He earned $673,735.

Bedouin

Unlike the plain Caterman, Bedouin, then twenty-three, was a flashy, near-white beauty. He competed primarily in claiming races, but he ran in the 1984 Kentucky Derby, finishing fifteenth. Two years later he won the ninth race of a Pick Nine at Santa Anita that paid a record $1.9 million. And on Bedouin's sixth birthday, March 14, 1987, he carried Laffit Pincay Jr. to the jockey's record seventh victory of the day at Santa Anita.

Bedouin won or placed in twenty-four of sixty-seven races and earned $311,394 before an injury ended his career. According to the CERF Web site, a veterinarian, Greg Ferraro, agreed to operate on Bedouin for free on the condition that he then be retired to CERF. The popular gray gelding was cheered into retirement at Santa Anita on Fan Appreciation Day in 1988. Track announcer Trevor Denman called him "the epitome of the bread-and-butter racehorse."

Caterman

Bedouin

"He's absolutely gorgeous," Belcuore said in 2004. "They say that when he was a two-year-old they brought him into Santa Anita in a van, and when he got off everybody stopped to look he was so magnificent."

Bedouin assumed the important role of CERF mascot. He traveled to fund-raising events at various tracks. He usually tolerated visitors, including children, with grace. But when socializing became tiresome, Bedouin simply moved to the middle of his corral — out of reach.

In April 2006, at age twenty-five, Bedouin died — after eighteen years at CERF. He, too, was cremated and buried at the ranch. Belcuore posted an emotional farewell on CERF's Web site. It read, in part:

No words aloud or written can express the love, the trust and the friendship that I was blessed to have with Bedouin ... He was his own horse, if I may say that. He kept a distance from his fellow equines and those humans with whom he came in contact. He was most selective and trusted only a few ...

He really just tolerated all others, yet that intolerance and distance became a magnet that drew everyone to him. There was no mistake that he rose above his fellow equines in courage, majestic beauty and intelligence ... He was one of a kind.

Broadway Joan

1979–2006 CH. M. BY BOLD ARIAN — COURTNEYS DOLL, BY WAKEFIELD TOWER

She was obscurely bred, by Bold Arian and out of a Wakefield Tower mare. Richard Bomze, Philip DiLeo, and Michael Spielman purchased her as a two-year-old for $2,500. Bomze said that when trainer John Hertler realized she wouldn't make it as a racehorse, he recommended they not even try. Yet when the handsome chestnut lady was paired with an unknown stallion — a near-rogue named Compliance — Broadway Joan was world class.

Compliance?

"It was strictly a matter of we had the stallion," Bomze said. "We weren't that involved in racing at the time."

Bomze and Spielman owned Compliance. Despite the stallion's impeccable breeding — he was a full brother to Try My Best and El Gran Senor — he was unaccomplished and aggressive. Windfields Farm had been happy to sell him, Bomze recalled.

While breeders spend years plotting matings, the Broadway Joan–Compliance match proved that legendary horses can come from the unlikeliest of pairings.

Their first foal was a winner, and their second was Fourstardave. Foaled in 1985, the New York-bred won twenty-one of one hundred starts, including thirteen stakes, and earned $1,636,737. His crowning achievement was winning a race at Saratoga for eight straight seasons, with five of those years including at least one stakes victory. Unprecedented, that feat earned him the nickname "Sultan of Saratoga."

Broadway Joan and Compliance produced Diane Suzanne next, and the lovely distaffer earned more than $130,000. Next from the pair came Fourstars Allstar, the first American-based horse to win a European classic. He captured the group I Irish Two Thousand Guineas, won eight additional stakes, competed for six seasons, and earned $1,596,760.

Two foals later Broadway Joan and Compliance produced Fourstar Brother, who won three races and earned $120,039. Bomze remembers a season at Saratoga when Fourstardave, Fourstars Allstar, and Fourstar Brother shared trainer Leo O'Brien's barn.

After all this success with an obscure stallion, imagine what Broadway Joan could do with the best. Bomze did.

"The biggest mistake I made with her was that when I saw how well she did with Compliance, a Northern Dancer, I said to myself, 'Who's the best Northern Dancer in the world?' Well, Sadler's Wells," Bomze said. "So, wise guy that I am, I called Coolmore Stud and said I want to send this mare over to Ireland. If I got such good stuff out of Compliance, why wouldn't I do better with Sadler's Wells?"

Broadway Joan and Sadler's Wells met six times. Two of their foals never raced, one never won, and the best, by far, earned $72,392. One, however, named Pittsburgh Phil, was a minor stakes winner over hurdles.

At age nineteen, Broadway Joan was shipped back stateside to Kentucky. By then DiLeo had become partners with investment banker William J. Punk Jr. on several horses, including grade I winner Ordway. When DiLeo and Punk decided to breed Broadway Joan to Ordway, Bomze bowed out.

Broadway Joan's 2000 Ordway filly, Broadway Lady, was stakes placed and earned $110,300. The mare's final foal, Broadway Chief, also by Ordway, was unplaced in five starts.

Broadway Joan ended up at Suzi Shoemaker's beautiful Lantern Hill Farm near Midway, Kentucky. The aging mare was bred to Grand Slam, Hennessy, and Thunder Gulch but didn't take. DiLeo and Punk pensioned the chestnut lady.

"We kept her as long as we could, and we took good care of her," Punk said.

"It's expensive, but a horse like that, you owe it to her."

Broadway Joan became best friends with Priceless Countess, Ordway's dam.

"They were out in a small paddock together, and they were roughly the same age," said Rachel Holden, Lantern Hill's farm manager. "They were like Velcro twins."

The day I visited Lantern Hill was a cold one, and the bitter wind bothered us humans more than it did the woolly mares. The farm is a gem, and Shoemaker and Holden are natural horsewomen. I immediately felt at home.

I had long wanted to meet Broadway Joan, as her story is legend in New York. She was honored as the state's best broodmare an amazing three times, and her courtship with the smoldering Compliance made her story even better.

She and Priceless Countess were waiting in the barn. Priceless Countess wasn't happy with her temporary constraint. Her eyes were large and nervous, and, despite the cold, she was sweating, weaving, and calling outdoors.

She relaxed after returning to her paddock. Broadway Joan didn't mind the change of routine, and the senior beauty posed with grand comfort.

In the spring of 2006, Priceless Countess passed away. Although Broadway Joan never replaced that friendship, she shared her remaining days with a mare named Smiling Neatly.

Then, on August 17 that same year, Broadway Joan showed signs of tremendous discomfort. A vet was summoned. The twenty-seven-year-old mare was colicking, and the difficult decision was made to put her down. She was laid to rest next to her old companion, Priceless Countess.

"She became quite the queen of the farm," Holden said. "In summer, she had to have her hay and feed on the same side of the stall as her fan. And she didn't like breakfast, so she got three feeds at night.

"She was ridiculously spoiled, and she reveled in it. But she was so quiet, never a problem. She really enjoyed her retirement."

Carabid

Winter battled on gamely in upstate New York in March 2003. In a stall at Mill Creek Farm, a mare named Carabid was entrenched in her own fight. While her gentle eyes glowed brilliantly, Carabid was under a death sentence.

The snow-shrouded barn was silent — save occasional howling winds — as other mares and foals romped in the snow during the day. Yet Carabid and her young filly stood confined. Carabid hobbled noticeably, her injured leg encased in a splint. Despite the aid of Bute, her head occasionally drooped in discomfort.

When Carabid's filly was weaned, everyone knew the mare would have to be euthanized.

❧

On September 28, 2002, Carabid stepped on a fence staple. It penetrated the bottom of her right front foot into the deep flexor tendon and the navicular bursa. Anne Morgan, who owns Mill Creek Farm with husband Tim Little, summoned veterinarians from the Battenkill Veterinary PC. X-rays were taken, but no break was evident. The staple was removed, and the area around the injury cleaned and bandaged.

Several weeks later, however, Carabid remained uncomfortable. She was shipped to the clinic, examined, and anesthetized for surgery. Dr. Steve Sedrish cut into the bottom of her hoof to let it drain. Additional X-rays had revealed a horizontal split in the navicular bone, a small bone in the heel. The top piece of the bone had pulled away from the lower and shifted.

"I've been doing this for twenty-five years, but I've never seen a horizontal fracture of the navicular bone," said Dr. Kurt Lutgens, Battenkill's owner. "It was split like a piece of wood."

Carabid's prognosis was bleak. The injury could not be repaired surgically, and stress would eventually cause the foot to collapse. The Mill Creek family was crushed. Carabid, whose barn nicknames ranged from Carrie to Care Bear to Bear, had been a farm favorite for a decade.

Anne and Tim had founded the farm, near Saratoga Springs, in 1990. One of their early joint acquisitions, in 1993, was a four-year-old bay filly by Carodanz out of the Bold Bidder mare Tender Bid. Named Carabid, she had not achieved racing success, but Tim hoped that with different training tactics her performances would improve.

Carabid was durable and kind, with an intelligent way and trusting eyes. Yet she did not improve on the track. In thirty-four starts over four years, she had but one win, one second, and four thirds. She earned $35,138. Anne and Tim hoped she'd do better in her second career. She did.

"She was a great mother from the beginning," Anne said. "When she had her first baby, she found her niche in life."

Carrie's first foal, Carable, earned several minor checks, and Carabid's second, Coast to Coast, earned many. He bankrolled $155,310, winning three races and placing nine times. Riveting Rosie earned $19,572, and then came Cajun Kelly, a winner who earned more than $50,000.

As the foals kept coming, Mill Creek's love for Carabid deepened. One day, when Anne could not entice yearling fillies to come in from the paddock, she slid baling twine through Carrie's halter and hopped aboard, bareback. The yearlings' curiosity took over, and they followed Carrie and Anne back to the barn.

When Carrie colicked one cold winter day, Anne and the family fashioned a makeshift stall in the garage. The car was moved out and Carabid in. Anne and Tim's children — Samantha, then five, and Michael, ten — helped by providing an abundance of attention and love.

"She was hanging out with the kids," Anne said. "I knew it'd be the best place for her, and she'd be sensible about it. Some horses have class, and some horses don't. If you look at her, she's just got it."

In 2002 Anne and Tim sent her to Lycius, a handsome group I-winning son of Mr. Prospector, and they eagerly awaited her next foal. Then came that fateful September day when Carabid turned up lame. The injury became infected, and Carabid was in pain, yet she was also six months pregnant. A difficult decision was made. Mill Creek and Battenkill set their sights on nursing Carrie through her pregnancy and, if possible, the foal's weaning.

"I've had to put horses to sleep that I loved," Anne said, "but the idea of putting her to sleep with that baby in her belly was just sickening to me. We willed her to live. It became like our mission here at the farm."

Said Dr. Sedrish: "Our best expectation was to keep this mare around long enough, if she'd stay comfortable enough, to wean the baby."

The next months were painful for everyone. Carabid could not place weight on her injured leg, and despite medication, her body was often warm with discomfort. Several procedures were needed to keep the injury draining, and infection held on. Her heel was nerved to lessen her pain. Laminitis was a concern, and her healthy leg was supported with a standing bandage.

Carrie was fitted with a Kimsey splint, an effective yet cumbersome device that shifted her weight to her toe. The splint, however, left raw rub marks, and an alternative was needed. Battenkill's Dr. Sarah Thompson came up with an unusual idea involving PVC pipe.

Plastic piping was cut into pieces slightly longer than the distance between Carabid's knee and hoof. It was secured with padding and duct tape along the front and back of her leg. That displaced the mare's weight to the piping and the sound foundation of her knee joint.

Anne and barn manager Cara Preddice tended to Carabid daily in the shed row. They removed the old bandages, cleaned the area, and rebandaged the leg. Carrie was a model patient. She was otherwise stall bound, but well-wishers offering carrots often visited her.

Autumn turned to winter, and her foaling date approached. Just days before

her due date, however, Tim didn't like what he saw when he looked into Carabid's usually brilliant eyes. He called Dr. Lutgens, Mill Creek's reproductive vet, who came out and agreed that something was amiss. He manipulated the foal into position, and at about 9 a.m., January 27, 2003, he administered a shot to Carabid to induce labor.

Carabid did not lie down, yet she gave birth an hour and a half later to a fine chestnut filly with large eyes and a thin blaze. But the birth sack was discolored. Had they waited for the foal to be born on its own, it probably would not have survived. By three the next morning, however, the filly had became unusually lethargic, and Anne called the vets again.

They treated the foal but she needed to be shipped to the clinic. It was bitterly cold, and Anne wrapped the baby in a comforter from their bed. The mare and her newborn were loaded onto a van. Without even taking time to put on warm socks, Anne threw a pair of boots on her bare feet and hopped in, cradling the bundled-up filly.

After four days of intensive treatment, the filly and Carabid returned to the farm.

"By the time we brought the filly home," Anne said with a grin, "she was a regular little terrorist."

The filly was healthy, bold, and curious. And her eyes were unusual, with white rims and long lashes. She looked sort of like an armadillo, or a turtle. They nicknamed her The Reptile.

So began the long winter for Carrie and The Reptile.

It was early February when I began visiting the stall-bound pair. As a regular visitor to the farm, I'd met Carabid and admired her attractive foals. I had photographed them and used the bright-eyed Carrie as a model. Yet I'd not seen her like this.

I slipped into the stall where Carabid stood in a far corner. The bay mare's ears flicked toward me, then back. Her bay coat was darker than usual, and

Anne Morgan, right, and Cara Preddice tend to Carabid in March 2003. Bottom right, Carabid and her filly get some exercise as Morgan observes.

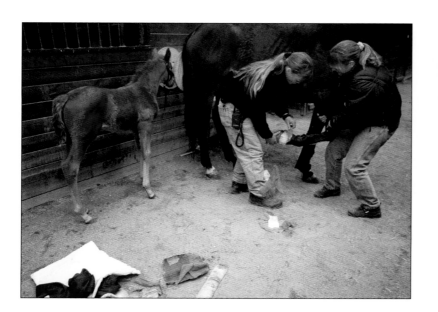

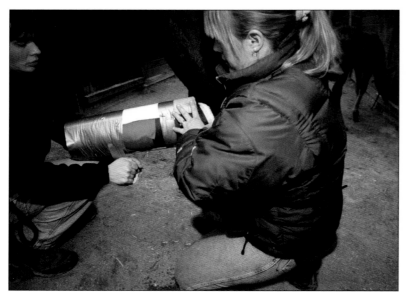

dull, and she was a bit underweight. In the straw a small form was curled up in a powder-blue blanket. Her head popped up: The Reptile. She scrambled to her feet and moved boldly forward. Her face was unusually long and her eyes wonderfully mischievous. Her golden mane flowed in soft curls, and her tail swished.

Carrie's ears popped up at the snap of a carrot, and she hobbled forward. She quickly took the carrot from my hand.

Carrie had trouble reaching her back, as even healthy horses do, so I ran my hand down her neck and across her back to her rump and scratched. Her head dropped, and her eyes closed. She moved nearer her foal and began scrubbing her teeth gently on the filly's hind end. The filly, in turn, scrubbed her teeth along Carabid's shoulder and body.

Carabid's situation, however, was heartbreaking.

When schedules and weather permitted, farm workers led the limping mare and her foal to a nearby paddock. Carabid stood patiently on the shank as The Reptile reveled around her. Most of their exercise took place inside, however. Workers closed both ends of the barn and let the two girls loose in the shed row. Carrie jogged a bit, and her foal darted here and there, almost literally bouncing off the walls.

Everyone understood what weaning time meant for Carrie. Her hoof, supported slightly off the ground, was growing oddly, and her leg was no longer straight. She was careful, however, using a wall to slide down to a lying position and never putting herself into a spot from which she could not rise.

Since December Anne had pestered the nybreds.com Web site coordinator to choose Carabid's baby for its monthly "Name the Foal" contest. In February 2003, The Reptile made her debut online. Racing fans submitted more than three hundred names. From that widely varied list Anne and Tim picked one. The Reptile, by Lycius, became Shesdelycius.

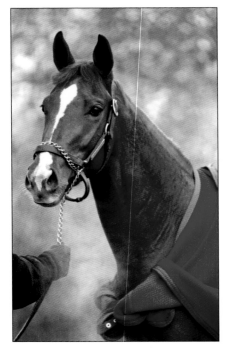
Shesdelycius in October 2005

The seemingly endless winter finally waned, and Carabid was in less discomfort. She'd adjusted her lifestyle to her injury, and the splints had kept most of her weight from her broken bone. By April, everyone noticed that Carrie looked better. Like the outside world around her, she was coming back to life.

As spring melded into summer, an untethered Carabid and her filly were let into a paddock as the staff kept close watch. Again, Carrie showed common sense, and soon her days in the paddock were spent without surveillance. She gained weight, and her winter coat shed out to rich bay dapples.

The braces eventually gave way to a standing bandage, and then came the day when the final bandage was removed. Carrie stood, without bandages, for the first time in nine months.

A near-miracle had occurred. Although a pronounced limp would always be a reminder of Carabid's ordeal, enough scar tissue had formed to hold her foot together. Her death sentence had been lifted.

"She never gave any indication that she wanted to give up," Anne said. "Horses that are sick or injured, they give up. You can see it in their faces. She wanted to live. She really did."

Said Dr. Sedrish: "I would have given this horse zero chance to live. She definitely qualifies as a remarkable survivor."

Shesdelycius was soon kicking up her heels in joyous merriment with her buddies, her blazed face generally showing the way. At the age of two, Shesdelycius was sold to Neal Galvin.

Galvin purchased Shesdelycius due to Carabid. "I've been going to Mill Creek for a long time with mares. When I saw Carabid, I saw how tough she was. She was gutsy."

Shesdelycius races for Galvin's Our Blue Streaks Stable. Through 2006, Shesdelycius had raced seven times — at Saratoga, Belmont, and Finger Lakes.

Her final 2006 start yielded her best result, a third, and she is scheduled to race in 2007.

Carabid's recovery was so remarkable that Anne bred her once more, and in 2005, Carrie foaled a gorgeous dark bay Cryptoclearance filly. But the added weight of pregnancy had been difficult on her, and Carrie became an official pasture pal. She settled into a life of leisure with two other infirm mares although, on occasion, they seemed to forget their handicaps. Tim marveled late one afternoon as the trio galloped at full steam, with nostrils flared and tails flipped above their backs in youthful abandon.

In summer 2006, however, several abscesses developed in Carabid's foot. For six weeks Anne soaked the foot while providing her Bute and antibiotics. On hot days, Anne aimed a fan toward the mare and secured her stall with just a crossbar. Carrie occasionally rubbed her hind end against the crossbar, popping it undone. But Carrie never had been stupid: She stayed in that open stall with its fan and promise of food.

Her condition improved, but in February 2007, farm workers found Carabid lame in her paddock. For several weeks Anne bandaged her foot daily as abscesses formed, yet the mare's condition did not improve. When Carrie stopped enjoying her carrots, Anne's hope faded.

Four and a half years after her initial injury Carabid's leg had deteriorated. She had no support system left.

On March 12, 2007, Carabid — Carrie, Care Bear, Bear — was euthanized at age eighteen. She was laid to rest by a beautiful pond, a white birch, and a spruce tree. A large stone was placed on her grave.

As news of Carabid's death spread, Anne and Tim received condolence e-mails and flowers. After all, Carrie had gained quite a following during her years at the farm.

"She got to be kind of a Barbaro in her own right," Anne said. "Strictly from a business point of view, she paid a lot of bills for me over the years when I'd sell one of her foals or get a breeder's check.

"In the grand scheme of things, she was an inexpensive broodmare. But she touched a lot of people, and a lot of people really liked her. She had a huge heart."

Carabid with "The Reptile"

Carnivalay

1981–2007 B. H. BY NORTHERN DANCER — OBEAH, BY CYANE

Jog, jog, jog, go, go, go. Stop. Rear. Go, go, go, jog, and … stop. Stand. Hey, look at me!

I've been prancing along this path to my paddock for many years now, but it never gets old. Nor do I, or at least I don't feel it.

I'm Carnivalay, and I live at Country Life Farm. You've probably heard of it — popular, family-run farm here in Maryland. And you've probably heard of me, too. I've been in lots of magazines, and there's stuff written about me in a book, *Country Life Diary*, by Josh Pons.

Josh lives here, too, and he has led me to my paddock many times. He's also helped me court the ladies (bless his heart). I haven't read his book, but I hear he told some secrets about me.

For instance, why did he have to tell everyone that for tall mares I needed an adjustable breeding ramp? So I'm not the tallest stallion. Neither was my daddy, Northern Dancer. He had a ramp, too, and he was only the best stallion in the world.

At least Josh gave me credit for being able to roll fully over and back again, and up and back until I'm coated in mud. Oh yeah, that's a good trick. I like that one.

Jog, jog, jog. Stop. Stand. Look around. Flick an ear one way, then another. Tense up. Keep standing.

I had barely started racing for Mrs. Jane Lunger's Christiana Stables when they brought me here. Only four starts, and they all happened in eighteen days!

My trainer, Allen Jerkens, didn't let rust grow on my horseshoes. I won one race and finished second once and third once. Not bad, huh? But my right front leg suddenly hurt — my cannon bone they said — and they put some screws in it. What an annoying time — stall bound. You know me. I hated that.

Mike Pons, Josh's brother, said that when they found me it was like the stars aligned, that it was eerie how much I looked like my sire. That was a good thing, looking like pop. People often mention it. And with my father *and* mother being famous, well, perhaps I should have been in show business.

My mother, Obeah, was a multiple stakes winner, and by the time I retired she'd already produced major stakes winners, the full siblings Dance Spell and Discorama. My full brother, Black Powder, was a stakes winner, too. Eventually, Mama had a foal more famous than any of us — Go for Wand. I still cry for her.

I'm a little guy, about 15.2 hands, but I'm as sturdy as Herschel Walker and as handsome as George Clooney. I'm bright bay, and people say I'm flashy. Bingo! I've got two white legs and a blaze as white as vanilla ice cream. It drips down my left cheek, and people like that. Mrs. Lunger said it was my smile.

Who wouldn't think I'd become a first-rate sire? Three foals from my very first crop were graded stakes winners. In 1990 I was named Maryland Stallion of the Year. Hot stuff! There's a plaque hanging outside my stall to prove it.

Somehow, my old barn mate, Allen's Prospect, eventually overshadowed me. I never understood why he got more girls.

Maybe it's because I'm a little nervous sometimes. But hey, I'm just always sittin' on go — like a racehorse should, right?

I'll let the stats do the talking. My average earnings per starter? Higher than Allen's. Graded stakes winners? I've got more. I've had four horses that

earned more than $600,000, and Allen doesn't have any. And, according to The Jockey Club, he had a whole lot more foals than I did: 1,071 compared to my 609.

I don't mean to knock him. After all, he was the state's leading sire six times, and he's the most successful sire in Maryland Million history. But a horse has got to look out for himself, doesn't he? I sired a really fast sprinter named Aggadan, who earned $860,306 and raced through 2006. That same year, my boy Mixed Up won the grade I New York Turf Writers Cup — at 2⅜ miles over a bunch of jumps.

By then I'd been retired. But I'll bet you figured this out already: I'm not the retiring type.

Ready to go. Tug on lead shank. Rear. Go, go, go, prance, prance, prance, go, go, go.

We're finally at my paddock. Oh man, I love being outside. Now let me loose. C'mon, c'mon, buddy, let me free!

Yippee!

Shake head. Bolt. Stop. Look back. Slip slowly to ground. Roll on one side ... roll on other side ... roll, roll. Rub chin in dirt, rub dirt all over. Jump up. Shake head, jog, slide to stop. Head down. Graze ... Look back one final time.

That's right. Look at me. I'm the one and only ... Carnivalay.

On January 9, 2007, Carnivalay died of an apparent heart attack. He was buried at Country Life Farm.

Christine's Ladies

Christine Hansen had already decided what she wanted to do for a living. The German teenager had taken riding lessons and ridden warmbloods, but her passion was Thoroughbreds. She wanted to breed, foal, and raise them.

She read, in a German horse magazine, that a magnificent equine center was being built in America: the Kentucky Horse Park. She told her parents:

"This is where I want to live when I grow up."

She began working toward that goal. She awoke early Saturday mornings and walked to the rail station for a twenty-minute train ride, and then walked twenty more minutes to the Frankfurt racetrack. There, she galloped horses and fueled her dreams.

Using her best high school English, she wrote to horse councils inquiring

Christine Hansen with Pukka Princess, 24

about equine programs. She learned about the Kentucky Equine Institute (KEI) program, located at, of all places, the Kentucky Horse Park. That's all it took. She moved to Lexington after high school for the park's six-month program.

After completing the program, she decided she wanted to stay in Lexington, and she attended the University of Kentucky, graduating with a degree in animal science. Christine worked at farms and eventually began buying horses of her own. Now, she owns Montessori Farm LLC and works in Nicholasville, Kentucky, doing exactly what she dreamed of doing — breeding, foaling, and raising horses. In addition, she prepares clients' horses for the sales and cares for older mares, some of which she owns.

One of Christine's longtime clients is respected breeder Rob Whiteley. He

Solar at age 26

A Kiss for Luck at age 28

managed Carl Icahn's Foxfield for seventeen years. Now, at his Liberation Farm, the stakes winners keep coming.

"Whether we breed, race, ride, or simply keep horses as companions and pets, I believe we share a common responsibility to provide humane care for these wonderful creatures throughout their life cycle," Whiteley said. "Our obligations do not end when a horse stops being productive or otherwise 'useful.'

"Christine is truly an earth angel who attends to these classy ladies with love and attention to detail. All of the mares happen to be royalty, but Christine would love them the same even if they were by Deadbeat out of Two Dead Flies."

I've visited Christine several times, and three of the ladies I photographed are no longer living. Solar (1976–2004, by Halo—Sex Appeal, by Buckpasser) was a beautifully bred stakes winner and half sister to the stallions El Gran Senor, Compliance, and Try My Best. Pukka Princess (1978–2003, by Pukka Gent—Heavenly Turn, by Prince John) was a strong-willed five-time stakes winner. Engagingly (1978–2003, by Quack—Secrecy, by Gallant Romeo), Pukka's dear friend, was a lovely and gentle producer of the multiple stakes winner Media Plan.

Christine keeps four geriatric mares, whom she calls her "special needs mares," in one paddock together — A Kiss for Luck, Silver Valley, Water Lily, and Viva Sec. The latter two were featured in *Old Friends,* and they look as content now as they did five years ago.

In the center of their paddock are the makings of several jumps. On occasion Christine saddles up a young paint gelding and rides him into

Silver Valley at age 28

Viva Sec at age 29

the paddock.

"I can ride with them in there, and they're rather bemused by the whole thing of me making this horse hop over these jumps," Christine said. "They'll stand there and watch me like it's the craziest thing they've ever seen.

"But if I'm making a circle and get too close to the group, Viva Sec will pin her ears and strut after me with that herding position they assume — with their nose out and that little snake-like movement of their head and neck — and she'll go after us. My gelding, who's a lot heavier than she is — and young — takes it very seriously, and he makes it very clear: 'Mom, we're getting out of here.'"

Water Lily at age 31

Raja's Delight, 29, left, with Tops in Taps, 24

Christine commented on each of her elderly ladies:

A Kiss for Luck (1979 dark bay/brown mare, by Reflected Glory—Painted Flag, by Dusty Canyon) — California's 1981 champion two-year-old filly, grade I Vanity Handicap winner, dam of millionaire Golden Cherry:

"She was more difficult and high-strung when she was younger — by younger I mean just over twenty. She has calmed down quite a bit … A Kiss for Luck had a very, very close friendship with my other mare [French Galaxy], and when I could tell it was time to put French Galaxy to sleep … about two weeks before, I put A Kiss for Luck in with the other older mares, and that worked really well."

Silver Valley (1979 chestnut mare, by Mr. Prospector—Seven Valleys, by Road At Sea) — minor stakes winner, eight-time winner, dam of top sire Silver Deputy:

"Very sweet, very kind, very easygoing mare. She doesn't complain about a whole lot. She's the only one out there who does seem to have bad days, when her age gets to her; her creaky joints get to her. But she always seems appreciative of your going out and doing small things, like putting a blanket on her."

Water Lily (1976 dark bay/brown mare, by Riverman—First Bloom, by Primera) — graded stakes winner, dam of grade I winner Talinum, the oldest mare at thirty-one:

"Lily stays quiet and easy to handle even if she doesn't like what's being done to her. She sometimes acts a little afraid when she is being approached or when her head is being touched. I often think that her vision is giving her trouble. So, while she might toss her head a bit in surprise, she is never unkind to her handler. The 'difficulty' lies in the fact that she may simply be very, very hard to catch if she thinks you are trying to put a shank on her in order to give her a shot or do some other not-so-pleasant thing."

Viva Sec (1978 dark bay/brown mare, by Secretariat—Viva La Vivi, by Royal Note) — multiple stakes winner, second dam of grade I winner Vicar:

"She's quiet now — we're not doing anything that upsets her now. She's never separated from her friends. It's those four [Water Lily, A Kiss for Luck, Silver Valley, Viva Sec], and we never separate them. If somebody has to come in because they are cold in the freezing rain, all four come in."

Lost Lode, 22, left, with Letty's Pennant, 25

Letty's Pennant (1982 dark bay/brown mare, by Bold Forbes—Nalees Flying Flag, by Hoist the Flag) — stakes-placed dam of graded stakes winner R. Associate and eight other winners; second dam of Raging Fever, Stormin Fever, and minor stakes winner Roaring Fever; friend of Lost Lode:

"Letty's Pennant is not difficult to deal with, but she's shy, timid, and hard to catch. She is especially hard to catch in the stall. She's such a sweet mare; she would never hurt anybody intentionally. But she will turn her butt to you in the stall, and you have to start scratching her over her tail, and you have to work all the way up along her spine. Then you can catch her. But if she doesn't get that spine massage, it's not happening."

Lost Lode (1985 chestnut mare, by Mr. Prospector—Past Forgetting, by Messenger of Song) — stakes winner, dam of stakes winner Find the Treasure, friend of Letty's Pennant:

"The best thing is that [Letty's Pennant] is buddied up with Lost Lode, because that's the only way we can catch her. Lost Lode is a lot like Silver Valley — a

sweet, dear mare who won't complain about anything, and quiet in the barn."

Tricky Squaw (bay mare 1983, by Clever Trick—Black Apache, by Gainsworth) — multiple graded stakes winner, dam of stakes winner Tricky Six, second dam of grade II winner Stanley Park:

"She seems to have a more developed sense of personal space than most horses. When you violate that personal space and get too close, she is not satisfied simply to move away from you. Her facial expression makes it quite clear that she expects you to move out of her space, not the other way around. And it's advisable to do so.

"The same applies when you lead her on the shank. Just suggest a direction, and she then graciously allows you to walk next to her. Funny thing, she never gets hard to catch; I guess she has the confidence to believe that whatever an encounter with a person brings, it's never really anything to be afraid of. We are the servants who provide her with feed and shelter, so why not come up to the gate."

Tops in Taps (1983 bay mare, by Topsider—Lightning Carol, by Lightning

Orphan) — stakes winner, pasture mate of Raja's Delight:

"She's not really a dominant mare, but she clearly is Raja's leader. Tops will get pretty nervous when we put her in the stall for vet work. She's not a difficult mare; she just really doesn't want to be inside. She wants to be outside in her natural element."

Raja's Delight (1978 chestnut mare, by Raja Baba—Evening Dance, by Dr. Fager) — stakes winner, pasture mate of Tops in Taps:

"Very docile, very sweet, very gentle. Sometimes she's not really sure about being caught, but when you have her, she is always an absolute doll. She's a very, very quiet, easygoing mare. One of my employees, a few years ago, put her one-year-old daughter on her back."

As our conversation ended, Christine said: "I really, really enjoy these older mares, and I think it's part of our responsibility, having animals, to take care of them. In some ways their personalities come out even more once they're old.

Tricky Squaw at age 24

"It's the same with my dogs, some of which will be sixteen and older. Sometimes, even if they don't look as attractive when they're older, I love them even more."

❧

Lost Lode, in foal, died the morning of February 24, 2007. A cause of death was never found. Her friend, Letty's Pennant, mourned for days, walking the fence line and keeping to herself. To help ease her loss, Christine moved Letty's Pennant to a separate property where Raja's Delight and Tops in Taps share a paddock. All three seem happy with the arrangement.

Tricky Squaw, the only other mare in foal for 2007, foaled a lovely bay Thunder Gulch filly on March 24, 2007.

Engagingly at age 24

Clabber Girl

1983 CH. M. BY ALYDAR — JEDINA, BY WHAT A PLEASURE

Clabber Girl made her million dollars the same way Smith Barney did: She earned it. Graced with talent, the lovely Alydar filly raced at a time when the distaff ranks were rich in quality. Finding the right spots took effort.

"She had a frequent-flyer ticket," said her owner, John Nerud, laughing. "She made a million dollars, and I paid $500,000 in airplane fees."

At ninety-four, Nerud is a fountainhead of knowledge and an unsurpassed spokesman for the sport. In 2007 he received the Eclipse Award of Merit, an honor saved for racing's most revered and influential people.

Born on a cattle ranch in Nebraska, Nerud received his first horse at age five. He was a restless sort, riding in match races and rodeos. After trading a workhorse for a Thoroughbred, he began training racehorses. By 1957 he was the respected trainer of Belmont Stakes winner Gallant Man.

About that time he teamed up with William McKnight, chairman of the board and majority stockholder of 3M Company. Between Nerud's business and horse sense and McKnight's resources, McKnight's Tartan Farms became a world force. Its success peaked with Hall of Famers Ta Wee and Dr. Fager. Nerud's expertise filled such roles within the Thoroughbred industry as well-respected breeder, prominent trainer, and president of Tartan Farms.

For Nerud, the line to Clabber Girl started with a daughter of Cequillo, whom he obtained from McKnight to settle up a partnership. "I've had four generations," Nerud said. "Cequillo had a great pedigree but not much of a race record. I took a daughter of hers and named her Grand Splendor. I bred her to Dr. Fager and got a mare called Killaloe, who was born on St. Patrick's Day. Then I bred Killaloe to What a Pleasure and got Jedina. Then I bred Jedina to Alydar and got Clabber Girl."

Killaloe also produced the immortal sire Fappiano, the French group I winner Torrential, and Bought Twice, the dam of 2000 Belmont Stakes winner Commendable. Clabber Girl's dam, Jedina, a minor stakes winner, is also the second dam of Kentucky Oaks winner Keeper Hill.

Nerud and his wife, Charlotte, often drove to Tartan's property near Ocala, Florida, to visit the horses, including Jedina and her 1983 Alydar filly. Among the countless billboards they passed were those touting Clabber Girl Baking Powder, a brand that competed for decades with Calumet Baking Powder. Because Alydar resided at Calumet Farm, Nerud named his Jedina filly Clabber Girl.

Nerud's son, Jan, trained her early on, but then she was shifted to the California barn of D. Wayne Lukas. Clabber Girl traveled far and wide, racing at seven tracks and registering eight wins, twelve seconds, and six thirds.

She set a track record at Hollywood Park on the West Coast — 6½ furlongs in 1:15⅗. And in her nineteenth stakes appearance, she became a grade I winner in the 1988 Top Flight Handicap at Aqueduct on the East Coast.

She won two other stakes — the grade II Chula Vista Handicap and the grade III Rancho Bernardo Handicap — and finished second in the 1987 Breeders' Cup Distaff.

It took thirty-nine races, but Clabber Girl retired a millionaire. Her earnings: $1,006,261.

Clabber Girl was boarded at Lane's End Farm in Kentucky for several years, and her first five foals were by such stallions as Cox's Ridge, Private Account, and Seattle Slew. The results were discouraging.

Nerud, an early and avid supporter of New York's breeding program, moved Clabber Girl to that state's Sugar Maple Farm. For the past decade Nerud's sire, A. P Jet, also at Sugar Maple, has been Clabber Girl's main man. They've collaborated on three winners, including Wing Man, who has earned more than $260,000, and the stakes-placed Running Dog, who has earned more than $160,000.

Clabber Girl's two-year-old A. P Jet filly, Curtains, was in training early in 2007, and Nerud planned to keep her for his broodmare band. At twenty-four, Clabber Girl entered 2007 in foal to Performing Magic. After that, Nerud planned to pension her.

Clabber Girl is an absolute beauty. A deep chestnut with a broad star and two hind socks, she lacks the strong, straight face often associated with Alydar. Instead, the side of her face is unusually dished. She resembles an Arabian with her broad jaws and finely tapered nose. Her eyes are kind and her manner relaxed. She is class through and through.

"Clabber Girl's been a wonderful thing for me," Nerud said. "She's been something to me all of her life. Before, she won me a lot of money. She's a beautiful mare and always was a very kind mare. She's a wonderful old gal."

Opposite: Clabber Girl with her 2005 A. P Jet filly, Curtains

Class Play

1981 CH. M. BY STAGE DOOR JOHNNY—FLYING BUTTRESS, BY EXCLUSIVE NATIVE

When Doug Koch noticed Class Play's name in a sales catalog, he picked up the phone. An astute observer of quality and class, he knew the seventeen-year-old broodmare, her racing career, and pedigree.

Koch called the agent, Mare Haven Farm, in Kentucky. Class Play hadn't even arrived for sales preparation, but he asked whether the owner might sell her privately. Koch got the answer he wanted and soon found himself at Mare Haven.

"I got there about the day the mare arrived from Ohio," Koch said. "She must have been out in a field. She had burdocks throughout her mane, her feet were in terrible shape, she was a hundred pounds underweight, and she had this horrible Hannibal Lecter–like cribbing device on, like nothing you've ever seen."

Since belonging to the businessman Peter Brant, who raced her and bred her early foals, Class Play had changed hands several times. For either $20,000 or $22,000, Koch recalled, she changed hands once more, taking up residence at Berkshire Stud, Koch's showplace farm in Pine Plains, New York.

Class Play was beautifully bred. Her sire, Stage Door Johnny, was a visual powerhouse and a major source of stamina. In 1968 he won the Belmont Stakes. Class Play's dam, Flying Buttress, was the first yearling that trainer Frank Whiteley purchased for Brant. Her pedigree was loaded with black type, and she became a winner and produced four black-type winners: Pillaster, Lutyens, Lamerok, and Class Play.

Class Play was a grand race mare. She raced twelve times, winning five and finishing third twice. She earned $279,070 racing against the era's toughest mares. Class Play won on dirt and turf from a mile to 1½ miles. Her crown-ing achievement came at the longer distance in the grade I Coaching Club American Oaks — a 1½-length score over Life's Magic and Miss Oceana. *The Blood-Horse* described Class Play as "a big, long, lanky filly."

She also was difficult. The blaze-faced chestnut was competitive and high strung, and her smoldering ways didn't end when she began producing. She simply became a bit less lanky.

While her foals weren't of stakes quality, one of her daughters has produced a grade III winner, the New York champion Incurable Optimist. Another grandchild, Reenact, won an Australian group I.

She was barren when Koch brought her to New York in 1998. The next season she got pregnant by Spinning World, but on Kentucky Derby day she colicked and underwent emergency surgery. About a month later she lost the foal. The next year she suffered from Mare Reproductive Loss Syndrome.

In 2001 she was bred to Distant View — six times — yet didn't get pregnant. A shift to Stravinsky worked, but she lost her pregnancy after thirty-five days. Finally, in 2003, she produced a handsome Stravinsky colt. Named Rigoletto, he eventually was sold overseas.

Despite Class Play's cantankerous ways, she was a gentle and doting mother with a foal at her side. The defiant look in her eyes changed to one of contentment.

In 2004 Class Play delivered a powerful chestnut Fusaichi Pegasus colt named Nobu, who sold at the Keeneland November sale for $100,000. Bred one last time in 2006 to Holy Bull, Class Play aborted.

"So that was her story. Of course, we were trying to get a filly out of her. But you know how life works," Koch smiled.

Nowadays, Class Play and a fellow pensioner, Notice Me, baby-sit younger

mares. The two elders — the "old biddies," Koch chuckled — generally stay outdoors, and they prefer it that way. As she has aged, Class Play has become easier to work with. And despite the intimidating mask she wore when Koch bought her, Class Play is not a cribber.

Koch, a veterinarian since 1976, provides much of the mare's medical care. She has lymphosarcoma and lumps under her skin. While noticeable, they are not life threatening. When a fellow veterinarian suggested that Koch keep track of the lumps to monitor any changes, he traipsed out to the field, pen and paper in hand.

"I went over and lifted her tail up to draw where the lumps were, and, bam, she kicked me right in the knee," Koch said.

It's a comfort — except perhaps to Koch — to know that while Class Play has mellowed, she hasn't given herself totally over to old age.

When she's not entirely trusting of someone and they reach for her halter, she lifts her head surprisingly high. The message is as clear as a kick in the knee: Leave me alone. However, she generally makes an exception for one person — Koch. Class Play allows him to catch her and work on her when necessary.

"When she does let me do what I need to do, she will often sigh, put her head down, and her face looks like she is saying 'OK, I know I am a nut, but I trust you and you saved me,'" Koch said. "At least that is the anthropomorphized version."

While she has lost some tone and gained some lumps, she is still a powerful, long-bodied chestnut with an unusually compelling eye. Her blaze extends down between her nostrils to a small spot on her lower lip. Her temples are

flecked with white. Her feet are tender.

"No other mare on the farm wears shoes, except the old retired pensioner we have to put shoes on all the time," Koch said, smiling. "So I've got to pay the $100 every six weeks to get shoes on the old nut job."

Why does he keep her?

"We don't put anything down unless they have to be put down," Koch said. "Any mares who've raced for us or that we have here that get to that age, we just pension them.

"She'll be here until we plant her. It's great to have her. She's a grade I classic winner. There aren't too many of those around. And, she's just one of those personalities. When she goes, the world will be a lesser place without her."

Count On Bonnie

1981 B. M. BY DANCING COUNT—BUENA NOTTE, BY VICTORIA PARK

Marvin Little Jr. will always remember the night Count On Bonnie, who would forever change his life, was born. It was May 1981, and his wife, Mary, had undergone cancer surgery that day at Johns Hopkins Hospital in Baltimore. After the doctor informed them that the cancer was completely removed, Little drove home to Newstead Farm in Upperville, Virginia.

That evening, his broodmare Buena Notte went into labor. Little had purchased the in-foal seventeen-year-old mare the previous October, hoping she would produce a filly.

During the foaling, however, things went amiss. Somehow, the foal's lungs became inflated, making for a difficult delivery. But Little, after stepping in to help, got the filly he'd wished for.

"If the doctor had told Mary he didn't get all the cancer, I would have stayed with her that night," Little said. "And there probably wouldn't be any Count On Bonnie."

Buena Notte was Little's first broodmare. He and his wife had worked nineteen years to accumulate $15,050 in savings. Unbeknownst to Mary, Little bought Buena Notte at auction for $15,000. Her pedigree traced back to Federico Tesio's Italian Derby–Oaks winner, Fausta. Little liked that. She had also produced a solid racehorse in Puerto Rican champion Shake Shake Shake.

When the bill from Fasig-Tipton arrived, Little said, his wife chastised him: "Now we can't even go to the grocery store. We only have $50."

Buena Notte had no more foals, coming up barren several times. The Littles took care of her until she died at thirty-four. But Count On Bonnie more than paid the grocery bills.

Little grew up working with mules and planned on working in the steel industry after a four-year stint in the Navy. When a steel strike thwarted that plan, he took a job cleaning stalls at Clovelly Farm in Kentucky. The manager Lars LaCour, one of the country's most knowledgeable horsemen, kept old copies of *The Blood-Horse* and *Thoroughbred Record*. Little borrowed them in armloads.

"Everything I read about a horse went in my head and stayed forever, and everything I read about anything else went in one side and out the other," Little said.

After five years Little moved to Newstead Farm, where he served as manager for twenty-one years.

Newstead bred many top horses. Among its finest was six-time grade I winner Miss Oceana, a regally bred Alydar filly who came along the same year as Count On Bonnie. Count On Bonnie, by Dancing Count, was not the standout.

"She always ran with Miss Oceana, so Miss Oceana was the one that always stood out," Little chuckled.

His daughter Marilyn broke Count On Bonnie, and another daughter, Teresa, named her by combining the names of the sire and dam.

Despite being offset and crooked in the knees, Count On Bonnie showed promise training with Steve DiMauro. But a knee chip slowed her down. She underwent surgery but still, eventually, pulled up lame. Little retired her, and Count On Bonnie soon headed to the breeding shed.

Her first foal was euthanized after suffering from an OCD lesion in his shoulder. The next year Count On Bonnie came up barren. But the third year, after being bred to Woodman, an Irish champion racehorse and popular stallion at Ashford Stud, Count On Bonnie delivered a stunningly handsome

bay colt. The blaze-faced beauty won the 1991 Preakness and Belmont, was named champion three-year-old colt, and earned nearly $3 million. His name? Hansel.

"Almost from the minute he was born," Little said, "he was just the most beautiful horse I ever saw."

About a week after Hansel's birth, Little moved to a new farm — his own — in Kentucky. Count On Bonnie and Hansel were the first of Little's horses to step foot upon Meadowlark Valley Farm.

Hansel was the first horse Little ever sold — for $150,000 at the 1989 Keeneland September yearling sale. It was a sizeable sum, well above his sire's sales average. Little sold Count On Bonnie's next foal, a Sportin' Life colt, for $35,000 — again, well above the sire's average.

Although seven of Count On Bonnie's last eight foals were by Woodman, none approached the status of their famous sibling. The best was Lahint, a grade III winner.

Little recounted what the rest of Count On Bonnie's foals sold for:

A filly sold for $350,000 … A colt sold for $725,000 … A colt sold for $450,000 … Two sold privately … Fifty percent of one sold to a friend … A colt sold for $650,000 …

Little kept the final two but eventually sold one, a 2000 filly named Magpie, in foal to Unbridled's Song, for $425,000.

"Wow, what big numbers," Little said, laughing. "I'd have been shaking stalls, probably, if it wasn't for Count On Bonnie. I've got a 150-acre farm, and I own four houses and about fifteen broodmares, and she bought it all for me."

Count On Bonnie did not produce another foal after Magpie despite several efforts, and the beloved mare was pensioned. She didn't fade into retirement. "She throws fits, you know," Little said. "She'll be in a certain paddock that she doesn't like, and I'll have to move her into another one. She always gets what she wants. She's living the good life. I hope she lives as long as her mama did."

She is the oldest mare there and stays outdoors with four other broodmares. She eventually will be buried on the farm, Little said, and a marker will be placed on her grave.

"She was a gift from God," Little said. "That's exactly what she was."

Count On Bonnie with Marvin Little Jr. and Marilyn Little

Crafty Prospector

1979 CH. H. BY MR. PROSPECTOR — REAL CRAFTY, BY IN REALITY

On March 15, 2007, Brookdale Farm near Versailles, Kentucky, announced Crafty Prospector's pensioning. While not known for siring record-priced sales yearlings or classic winners, Crafty Prospector quietly compiled remarkable statistics.

"He was a real racehorse sire," said Brookdale's Fred Seitz Jr. "It's incredible the numbers he's put up."

When he entered stud in Florida in 1984, his strong face — reminiscent of his sire, Mr. Prospector — wouldn't earn him the title "pretty boy." But Crafty Prospector had a powerful body, a solid pedigree, and an exceptional race record.

He won seven of ten starts and was never off the board, winning from six furlongs to 1 1/16 miles. He also finished second, by a neck, to champion Christmas Past in the grade I Gulfstream Park Handicap at 1 1/4 miles.

Before his first foals raced, his stud fee at Happy Valley Farm was listed at $15,000. After nearly every foal from his first crop won, his fee quickly became "private." On January 30, 1990, Crafty Prospector took up residence at Brookdale Farm. He's lived there ever since.

For more than a decade his foal crops numbered in the fifties and sixties. He sired eighty-nine stakes winners, including twenty-eight group or graded events. At the time of his pensioning, his progeny earnings topped $88 million, and his

average earnings per starter was nearly $100,000.

Crafty Prospector's most famous runner, Agnes Digital, was Japan's 2001 champion older horse. He earned more than $6 million. Stateside, Crafty Shaw won nine stakes and earned more than a million dollars, and Crafty C. T. and Crafty Friend are both grade II winners. All are now stallions.

Crafty Prospector's numbers waned the past three years, and in 2006 he covered thirty-three mares. That June he colicked and underwent surgery at Rood & Riddle Equine Hospital. He recovered quickly, yet he did not breed in 2007.

Said Seitz Jr.: "He's twenty-eight years old, and he still acts like a young horse. He's almost too tough on himself. He'll go out and run himself in the paddock every once in a while. I just don't think he knows that he's aging."

Perhaps the greatest compliment came from respected breeder Rob Whiteley, who told *The Blood-Horse*: "This is brash on my part, but I think Crafty Prospector is probably the greatest stallion ever. I helped arrange for him to go to Brookdale and I bred to him a lot. I think he had thirty-one winners from thirty-five foals in his first crop."

"He was pigeon-holed as a sire of sprinters and never received the respect or appreciation he deserved. Bred correctly, they can go a distance of ground, and on turf, too. If I was in racing instead of commercial breeding, half my barn would be Crafty Prospectors."

Crystal Water

1973–2004 B. H. BY WINDY SANDS — SOFT SNOW, BY T. V. LARK

The Mojave Desert was dry with winter, as lonely silver cottonwoods shimmered above cacti and brush. Far in the distance the San Bernardino Mountains formed a stark background that seemed like the ends of the earth.

There, an old stallion stood proudly, tenuously, on legs barely supported by deeply sunken fetlocks. The wind shifted his long, unkempt mane, and his eyes appeared weary and worldly. His winter coat was thick, rich with tones of black and bay.

Like a wild mustang that had long since lost his harem, Crystal Water lived quietly, far from the crowd, in remote Lucerne Valley, California.

It was once so very different. In *The History of the Thoroughbred of California*, Mary Fleming wrote: "He cut an unforgettable figure on California tracks — a powerful, charismatic animal, singular in appearance, who fought like a demon possessed when confronted with a battle to the wire. Horses simply could not pass him once he owned the lead in the stretch. He would not let them."

Crystal Water raced for his breeder, Connie M. Ring. Mrs. Ring bought her first Thoroughbred in 1947, and her husband, George, quickly climbed into the business with her. Their Three Rings Ranch raced such standouts as Olympiad King, Fleet Rings, and Windy Sands.

Fleet Rings, winner of the 1949 Hollywood Lassie and a tremendously important broodmare for the farm, produced just one foal, a daughter named Winter Snow. Winter Snow produced Soft Snow, and Soft Snow, when bred to the Rings' house stallion, the multiple stakes winning Windy Sands, produced their best racehorse.

From Soft Snow and Windy Sands came Crystal Water.

Despite racing against the likes of Ancient Title, J. O. Tobin, Majestic Light, and Vigors, Crystal Water won nine of twenty-five starts. Six wins came in stakes, and five were grade Is: Hollywood Derby, Hollywood Gold Cup, Santa Anita Handicap, Californian Stakes, and Oak Tree Invitational.

Crystal Water was a powerhouse, and fans loved him. His thick body was heavily muscled, as if sculpted; his strides pounding; and his black mane whipped when he sailed homeward. Trained by Roger Clapp, he won under 129 pounds, on turf and dirt, with and without blinkers, and under top jockeys such as Willie Shoemaker and Laffit Pincay Jr. He set a track record in the 1977 Santa Anita Handicap of 1:59⅕ for the 1¼ miles. And on turf, he equaled the nine-furlong world mark of 1:45⅕.

In 1978, when Crystal Water lost a step or two, the five-year-old was sent home to stud at Three Rings Ranch near Beaumont, California. He sired stakes winners in his second and third crops, yet by 1984, as Mrs. Ring scaled back her operation, his matings numbered in the single digits. George Warwick bought Crystal Water and moved him to Clear View Farms in nearby Apple Valley.

"He had some age on him by the time we bought him," said Duane Neumann, Warwick's partner and the farm manager. "But we probably bred more mares to him during the first two years than he had gotten his entire career."

The still-powerful, magnificent stallion sired fifteen or more foals in each crop through 1993. While this outstanding racehorse sired useful runners — his sire-production index was higher than average — he never produced "the big horse." From his twenty-two crops came nine stakes winners. His most important runner, perhaps, was Glacial Stream, who won the grade

II Malibu Stakes and earned $273,203. His leading earner, the stakes-placed Canyon Crest, earned $421,720.

After Warwick's death in 1991, Neumann took charge of Crystal Water. His final crop, which numbered one, came in 2000.

I flew out to visit Crystal Water in January 2004. The road to Neumann's small farm in Lucerne Valley was unpaved and lined with weathered telephone poles, steel windmills, and scrub trees. Mountains rose on both sides — some barren, some snow-traced. Cold winds pushed dark, rolling clouds over otherwise brilliant blue skies.

Neumann and his daughter, Sherri, led me back to see Crystal Water. He stood in a pen, resting with one hind leg cocked. Sherri snapped a lead shank onto his halter and led him into a larger paddock for photos.

Freshly turned thirty-one, Crystal Water seemed surprised — and delighted — by this change in his daily routine, the highlight of which was usually Neumann's wife, Linda, feeding him lots of carrots. Or, as Neumann said, smiling: "There's not too much to his routine anymore except for sunshine and lollipops."

Crystal Water began to bellow, perhaps thinking he was getting another opportunity at stud. He was a sight to behold, this five-time grade I winner, ouchy on geriatric legs yet still eager to test those legs if given the chance. Although no mares appeared, he puffed up the best he could. When he lifted his lip to sniff the wind, he proved that he was, indeed, "long in the tooth."

But still, more than a quarter century after turning heads at the track, Crystal Water, the ancient stallion, remained a thing of beauty.

Six months later, in July 2004, Crystal Water died.

Cupecoy's Joy

1979–2004 B. M. BY NORTHERLY — LADY ABLA (ARG), BY ALSINA

Cupecoy's Joy was described in stories as nutty, temperamental, wild, a freak, a crazy horse. Her racetrack stall was padded, she ate twice as much as a regular filly, and she took great joy in biting innocent passersby. She dumped exercise riders as a matter of course, ran into a horse once, and even broke loose in the Belmont paddock before winning a grade I.

Yet her antics, combined with her winning spirit, endeared her to the public. The fact that the flamboyant New Yorker Robert Perez owned her only added to the appeal. He bred the leggy filly and raced her in partnership.

Perez bought her dam, Lady Abla, in Argentina for about $35,000 and won a stakes with her a few days later. He shipped her to the United States, where she ran against the champion Proud Delta, finishing seventh in the grade I Top Flight Handicap. While training toward her next start, she fractured her left front ankle, and Perez retained her for breeding.

While Lady Abla would always carry a pronounced limp, she also carried eleven foals. Cupecoy's Joy, by far, was the best. The bay Northerly filly, with refined features and a long blaze, was born and raised at Leeward Farm in New York. Farm owner Anne Lise Coleman remembered Lady Abla giving birth in a paddock the morning of June 8, 1979.

"She had a perfectly normal, healthy filly that literally landed running," she told *The Blood-Horse*. "The only remarkable thing we noticed was that the filly had a certain sparkle. It's hard to define, but that's the only way you can put it."

Although Cupecoy's Joy raced at two, it was at three she became a celebrity. After finishing third in the Spiral Stakes against males, her owners sent her to the Kentucky Derby. At 8.90-1 as part of the mutuel field, she led for more than a mile but faded to tenth.

The filly then headed to Pimlico. By then, reporters were beginning to take notice, not so much for the filly's racing ability (they would notice that soon enough) but her temperament. She was tough to gallop — a real handful — and she was fun to watch.

Perez, reportedly unhappy about the lack of seats provided him for the Preakness, scratched Cupecoy's Joy the morning of the race and took her back to New York. Two days later she lost the seven-furlong Albany Handicap for state-breds by a neck to a colt.

Five days after that she headed postward for the one-mile Acorn Stakes against some of 1982's finest fillies, including Broom Dance, Nancy Huang, Christmas Past, and Before Dawn. Cupecoy's Joy grabbed the early lead and won by 2¾ lengths. Her time, 1:34⅕, broke Ruffian's stakes record.

"Best filly in the country," Perez declared. And to show that a New York-bred in open company was nothing to laugh at, he had a blanket made for his grade I winner that read: "Yes, I am a New York-bred."

The Blood-Horse's "What's Going On Here" column soon sang Cupecoy's Joy's praises and summarized what happened next:

"She is in the first crop by a well-bred stallion that stood for $4,000 and was sold to Japan … She is out of a mare that broke down on the race track, and has an Argentine pedigree full of names nobody knows anything about …

"And she is indestructible. Could fall down into a cistern and come up with a mouthful of hay … She slipped her bridle in the paddock just before the Mother Goose, had three or four men hanging on her neck trying to keep her from running off, a hassle that would finish your ordinary filly; but she went right on, won as calmly as you please.

"Then on Tuesday before the CCA Oaks, she flipped her rider in the morning and galloped around the barn area for a while. Two mornings after that she ran smack-dab into another horse on the race track, and came out with only minor cuts above a knee.

"For all that, she broke from the gate running in the CCA Oaks, went the first mile in 1:36⅕, which was a full second faster than her pace in the Kentucky Derby; and she still was right there after 1¼ miles in 2:02⅕, a tick faster than Gato Del Sol's winning time in the Derby. In finishing second at 1½ miles … well, she can sprint, she can stay, and volcanic eruption will not rattle her. She has to be one of the gamest fillies of all time."

Perez entertained some tempting offers for his darling during her Triple Crown run, including one for $3 million, he said. But he held on to her.

Cupecoy's Joy raced only three more times. She ran last in the grade II Sheepshead Bay Handicap after kicking herself during the race and damaging tendons in her left front leg. Minor surgery was required. She attempted a

Cupecoy's Joy with her 2003 Senor Speedy colt

comeback but ran a well-beaten ninth in the grade II Meadowlands Cup behind such top handicap males as Mehmet and John Henry. In her career finale, a minor stakes against females, she ran sixth. It was her fourteenth start at age three. She retired with twenty-two starts, six wins, seven seconds, four thirds, and earnings of $377,960.

For her second career, Perez paired his star with some impressive leading men, including Liloy, Alydar, Criminal Type, and Capote. Yet the resulting foals, some of which won, were no Cupecoy's Joy. In 1995 Perez sent her to his own stallion, Senor Speedy. They partnered five times. Only one of their foals won, and he proved to be Cupecoy's Joy's best. Sicilian Boy earned $140,172 and placed in the state-bred Kingston Stakes.

In 2003 I visited Cupecoy's Joy, then twenty-four, on a sweltering July day at Perez' Haras Lucy Grace near Otisville, New York. The years had not been overly kind to her, or, as likely as not, she had not been kind to them. While she tended lovingly to her foal, a sweet chestnut colt with a large blaze, Cupecoy's Joy appeared tired.

Yet there was no mistaking that famous blazed face. She had attained an unmistakable aura of aged beauty, and she would always be a queen in my eyes. In describing her, farm manager Jaime F. Martin said: "She's very nice with a baby, but she's hard to catch without one. She's very independent. But you don't want a horse that just follows you around."

e⁄ɔ

The once flighty, entertaining Cupecoy's Joy died the next year and was buried on the farm, and her adorable 2003 colt was never named. Perez soon reduced his involvement in racing, and a major dispersal of his horses took place at Timonium in February 2005. Among the offerings were Cupecoy's Joy's half sister Cupe Sister, her daughter Cupid's Joy, and a granddaughter, Million Bundle. None met their $1,000 reserve. Another daughter, Speedy Lucia, sold for $1,000. Several that did not meet the reserve were supposedly given to a 4-H riding program.

Perhaps Cupecoy's Joy was a shooting star — blazing, and then burning out without leaving a noticeable trace. But, oh, how brilliantly she burned.

D'Accord
and the Mares of Akindale Farm

The story of D'Accord and the aging mares at Akindale Farm reflects the story of John Hettinger, the farm's owner. The horses can rest assured that they will live out their days at the New York farm, that they will never know the terror associated with death by slaughter.

Why?

"Because I am a responsible human being," Hettinger said. "I do not buy the hypocritical, self-serving arguments that have been offered in favor of slaughter. I think they're all very transparent, and I think that they all foster irresponsibility in our industry."

After thirty-four years in the horse business, Hettinger is leading the movement to ban horse slaughter in this country. He came to his activism from a position of influence as, among other titles and distinctions, majority stockholder with family members of Fasig-Tipton Co., chairman emeritus of the Grayson-Jockey Club Research Foundation, and recipient of a Special Eclipse Award in 2000.

He led the drive for auction companies to raise minimum bids to $1,000, placing horses out of reach of the "killer buyers." In conjunction with Fasig-Tipton, he founded Blue Horse Charities, which subsidizes groups that find homes for horses as an alternative to slaughter. Also, he offers a guarantee with all the homebred horses that he sells. If the owner doesn't want them, then Hettinger will pay twice the "killer price" and pick them up the day he receives the phone call, at no expense to the owner.

CHAMPION OF THE FARM

D'Accord has resided at Hettinger's farm in Pawling, New York, for about two decades now, with brief stints elsewhere. The strapping, dark bay stallion, by the immortal Secretariat and out of champion Fanfreluche, was bred by Mr. and Mrs. Bertram Firestone in Virginia. His full brother, Medaille d'Or, and half siblings L'Enjoleur and La Voyageuse were Canadian champions. His half sister Grand Luxe was a multiple stakes winner.

D'Accord won five of ten starts, including Keeneland's grade II Breeders' Futurity. When Hettinger heard he was retiring, he contacted the Firestones about standing the horse in New York. D'Accord was soon on his way to Akindale.

"His three first runners were winners," said farm manager Kate Feron. "I remember we were so excited. He was just the champion of the farm. He could do no wrong."

La Belle Fleur (1977 b. m. by Vaguely Noble—Princess Ribot, by Ribot), left, with Move It Now (1977 b. m. by Timeless Moment—Warfingers, by Warfare)

D'Accord (1979 dk. b/br. h. by Secretariat—Fanfreluche, by Northern Dancer)

My Sika (1978 dk. b/br. m. by True Knight—Warfingers, by Warfare)

He did little wrong for years, producing quality runners despite limited opportunities. D'Accord's average earnings index of 1.67 and comparative index of 1.6 mean he not only produced runners that earned more than the national average but also "moved his mares up." Their offspring with him were better than with other stallions.

"Every graded stakes winner I ever bred was by him," Hettinger said. "And if he'd ever gotten a mare worth more than $15,000 in New York, you might have to rewrite the history of racing."

For Hettinger, D'Accord sired three crackerjack fillies: multiple grade II winner Lady D'Accord, who earned $590,138; grade II winner Warfie, who earned $418,490; and grade II winner Yestday's Kisses, who earned $229,614.

D'Accord produced other excellent stakes winners, too. Montreal Red won the grade I Futurity and two other graded stakes. D'Accord's leading earner was North East Bound, who won ten stakes and earned $1,363,228. Unfortunately, the same year that North East Bound began winning stakes D'Accord was pensioned because of declining fertility. His final crop, in 1999, consisted of one foal.

Eight years later D'Accord is still champion. Kate Feron and Karin Mil-

Three Hour Lark (1982 dk. b/br. m. by Super Concorde—Pink Lark-spur, by Vertex)

lard, who have both worked at Akindale for some twenty years, care for him. For thrills he sticks out his tongue at them — literally — in hopes that they'll amuse him by tugging on it.

When I visited in 2005, Kate and Karen led D'Accord into his snow-laden paddock and turned him loose. From the tip of his flared nostrils to the end of his raised tail, he was grand. He charged cheerily from Kate to Karin, and then from Karin to Kate, skidding just shy of them, scattering the snow and then dipping his nose toward them in greeting.

"D'Accord is just a big kid," Kate said. "He would never hurt anybody because he was being mean. He might bowl you over because he's big, and strong, and pushy, but he doesn't really have any mean bones in his body.

"One time, a yearling got loose over by the stallion barn with the shank hanging. So of course, you know, when they have the shank they go running for their lives. He came running down, and he jumped right into the field with D'Accord. That was the 'big' yearling, of course, and the old retired stallion could potentially kill him.

"He ran around the field a little bit, then he ran up to D'Accord. I think he thought D'Accord was going to comfort him. D'Accord didn't hurt him, didn't bite him, didn't do anything. He just arched his neck and sniffed him a bit. But we caught him, as D'Accord had [the yearling] stopped close to the gate. He knew he was just a little horse and wasn't competition."

THE MARES

In another paddock not far from D'Accord's, geriatric mares roam in contented bliss. The roster is continually changing as pensioned mares die and others arrive. Many have intimate connections to D'Accord.

Move It Now (1977), is best known for having been left behind the starting gate before the 1980 DeWitt Clinton Stakes at Saratoga. The starter pressed the button before Move It Now, at 5-2, was loaded. Racing officials tried to rectify the error by writing another stakes with identical conditions, but as she trained for the race, Move It Now was injured and retired.

Hettinger bred Move It Now but sold her before her racing career for about $36,000. In 1989 he bought her back at auction for $40,000. Four matings with D'Accord produced three foals. All were winners, including the stakes-placed Movin Along. The least any earned was slightly more than $70,000.

"Move It Now is a cribber. She's like a chronic smoker," Kate said of the thirty-year-old. "Now, she's mellow, but she wasn't always like that.

"Move It Now always had the tastiest tail. She never had one because her kids were always chewing it off. Whenever she'd get excited and she'd run away, you know how they throw it up in air? It would be like one of those French hats … She's so chunky, and very cute. She's a fun mare."

One more cute touch: In her old age she has learned to straddle her waterer in order to scratch her belly.

La Belle Fleur (1977) was beautifully bred, by Vaguely Noble and out of Princess Ribot. Hettinger bought her for $200,000 when she was four. He bred her to D'Accord twice, but one foal was born dead, and the other raced but died at four. Bred to Sir Ivor, however, La Belle Fleur produced the multiple stakes winner Chase the Dream.

"La Belle Fleur was a goofy, goofy mare, as goofy as they come," Kate said. "She was the kind of horse who would pull a piece of paper off a feed bag. That piece of paper would then be in her mouth, and it would be white and flapping, and she would then have a heart attack and take off."

Avichi (1978) was a mellow, kind broodmare who loved her babies. She was New York Broodmare of the Year in 1992.

Avichi and D'Accord produced Lady D'Accord. When Lady D'Accord was young, she got hurt in a field and couldn't be sold. Hettinger kept her, and she thanked him by winning two grade IIs and earning nearly $600,000. She's still an active broodmare at Akindale.

Avichi's other matings with D'Accord were not successful, but with Turkoman she produced the popular graded stakes winner Missymooiloveyou.

Three Hour Lark (1982), by Super Concorde, was named for the time it took the Concorde to fly from New York to England. She's a sweet mare, both stakes placed and a stakes producer.

"She's the kind you don't ever worry about," Kate said. "She's not the one who's going to run you over; she's not the one trying to beat up the other horses; she's not low enough on the totem pole that she can't survive. She's just the perfect horse.

"She has two daughters who are really similar to her, Three Pack and She La Rose, and we still have those two mares."

My Sika (1978) was one of Kate's favorites.

"She was another goof-bag and a half," Kate said. "She was Move It Now's [half] sister. P.G. Johnson trained her, and they actually thought she was better than Move It Now. But she was so neurotic that when she was at her first

Left to right: Sugar Gold (1980 dk. b/br. m. by Mr. Prospector—Miss Ironside, by Iron Ruler); Yestday's Kisses (1986 ch. m. by D'Accord—Rollrights [GB], by Ragstone [GB]); Avichi (1978 b. m. by Damascus—Court Circuit, by Royal Vale)

race at Aqueduct, in the middle of winter, the sweat was pouring off her. She was a nervous wreck. That was the end of her racing career.

"She would try to foal in secret. She would always wait until everyone was gone. One time I hid the pickup truck in the barn and watched her from the window, and I caught her at the point of no return. She didn't want to van, either. She'd do that cross-legged thing. You take like a little curve, and she'd act like you were speeding around a hairpin. She was just a kooky girl."

My Sika produced her best foal after a mating with D'Accord. Their daughter, Warfie, won the grade II Long Island Handicap.

Sugar Gold (1980), a kind mare, eventually went blind, and her final four foals wore bells around their necks so she'd know where they were. When she was pensioned, farm workers placed a bell around another old mare so Sugar Gold would know she still had company.

Her best D'Accord foal was the multiple stakes-placed Memories of Linda, who earned $333,139. She also produced Hettinger's graded stakes winner Prospector's Flag, who lives on the farm; Kechi, a fourteen-time stakes winner; and the stakes-winning Vamos Al Oro.

Avichi, La Belle Fleur, My Sika, and Sugar Gold have died. Move It Now and Three Hour Lark were recently joined in the pensioners' paddock by D'Accord's daughter, the homebred Yestday's Kisses (1986), the dam of two stakes winners.

"She can be a little grouchy," Kate said of Yestday's Kisses. "She has moments where she's a happy mare, but lots of times it's 'if I'm here and doing my own thing, please don't bother me.' "

Hettinger provides for them all — the gentle, the goofy, the grumpy, the kook. What's more, he lets the Thoroughbred Retirement Foundation use sixty-five of his acres for boarding and retraining horses. Many were rescued from slaughter at the New Holland, Pennsylvania, auction.

"There are some ninety-head that I'm feeding now. I don't expect to be feeding these horses forever. But as they transition from racehorses to horses with another useful purpose, they're here. They're not all through the Thoroughbred Retirement Foundation, although some are. We deal with anybody."

As Hettinger told *The Blood-Horse* in an interview about horse slaughter in 2006: "The horse gives his life to you. The horse is your companion for ten, fifteen years. Then you turn around and betray it. For me, this is not an animal-rights issue. It's a betrayal issue. Horses have a name. How many steers have names? How many chickens have names? This is all so obvious."

Darby Dan's Queenly Quartet

History reigns at Darby Dan Farm. And not only does Darby Dan have its own storied past but so, too, did its predecessor, Idle Hour Farm. As such, it is easy to imagine that at night, when lights are dimmed and the Bluegrass countryside rests, the property's rich history comes to life.

Black Toney's memorial statue stands vigil, unblinking, as the immortal stallion strides coolly from his plot. Ribot, who once resided in a stall with walls designed for his rages, gallops with his tail on high. And Darby Dan's Soaring and Golden Trail graze noiselessly, gliding through blue moonlight and diaphanous fog, alongside Idle Hour's Blossom Time and Blue Warbler.

Each has left a mark here.

And as the moon pales toward the horizon and the skies shift slowly to dawn's pastels, those immortal Thoroughbreds retreat. Modern-day Darby Dan awakens.

❧

Among Darby Dan's recent history makers are five extraordinary mares — Graceful Darby, Love You By Heart, Plenty of Grace, Tribulation, and Memories of Silver — who each won Keeneland's Queen Elizabeth II Challenge Cup. The 1⅛ mile distaff turf stakes is one of Keeneland's premier autumn events.

No other farm can boast such a royal record, and the feat is even more impressive considering the race's inaugural running was 1984.

Although I study racing history, I was unaware of that accomplishment when calling Darby Dan in December 2003. I was simply asking to see one of my favorite old race mares, the gorgeous Love You by Heart. When she won at Saratoga back in 1988, I was bowled over by the blazed-faced filly with the beautiful name.

While asking, I decided to push my luck to see whether I might also photograph another older mare named Plenty of Grace. Yes, came the reply. Managing partner John Phillips wondered, however, might I be interested in photographing their four living Queen Elizabeth winners together: Love You by Heart, Plenty of Grace, Tribulation, and Memories of Silver? (Graceful Darby died in 2000, and her ashes were spread on the farm)

Why, yes. Yes, I would be interested. Very, very, interested.

The agreed-upon morning dawned to dark-gray, cloud-laden skies, and the chilled ground was laced with puddles from overnight drizzle. The weather forecast wasn't promising. While I would usually postpone such an important shoot, I had to fly home that afternoon, and this opportunity might not arise again. It was off to Darby Dan.

Soon, we witnessed a most extraordinary procession as four bay mares were led, willingly, from a barn behind the office. I snapped a few shots, but the photos did not match my mind's eye: Cars cluttered the background.

Phillips had carefully planned the moment. The portraits' stunning backdrop would be the famous columned mansion near the stallion cemetery. Phillips held Memories of Silver while fellow managing partner T. Wayne Sweezey handled Plenty of Grace. Farm administrator Carol Schmelz partnered with Love You by Heart, and then-broodmare manager Jennifer Shupe held Tribulation. All four mares behaved professionally and good naturedly.

Love You by Heart, then eighteen, was even grander than I had remembered. The long-bodied, classic Nijinsky II mare had certainly bulked up over the years. Her reddish-bay coat was thick, and while her stride was slightly hitched by an ankle fused long ago, she strode out comfortably. Her blazed face was instantly recognizable.

Queen Elizabeth II Challenge Cup winners Plenty of Grace, Tribulation, Memories of Silver, and Love You by Heart

Bred by Daniel Galbreath and raced by Darby Dan, Love You by Heart won the grade II Black Helen and Sheepshead Bay handicaps, the grade III Suwanee River Handicap and Nijana Stakes, and, of course, the then grade II Queen Elizabeth II Challenge Cup. She won eight of nineteen starts and earned $612,630.

She has produced one stakes winner from eleven foals, Makethemostofit, an Easy Goer filly who won the April Run Stakes. Her most recent foal, a two-year-old Aldebaran filly, sports the wonderful name Love You All.

Plenty of Grace, sixteen, was classically long bodied as well. Bred by John Galbreath and raced by Darby Dan, both her sire and dam — Roberto and Wings of Grace — exemplify Darby Dan at its best. Wings of Grace, the dam of Eclipse champion Soaring Softly, was a half sister to major producer Battle Creek Girl.

When Plenty of Grace ran in the Queen Elizabeth, she'd been racing primarily in New York and had won just two of seven starts. She went off at odds of 10.70-1 and came home a neck victor.

Over her five seasons on the track, she won five graded stakes, including the grade I Yellow Ribbon Invitational and the grade II Diana and New York handicaps and Queen Elizabeth. She earned $728,179.

While Plenty of Grace has produced no stakes winners, her daughter, Bonnie Byerly, is the dam of multiple stakes winner Diabolical.

"She's disappointed as a broodmare for us, and I could never understand it because she's absolutely conformationally gorgeous," Phillips said. "So it was probably the person who makes the mating decisions [me] that takes the blame."

The year after my visit, Plenty of Grace was sold at the Keeneland November sale for $100,000.

The next queen was the oversized Tribulation, thirteen, bred by Mr. and Mrs. J. Phillips (daughter and son-in-law of John Galbreath), A. Seelbinder, et

Love You by Heart (1985 b. m. by Nijinsky II—Queen's Paradise, by Summer Tan)

*Plenty of Grace (1987 b. m. by Roberto—Wings of Grace,
by Key to the Mint)*

al. While she was offered for sale as a yearling, she had a pronounced offset knee.
For a listed price of $35,000, she went back to Darby Dan. There she remains.

"More than any other horse we've raced, she had a characteristic that,
when you ask her to run — when you hit the quarter pole — you could
physically watch her lay her head flat and reach," Phillips said. "She length-
ened out her stride by lowering her entire frame down. She had a tremendous
explosion of power."

Yet Keeneland's bettors overlooked her when she stormed home two
lengths clear in her Queen Elizabeth. The day was cold, and Tribulation's win

*Tribulation (1990 b. m. by Danzig—Graceful Touch,
by His Majesty)*

John Phillips with Memories of Silver (1993 b. m. by Silver Hawk—All My Memories, by Little Current)

photo shows snow on the bushes. Raced by James W. Phillips and Arthur G. Seelbinder, she paid $44.80. She also won the grade III Boiling Springs and Gallorette handicaps. Winning or placing in nine of eleven races, she earned $379,300.

Her best offspring thus far was a chestnut Silver Hawk colt named Coshocton, who won Goodwood's Predominate Stakes in 2002.

Rounding out the quartet was Memories of Silver, a medium-sized bay with an attractive blazed face and happy eyes. She was bred by the Galbreath/Phillips Racing Partnership. Phillips chose to hold Memories of Silver for the photo, and his admiring glances toward the ten-year-old mare were a treat to behold.

"While they're all like your children, and you love them differently, Memories of Silver came at a very important time for my family," Phillips said. "She came on as a three-year-old and showed brilliance. My father died in early August [1996], and she went on [that month] to win those stakes races up at Saratoga [the grade III Nijana and Lake George]."

Her next start was the Queen Elizabeth. In front of an appreciative hometown crowd, the filly, owned by Joan G. and John Phillips, won in a stakes record 1:45.81. The record still stands.

"She was brilliant," Phillips said. "I always thought she was as good as they come, from a mile and an eighth to a mile and a quarter."

Overall, Memories of Silver won the grade I Queen Elizabeth II Challenge Cup and Beverly D. Stakes, and six other stakes. She earned $1,448,715. Her first two foals, British Blue and War Trace, both minor stakes winners, are now stallions.

The shoot was over in a matter of minutes, and each mare was then posed separately for a conformation photo and head shot. Each complied willingly although the skies remained dark and the lighting dismal. While the mares were certainly classic, the photos weren't.

As to the reason behind their Queen Elizabeth success, Phillips cited the farm's classic influences — the immortal Ribot, his sons His Majesty and Graustark, and Roberto. All four lie buried at Darby Dan.

On the female side, four of the winners descend from the farm's main foundation mares: three from Soaring (Graceful Darby, Plenty of Grace, and Tribulation) and one from Golden Trail (Memories of Silver).

The fifth, my beautiful Love You by Heart, a daughter of Queen's Paradise, descends from an E.R. Bradley family line. As such, her descendants grazed these lands, too.

"If one would put a label on Darby Dan mares, they almost exclusively hail from [Soaring and Golden Trail]," Phillips said. "Interestingly enough, the third [foundation mare] would probably be Queen's Paradise. But the farm, as it has transpired in the last twenty years, Soaring and Golden Trail [descendants] by far and away dominate the mares."

Five Queen Elizabeth win photographs hang side by side at the farm. And with the quintet now firmly ensconced in the farm's history — as Ribot, Soaring, Golden Trail, Roberto, and other descendants live on — Phillips looks toward the future.

"Did we start it with the intent of winning [the Queen Elizabeth]? No. The pedigrees started that process," Phillips said. "But after you win that race three or four times, then you begin to look at your fillies and say, 'Ah, there's my next Queen Elizabeth winner.'"

Darn That Alarm

1981–2003 GR. H. BY JIG TIME—EXTRA ALARM, BY BLAZING COUNT

D arn That Alarm was something — a model of contentment, a magnificent gray specimen, a successful and beloved stallion. When I finally met him, in March 2003, it was more than just a treat. It was an obligation. I owed him.

His eye-catching daughter, the multiple grade I winner Turnback the Alarm, provided me my first Eclipse Award for photography. Her elegant look and light-gray coat made her both an outstanding model and an inspiration. I spent days hounding her during the summer of 1992, finally capturing a memorable moment in a puddle's reflection.

The fact that her great name, or her sire's, could be my life's motto … well, that only heightened my appreciation.

Long before siring Turnback the Alarm, Darn That Alarm was a stellar racehorse for his owner, Robert Caporella, and his trainer, George Gianos. Caporella is part owner of Big C Farm in Reddick, Florida, the breeder of Darn That Alarm. Darn That Alarm's sire, the gray Jig Time, was a house stallion.

Three years before Darn That Alarm's birth, his dam Extra Alarm, also gray, produced a Jig Time colt named Jiggs Alarm. He raced four years, winning ten of fifty-three starts, including the Spectacular Bid Stakes, and earned $245,223.

Two years after delivering Darn That Alarm, Extra Alarm produced a Jig Time stakes winner named Strong Performance, who earned more than $250,000 and won the grade II Tropical Park Derby.

Darn That Alarm proved the best offspring from the Extra Alarm–Jig Time cross. That he remained in the Caporella family throughout his racing career was not due to a grand master plan. It was more a stroke of good fortune — the good fortune of running through a fence.

"The only reason we kept Darn That Alarm," Nick Gianos, Big C manager in 1984, told *The Blood-Horse*, "is they wouldn't accept him for the preferred sale [of two-year-olds at Hialeah] because his left hind is deformed. He and a dozen other yearlings got chased into the fence on the farm. The leg blew up like a balloon. It's still deformed."

Darn That Alarm's career began simply enough. The two-year-old finished third and second in his first two starts. In his third, in June, he was odds-on in a maiden event when "fortune" struck again.

"It was pouring down rain," Gianos said, "and he was never good in the gate when he was a baby … He got halfway in, reared up and spun around, dropped the jock, and took off running down the chute [the wrong way].

"When he got to the end of it he never broke stride, just crashed right through the fence and fractured both knees. He still managed to run back to the barn, on the macadam. It's a wonder he didn't fall and hurt himself even worse."

Darn That Alarm underwent surgery the following day. By late December, the resilient two-year-old again headed postward. Two starts later he broke his maiden, and on March 17, 1984, at odds of 39-1, he led from start to finish in the grade II Fountain of Youth Stakes. Among the vanquished were Swale and Carr de Naskra.

While that race turned out to be his biggest win, Darn That Alarm raced successfully through the age of six. He won the Weston Handicap at his home base, Calder, and the Miami Lakes Stakes at Hialeah. He placed second or third in thirteen other stakes, including runner-up finishes in the grade I Dwyer Stakes and Widener Handicap. All told, he won or placed in twenty-nine of forty-two starts and earned $415,456. With those im-

pressive numbers behind him, Darn That Alarm headed to stud for the 1988 season.

He originally stood at the Caporella family's Big C Farm, and it was there that he accomplished the remarkable task of siring two grade I winners in his first crop: Turnback the Alarm and Pistols and Roses. Turnback the Alarm won five grade Is: Coaching Club American Oaks, Mother Goose and Go for Wand stakes, and the Shuvee and Hempstead handicaps. Pistols and Roses won two runnings of the grade I Donn Handicap.

Darn That Alarm moved to Meadowbrook of Ocala Jockey Club for 1992, and while he continued siring successful horses, he never again sired a grade I winner. Next on his honor roll are two grade II winners: Foil, a lovely gray filly who earned nearly $500,000, and Darn Tipalarm, a popular steeplechaser.

It was at Meadowbrook that I finally met Darn That Alarm. He was twenty-two — and more wonderful than I could have imagined.

When I arrived at the barn, I peered from stall to stall while awaiting assistance. The structure was state-of-the-art stone and metal boasting a beautiful, world-class design. The stalls were airy and the place immaculate.

It was easy to pick Darn That Alarm out amidst the bays, dark bays, and chestnuts. He was tremendous — thick, near-white, with an eye that, even in his stall, drew you in. He stepped to the front and viewed me with interest. When farm manager Pete Cox brought him outside, he was downright joyous at having the chance to strut.

Darn That Alarm and Pete were obviously buddies, and the stallion minded his gentleman's every request. He circled once, then again, and again. Each time, he pushed a bit more to see what Pete would allow. Darn That Alarm arched his massive gray neck, and his wavy, gold-traced tail flicked. He tossed his head and asked for a bit more shank, then danced a bit higher. His chest swelled as he lowered his head.

Pete did not speak aloud to the horse — his hands spoke through the shank. Darn That Alarm knew when not to push any further. When Pete requested that

the stallion stand for portraits in the yard in front of the barn, Darn That Alarm became a statue.

Perhaps Darn That Alarm's back dipped a bit, but he was stunning — the ageless look that inspires legend. No signs of his old injuries were apparent — his broken knees or deformed hind leg. Had he only sported the appropriate brands, he could have passed for a Lipizzaner.

Darn That Alarm was heading to his paddock after the shoot, so I followed Pete and his happy charge. The aging stallion waited patiently for his release, and once free, he jogged with purpose to the far end of the paddock. There, he stopped and coolly considered a nearby stallion.

Pete called to him. Darn That Alarm looked back, tossed up his tail, and jogged dutifully across the paddock to Pete. He waited to see what was requested next. It's a rare stallion that trusts his keeper enough to risk his precious paddock time.

Pete petted him and then let him alone, and Darn That Alarm settled in, contentedly, to graze. Life was good for the old boy. The farm was idyllic as stallions grazed noiselessly in their respective emerald paddocks..

Two months later, however, tragedy struck, when Meadowbrook's showpiece barn caught fire in the late afternoon of May 6, 2003. The nine stallions were all inside. Several people noticed the blaze — six passersby and a farm employee — and tried to free the horses.

Four were saved, but the other five — Faygo, Reality Road, Star of Valor, Traitor, and Darn That Alarm — perished. While no official cause was found, the fire was ruled accidental. Darn That Alarm and Faygo, another Big C Farm homebred, were shipped back to the Caporellas' farm for burial.

With the fire grabbing the headlines, none of the five individual stallions got much coverage. In a few obituaries Darn That Alarm was called the "veteran" or "popular" sire. The *New York Times* described him as "a sire to 11 stakes winners," but most just mentioned his name.

But he was so much more than that. He was really something.

Dear Birdie

1987 CH. M. BY STORM BIRD — HUSH DEAR, BY SILENT SCREEN

Marylou Whitney had every right to be giddy in the 2003 Kentucky Oaks winner's circle. Her homebred filly Bird Town was draped in lilies after drawing away to a 3¼-length victory.

Marylou, all smiles, was impeccably fitted in a classic subtle-peach outfit. Topping off her regal look was a large button, colored in the Whitney Eton blue and brown, that read: *Bird Town.*

Although Marylou had stood in countless winner's circles, this was the first grade I victory for Marylou Whitney Stables. In just over a year's time Bird Town and her younger half brother Birdstone would add four more grade Is to the Whitney legacy.

And it all resulted from Marylou's passion for the sport, her belief in the Whitney bloodlines, and a mare named Dear Birdie.

When Marylou married Cornelius Vanderbilt (C.V.) Whitney in 1958, she married into one of racing's longest-lasting — and most successful — families.

C.V.'s grandfather William Collins (W.C.) Whitney launched the dynasty just before the turn of the century and by 1901 led the nation in earnings. He repeated as leading owner two years later. His carefully planned bloodstock purchases laid the foundation for generations of Whitneys.

When W.C. died in 1904, his son Harry Payne (H.P.) carried on. Between 1913 and 1930, H.P. led the nation in earnings six times, and he was eight times leading breeder. He won the Kentucky Derby with Regret and Whiskery. In 1914 he purchased about one thousand acres in Lexington and named it the Whitney Farm. Whitney horses still graze on that land.

C.V. "Sonny" Whitney took over when H.P., his father, died in 1930. C.V. topped the nation's owner standings from 1930 through 1933 and

again in 1960. By then, Marie Louise (Marylou) Hosford had made her stage entrance.

Marylou was hosting a television cooking show when she met C.V., but she dreamed of being a famous actress. They fell in love during the making of *Missouri Traveler,* a film C.V. produced featuring Marylou, Gary Merrill, and Lee Marvin. Hers was more than a beauty born of flowing golden hair and lively blue eyes. Marylou had an extraordinary zest for life. She was born to be special.

While cheering her husband's color bearers home, she evolved into the role of socialite extraordinaire, hosting famous Kentucky Derby and Whitney Handicap parties. She embraced the public and played up to the media. She donated millions of dollars to various charities and worthy causes.

Although a Kentucky Derby victory eluded C.V., his horses won two Belmont Stakes, four Kentucky Oaks, and such historic races as the Jockey Club Gold Cup, Travers Stakes, and Whitney Handicap.

C.V. occasionally named horses for Marylou, including Honey Dear, who was born in 1958, the year they married. He named Honey Dear's daughter, You All, for the colloquialism Marylou and her children picked up whenever they visited Kentucky.

C.V. had particular fun with You All's 1978 foal. When he thought Marylou was being a bit too chatty, he would occasionally tell her to shut up. She thought that wasn't very nice and asked him to say something else. The result: Hush Dear (by Silent Screen).

The lovely distaffer — an unusually long-faced chestnut with a thin stripe down her face — won two runnings of the grade II Diana and Long Island handicaps as well as the grade II Tidal Handicap against males. She won eleven races and earned $428,458 before retiring to the Whitney Farm in 1983. She did not remain there long.

The next year C.V., at age eighty-five, citing a lack of time and energy, announced he was leaving racing. Since he did not consider racing an appropriate sport for women, he transferred the Whitney colors to a nephew, Leverett Miller, and dispersed his horses at a successful Keeneland November sale. The highest priced Whitney mare was Hush Dear, who sold to Echo Valley Farm for $1.15 million. In 1987, Hush Dear produced a Storm Bird filly for Echo Valley named Dear Birdie.

C.V. Whitney died December 13, 1992, at ninety-three. By then Marylou, despite her husband's belief about women and racing, had become partners with Leslie Combs II in Blue Goose Stable. She eventually formed Marylou Whitney Stables, adding a brown hoop to the traditional Whitney colors, and started buying old Whitney broodmares and their descendants and bringing them home to the Whitney Farm.

Marylou noticed Dear Birdie in a sales catalog in late 1992. Dear Birdie had won only two of twenty races, but Whitney blood coursed through her veins, and that was enough for Marylou. She bought the mare before the sale for $50,000 from an old Arkansas friend, Juanita Winn. As it turned out, Dear Birdie was on a farm just down the road from Marylou's home in Kentucky.

Marylou didn't have much racing success early on, and she eventually sold off most of the Whitney Farm. Much went to the adjacent Gainesway Farm, where she still boards her broodmares. In 1997 she married John Hendrickson.

William T. Young, longtime friend of Marylou and respected owner of Overbrook Farm, later told *Keeneland* magazine: "Before Marylou married John, she got very discouraged with her horses. She was thinking about selling them."

John was a former chief aide to Alaska Governor Wally Hickel. Sagacious with an engaging sense of humor and keen business sense, John saw how much Marylou loved racing. They set their minds — and resources — on rebuilding a stable worthy of the Whitney name.

Dear Birdie's offspring weren't performing that well at the track, and many people advised Marylou to give up on her. Rather than sell her, Marylou gave

her to Miller in 2001. Before parting with Dear Birdie, however, Marylou bred her to Cape Town in 1999 and Grindstone in 2000. Marylou couldn't know that the resulting foals, Bird Town and Birdstone, would restore glory to the Whitney stable.

After Dear Birdie's 1998 daughter, Mountain Bird, finished second in the grade II Beaumont Stakes, Marylou decided to give Dear Birdie another chance. She soon bought her back from Miller, in foal to Silver Charm, for $60,000.

And so it came to be that, about six months later, on May 2, 2003, Marylou beamed with Bird Town in the Kentucky Oaks winner's circle. Before a crowd of 100,523, her homebred Dear Birdie filly had set a stakes record (1:48.64) and paid $38.40 to win.

Bird Town added the grade I Acorn Stakes the following month.

And on October 4 at Belmont Park, a scene played out reminiscent of a time when Whitney runners so often powered down that long homestretch and strode into the winner's circle. On that day, Bird Town ran second in the grade I Beldame Stakes and handed the Whitney torch to her younger half brother Birdstone, who authoritatively won the grade I Champagne Stakes.

Bird Town earned 2003 champion three-year-old filly honors and entered the Whitney broodmare band. The next year Birdstone, a small but determined bay colt, spoiled Smarty Jones' Triple Crown bid by capturing the Belmont Stakes at 36-1 odds.

After the race an ecstatic Marylou declared: "I've been in the winner's circle many times with my late husband, but this is not the same. This means so much to me because it's a homebred. You know how much I love Dear Birdie and all my horses."

Birdstone added the Travers Stakes, and Dear Birdie was soon crowned Kentucky Broodmare of the Year. All eleven of her foals to race are winners.

In 2006, the two-time grade I producer gave Marylou and John quite a scare. That year, the birth of her Unbridled's Song filly caused a tear deep in Dear Birdie's rectum, and by the time it was detected, she was in grave condition. Veterinarian Michael Spirito felt she had a 5 percent chance of survival and that "she was more dead than alive" during the subsequent long, difficult

surgery. Yet Dear Birdie bucked the odds and has recovered very well. She was not bred in 2006 but has been bred to A.P. Indy this season.

Like her dam, Dear Birdie is an unusually long-faced chestnut with large ears and a stripe down her face. Her nose is finely tapered, and she holds her head high. Small white spots dot her red coat. A powerful hind end accentuates her sturdy build.

She is strong-willed and not overly patient with frivolous things, such as our photo shoot. Gainesway farm manager Neil Howard led her into a large paddock adjacent to her barn. She could not stand still for long, and, instead, she danced, fretted, and whinnied toward friends in a nearby field. The only time she seemed pleased was at the end of our short visit as she was being led away.

Dear Birdie is one of Marylou's current band of twenty-five mares, twenty-four of which boast Whitney bloodlines.

As John Hendrickson told the press after Birdstone's Belmont, C.V. Whitney "sold all of his bloodstock, and then, when he passed away, he gave Marylou his entire fortune, and she spent half of that trying to get the stock back. She really deserves a lot of credit — all the credit."

Flying Pidgeon

1981 B. H. BY UPPER CASE—MISS MINNESOTA, BY MINNESOTA MAC

On October 13, 2006, a press release marked an era's end: "G1 SW Flying Pidgeon Retires to Old Friends in Kentucky." And so ended years of advertisements featuring the dark, long-bodied stallion peering toward the camera with that white-rimmed eye.

The ads intrigued me because Flying Pidgeon had not had many foals or overwhelming success with them. He was aging, his name seemed misspelled, and while his pedigree was classic, it was not overly fashionable. And then there was that unsettling eye.

Yet here was a horse loved on and off the track with a catchy name and a captivating story. How many horses have shopping centers named after them?

Even the way he got his name was fun. According to the book *The Names They Give Them*, his part-owner Armand Marcanthony, while attending the races, "was victimized by a flying pigeon. When he applied for the name, he inadvertently used 'Pidgeon' as he was a fan of actor Walter Pidgeon."

How the horse could fly down the homestretch. With a late charge that made him a fan favorite, Flying Pidgeon won twelve of fifty-six starts over five seasons and finished second or third twenty-two times. He won seven stakes, including the grade I Hollywood Invitational, and earned more than $1 million.

"He had a lot of arthritis in his back legs," recalled Luis Olivares, his admiring trainer. "When he came out of the stall, he looked like an eighty-year-old."

But after a couple of turns around the shed row and a jaunt to the track, Flying Pidgeon ran like the healthiest horse in the barn. Based at Calder, he won consecutive W.L. McKnight handicaps, setting a track record for 1½ miles on turf in the second one, and lost a third consecutive running by a fast-closing nose after being blocked repeatedly. He was inducted into Calder's Hall of Fame in 2000, and the track annually runs a race named in his honor.

Marcanthony, a developer, named an Ocala, Florida, shopping center after his popular horse. A statue of Flying Pidgeon in front of a wishing-well fountain stood vigil there for years.

At stud, Flying Pidgeon was initially an "easy sell." The come-from-behind turf specialist, a winner from 6½ furlongs to 1½ miles, was by Upper Case and out of a Minnesota Mac mare.

Marcanthony welcomed the dark horse with the odd eye to his Florida breeding farm in 1988 with a billboard that proclaimed: Home Of Champion Millionaire Flying Pidgeon. The stallion's first crop of twenty-seven foals included the stakes winners Flying American (earnings $374,502) and Pidgeon's Promise ($200,219). They remain his two top earners.

By 1996 Flying Pidgeon had sired four more stakes winners. Yet when Marcanthony, who owned 50 percent of the stallion, died that year, Flying Pidgeon's future was uncertain.

Enter Jane White, a syndicate member and Pennsylvania schoolteacher whose husband, Don, trains at Philadelphia Park. She put together a new syndicate and relocated Flying Pidgeon to Pennsylvania in late 1997. She had bred her mare to him early on, and he had given her two winners.

"I liked the idea of breeding my one and only mare, void of black type in five generations, to a millionaire," White said.

She came to love him. She put those ads — the ones with that compelling conformation photograph — in *The Maryland Horse* and *Mid-Atlantic Thoroughbred* even as Flying Pidgeon's stud career waned.

Through advertising, e-mails, and phone calls, White continued to promote the horse she so believed in. Flying Pidgeon continued to sire winners.

Flying Pidgeon with Maui Meadow Farm's Erika Lyman

And breeders, most of whom were not syndicate members, continued to send mares his way. After Jane took over, there was only one season in which his foal crop numbered less than ten. By 2003, however, the syndicate was down to four members. White carried on.

Flying Pidgeon's offspring began excelling in another arena — the jumper ring. By then, however, his career was nearing its end.

I visited Flying Pidgeon in 2005 at Maui Meadow Farm in Pennsylvania on a day when the wind was bitter cold and smelled of snow. Pidgeon was twenty-four with a slight dip to his back and a dark coat of thick fur. He strode out gingerly, yet, after warming up, he jogged around the pad-dock in kingly fashion. As the snow began to fall, I photographed that familiar white-rimmed eye, now more soulful than unsettling, through swirling flakes.

White moved Flying Pidgeon to New Jersey for the 2006 breeding season, but none of the mares he bred got in foal. That fall White sent out the press release: Flying Pidgeon was on the move again, this time to Old Friends, the farm in Kentucky for equine senior citizens.

"It has been a 10 year honor, privilege, and labor of love promoting this wonderful horse," White wrote. "I thank every one of you who has shown an interest in him over the years."

Forever Silver

1985–2005 GR. H. BY SILVER BUCK—DISABLED MAID, BY CORRELATION

The silver stallion danced from the barn as the winter's breeze caught his wild mane. Snow crunched beneath balletic hooves, and sunlight bounced from taut muscles. Despite the sun's warm tone, his coat reflected cool shades of blue, gray, silver, and white. His long, silver foretop billowed about his beautifully dished face and obscured his dark eyes.

While his papers said "Thoroughbred," the astonishingly beautiful Forever Silver was, visually, a Lipizzaner or an Andalusian. He was as magnificent a horse as I've ever photographed. On that cold December afternoon, his lively disposition belied the fact that he would die the following day.

He was one of my favorites.

Forever Silver was foaled in Florida on May 28, 1985. He had the misfortune of being born during the reign of a true New York star. Easy Goer defeated Forever Silver in the 1989 Suburban, Whitney, Jockey Club Gold Cup, and Woodward. Yet, when avoiding the three-year-old sensation, Forever Silver won three stakes that year: the grade I Brooklyn and grade II Excelsior and Nassau County handicaps. He earned slightly more than $1 million and was Silver Buck's second leading earner.

He entered stud in 1991 at Highcliff Farm in upstate New York with an exceptional race record and a fairly strong female line. Yet his sire, Silver Buck, was years away from siring the horse who would immortalize him: Silver Charm.

Forever Silver's largest foal crop — by far — numbered twenty-seven. He did not sire a stakes winner until 1996, and that horse, Nu Rival, didn't exactly send mare owners scrambling to sign contracts when he won the 2000 Thomas F. Moran Stakes at Suffolk Downs.

Still, as a regular Highcliff visitor, I was smitten with the gray beauty, and I photographed him often.

In 1996, after a snowfall, I took his picture for a Christmas card. He galloped around his paddock and then stood perfectly between two wreaths hanging on a barn wall. His shimmering coat still held rich dapples and dark points. By the time I photographed him in 1999, the dapples were muted.

In October 2002, Forever Silver was sent to the State University of New York at Cobleskill as a stallion in the school's animal science program. That year his best foal — his second stakes winner — was born. Named Carlow, she won several stakes, including the New York Oaks, and had earned $287,469 through May 2007. Forever Silver didn't impregnate any mares at Cobleskill, and his final foals — a crop of two — arrived in 2003.

By April 2003 Forever Silver had made his way from Cobleskill to the Cornell University Equine Park. I tracked him down there in late 2005, only to learn he was about to be euthanized due to a leg infirmity. Through the kindness of Carol Collyer, the park's director of equine services, I drove to Ithaca, New York, on December 7, 2005, to see my old friend one last time.

Forever Silver glowed in a dark but roomy stall in a converted dairy barn. He was eager to do something, and when he saw a horse far down the row he let out a stallion scream and bounced against the door. He tossed his head and postured, unaware that the animal was a gelding. Forever Silver certainly never lost his libido.

But, despite his exuberance, he was no longer breeding. He was a research animal now, and his semen was collected regularly. The staff collected through chemical ejaculation, which was painless and could be performed as he rested. Therefore, Forever Silver would not injure himself by

becoming overly stimulated.

A Cornell staff member explained: "During his stay at Cornell, Forever Silver's semen was used for cutting-edge research on sperm capacitation; that is, the molecular changes that sperm must undergo to fertilize a mare's egg. His contribution helped greatly in advancing our knowledge on basic sperm physiology, which might ultimately lead to better understanding subfertility in stallions and to the success of in vitro fertilization in the horse."

Despite his infirmity, Forever Silver literally bounced from the barn when he was led outside for photos. He clearly relished the crisp air and its promising scents, and although he was twenty, he shook with power while grudgingly obeying the man at the end of the lead shank.

A bright red bandage shrouded his left hind leg, his ankle swollen with tissue damage and severe arthritis of the fetlock. He rested with his leg cocked. The red cloth contrasted sharply with his silver-white body as he soaked in his last sunlight and snow. The following day, he would be euthanized and used for further research.

After the shoot Forever Silver powered his way back into the barn. Once in his stall, he again pushed at the door and peered down the row hopefully. I offered him carrots, and he quickly swept them away. Yet I was an afterthought to him. I took a few last photos. He barely noticed my leaving.

On my drive home that night, snow squalls and dark, barren roads amplified the emptiness. The sun-splashed day and the magnificent silver stallion seemed an illusion.

Franks' Friends

Dave's Friend & Grand Espoir Blanc

John Franks owned thousands of horses and won four Eclipse Awards as outstanding owner. Yet he wrote this about Dave's Friend: "He's the greatest and most dominant horse I've ever owned," underlining "dominant" for emphasis.

Franks purchased Dave when the gelding was six and campaigned him through age eleven. Primarily a sprinter, Dave won seventeen stakes and thirty-five of seventy-six starts in a nine-year campaign. He set or equaled six track records.

Dave earned $1,079,915 during his racing career and was crowned Maryland's champion three-year-old, champion older horse, and Horse of the Year. When he retired in 1986, he was the all-time leading Maryland-bred earner.

Daily Racing Form's book *Champions* included only a few modern horses that didn't win a national championship. Alydar was one. Dave was another.

If Dave was Franks' greatest horse, then certainly his most unusual was his homebred Grand Espoir Blanc. By a bay sire out of a bay mare, he was born in 1984 and became only the fifth white Thoroughbred registered by The Jockey Club and only the second male.

In his office Franks hung a photo of his white horse facing one of Dave's Friend. "I'm trying to make him pick up a little of that speed," Franks said.

It didn't work, although Grand Espoir Blanc (Great White Hope) won three of sixteen starts and earned $35,530. After retirement he was trained for dressage because he was such a beautiful mover. Yet difficulty with his eyesight — a growing sun sensitivity — eventually squelched that plan. Grand Espoir Blanc won at several levels before complications set in, said Alan Fox, his dressage trainer.

Grand Espoir Blanc's sensitivity to light made him uncomfortable and nervous in show situations. Fox tried applying black streaks beneath the horse's eyes — as human athletes do — but that wasn't allowed in dressage competition. "Whitey," as he was called, was retired for good. His last public exhibition — on longe lines — served to raise money for handicapped children. Then, he was sent back home to Franks' farm in Shreveport, Louisiana.

Franks adored his horses, and Dave's Friend and Grand Espoir Blanc grazed side by side. Franks often stopped his car on the way to work and entered their paddock, pulling peppermints, which Dave especially loved, from his pockets. After Franks died on December 31, 2003, his Ocala, Florida, farm was quickly sold, and his horses auctioned off. Dave, however, stayed on the Louisiana property.

Grand Espoir Blanc was given to one of Franks' trainers, Sherry Milligan, and the horse lived in a training barn behind Louisiana Downs. He often stayed indoors, because the sun burned his skin and irritated his eyes.

Milligan loved the aging beauty.

"I have a granddaughter who's ten, and two that are four," she said in 2005. "I've had them on him, and he was as kind as could be. They're enthralled with him, like something from a cartoon."

Dave, meanwhile, had a large paddock to himself and put on weight after the younger, fast-eating Grand Espoir Blanc left. Cows grazed in an adjacent field, and Friday, the faithful barn cat, traipsed about, but Dave was the only horse on the property.

"Dave was on social security for twenty years, and he received the best care that could be given," said Johnny Whittington, farm manager and Dave's caregiver. "However, his care was not an exception, but the rule. Mr. Franks had a big heart when it concerned the welfare of his animals."

Franks had insisted that Dave's alfalfa be free of dust because the horse suffered from Stridor disease, a constriction of the pharynx. A tracheotomy

Grand Espoir Blanc (1984 wh. g. by One for All—Erasure, by What a Pleasure)

Dave's Friend (1975 b. g. by Friend's Choice—Duc's Tina, by Duc de Fer)

in the mid-1990s helped, but Dave still sometimes labored to breathe. He held his head low as it was easier to breathe that way, and Johnny equipped the barn with fans and misters to help Dave get through the stifling Louisiana summers.

Although it retained some vision, Dave's right eye was clouded, the result of a stick piercing it during a tornado in 1999. He received senior feed, and the blacksmith and vet visited him regularly.

Before my visit in March 2005, Johnny sent a note in which he joked: "It is a challenge to make Dave look like the racehorse he once was."

That was true, of course, but thirty-year-old Dave, a willing and curious model, still looked wonderful. Johnny led him past brilliant red tulips to a scenic spot where a magnolia tree burst with pink flowers. Dave's winter coat was thick, but there was no hiding his class or solid conformation. Johnny, obviously proud of his aging friend, petted Dave often and smiled broadly.

When we finished, Johnny led Dave back to his paddock. Yellow flowers poked above the early spring grass. Dave eyed us kindly as he ambled by — perhaps hoping to hear the crinkle of a peppermint wrapper — and then

Dave's Friend with Johnny Whittington

wandered to the back of his field. As he had for two decades, he lowered his head to graze.

❧

Grand Espoir Blanc lost coordination in his hind end in late 2005, and, on December 15, 2005, he was unable to rise. He was euthanized and buried on Sherry Milligan's farm. He was twenty-one.

Dave's Friend's health deteriorated quickly during the summer of 2006. The heat made breathing difficult, and he went off his feed. Johnny made the heartbreaking decision to euthanize Franks' beloved old friend. He dug a grave on the farm at a spot that he and Franks had picked out years before.

"The spot is in the general area that we had buried other horses that were lost over the years," Johnny said. "Mr. Franks felt that Dave would like to be in close proximity to others, and it is in a location that we felt could never be utilized or tampered with."

Dave's Friend was euthanized on June 14, 2006. He was thirty-one.

Fran's Valentine

1982 DK. B/BR. M. BY SAROS (GB) — IZA VALENTINE, BY BICKER

George Strawbridge Jr. shall never forget the first time he laid eyes upon Fran's Valentine.

"It was just, 'Good God. This is what Ian Balding's talking about: The look of eagles,' " Strawbridge said. "It was the first time I'd seen that look. It was such an extraordinary, heart-stopping moment.

"I was in love with her from the first time I saw her."

Strawbridge was no novice awestruck by his first Thoroughbred. He is a universally respected horseman with countless international breeding and racing successes. He bred or owned such grade/group I winners and champions as Waya, Selkirk, Silver Fling, Tikkanen, and Treizieme.

Through his Augustin Stable, Strawbridge is the nation's all-time leading steeplechase owner. He is a founding member of the National Steeplechase Foundation and has served as president of the National Steeplechase Association. His father, George Strawbridge Sr., was NSA president as well.

Yet Strawbridge had never seen that look of eagles he found in Fran's Valentine in 1992. He purchased the gorgeous dark bay lady, then ten, for his broodmare band.

"She was from a bit odd family. She wasn't classically Phipps-bred," Strawbridge said. "But she was such a hard-knocking, tough, overcome-all-obstacles mare. I just admired that so much."

Fran's Valentine was a California-bred by Saros and out of the Bicker mare Iza Valentine. She was bred and raced by Earl Scheib, the renowned auto paint and body repair shop owner who boasted in national ads: "I'll paint any car any color for $29.95."

Fran's Valentine launched the inaugural Breeders' Cup with a bang. In only the second Breeders' Cup race, she powered home first in the Juvenile Fillies at 74.80-1. Unfortunately, she powered over-aggressively, slamming into a filly named Pirate's Glow. She was disqualified and placed tenth.

She remains the only Breeders' Cup winner to be disqualified.

The California-based distaffer made up for that youthful indiscretion. She won or placed in graded stakes from ages two through five and won her three grade Is as a three-year-old: Hollywood Oaks, Santa Susana Stakes, and Kentucky Oaks. She finished first in thirteen stakes (including the Breeders' Cup), won thirteen of thirty-four starts, and earned $1,375,465.

Fran's Valentine produced three foals before Strawbridge marveled at her regal beauty. Two of the three failed to win a race, and the third raced primarily in claiming company.

For Strawbridge, however, Fran's Valentine's 1993 colt, With Fascination, won the group III Prix de Cabourg and placed in two group Is. Her 1994 foal, With Fire, won or placed in twelve of sixteen races and finished third in a French group III.

And then, in 1995, Fran's Valentine produced the gray Relaunch gelding With Anticipation. Sporting Augustin Stable colors, With Anticipation raced competitively for eight seasons. As he racked up wins and his coat grew ever whiter, he became a tremendous fan favorite.

The powerful turf specialist won five grade Is: the United Nations Handicap and two runnings each of the Sword Dancer Invitational and Man o' War Stakes. He finished second in the 2002 Breeders' Cup Turf, set a course record in his United Nations win, and won or placed in thirty-two of forty-eight races. His earnings topped $2.6 million.

Fran's Valentine produced four more foals, but none approached her earlier runners. She was pensioned at her longtime home, the beautiful Derry Meet-

Fran's Valentine, left, with farm manager Bobby Goodyear and Selkirk's dam, Reiko, in September 2005

ing Farm in Cochranville, Pennsylvania, where Strawbridge boards most of his broodmares.

Founded by Strawbridge's longtime friend Marshall Jenney, Derry Meeting is a world-class facility of rolling hills and spacious paddocks. Countless top-class horses romped in those paddocks, including Storm Cat and Danzig. Both were foaled there.

When Jenney died in 2000, the farm continued under the attentive watch of his wife, Bettina, a lovely woman of quiet grace and perseverance. And when beloved farm manager Robert Goodyear succumbed in 2005, his son, Bobby, took on the position.

Fran's Valentine spends much of her time with fellow pensioners, including elderly group I winner Silver Fling and a young Clydesdale cross called Bud,

along a fence line behind Goodyear's house. After all, someone might pass by — Bobby or his wife, or a farm worker, or Mrs. Jenney on her daily walk. And those who pass might — just possibly — bring carrots.

While she doesn't particularly care to be bothered, she is tolerant of most intrusions and watches the days' events with interest.

"She's doing great," Goodyear said. "She stays to herself, but she always likes to know where everybody is."

Now twenty-five, she is exotically and uniquely beautiful with a long back and sturdy build. Her near-black coat is accentuated by a sharp blaze. The reddish tones of her sun-bleached mane and tail accentuate her captivating liquid brown eyes.

When I photographed her, I, too, was thunderstruck. Fifteen years after Strawbridge first gazed upon her, she still had that look of eagles.

Gem Twist

1979–2006 GR. G. BY GOOD TWIST — COLDLY NOBLE, BY NOBLE JAY

Gem Twist is as immortal in the jumping world as Seattle Slew and Secretariat are in racing. The Thoroughbred gelding won an unprecedented three Horse of the Year titles, earned two Olympic silver medals — both individual and team — and was crowned the "World's Best Horse."

His breeder and trainer was the celebrated equestrian Frank Chapot. In 1979 Gem Twist was born at Frank and wife Mary's Chado Farms in Neshanic Station, New Jersey. Chapot is a household name in the show-jumping world, and both Mary and Frank are enshrined in the Show Jumping Hall of Fame. Frank's riding style, according to the hall's Web site, was "a combination of electrifying speed, utter determination, and intense competitiveness." That describes Gem Twist as well.

Gem Twist's sire was Good Twist, one of Chapot's most talented mounts. Unusually determined, the small and speedy gray won twenty-one international classes. He descended from the immortal show-jumping foundation sire Bonne Nuit.

When Gem Twist was two, Chapot sold him to Michael Golden, an amateur jump-rider from nearby Chester, New Jersey. Golden had been taking lessons from Arlene Orr, an instructor who in her youth had been a student of Chapot. When Golden decided it was time to have his own jumper, they went to see Chapot.

Chapot let them take two horses back to Orr's farm in Chester for a week's tryout. Golden and Orr rode them both, and Orr recommended the gray gelding named Icey Twist. Golden bought him.

"Since he was my first horse, he was going to be my gem," Golden said. "We legally changed the name to Gem Twist [with the U.S. Equestrian

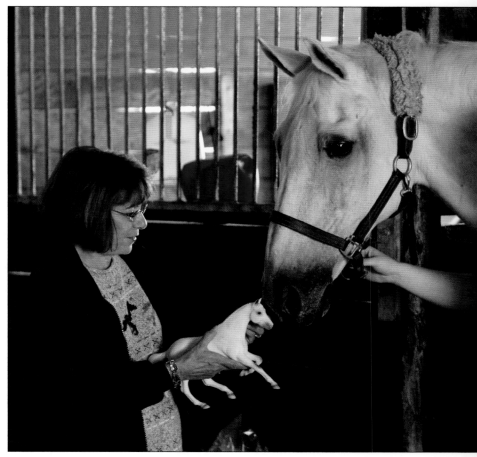

Gem Twist investigates one of two Breyer Gem Twist releases.

Team but not with The Jockey Club, which still lists him as Icey Twist]."

Golden and Orr rode Gem Twist for two years, but they realized he had extraordinary potential. Golden, who retained ownership of Gem Twist throughout his life, sent him back to Chapot for training.

"It's pure good fortune that I ended up buying, as my first horse, a young horse that turned out to be maybe the horse of the century, certainly one of the great show jumpers in the world," Golden said. "I was smart enough to recognize that I was associated with one of the greatest minds in show jumping in Frank Chapot. I have such an admiration for everything that he stands for: integrity, honesty, and protection of the athlete — in this case, the horse."

When Gem Twist was five, Chapot teamed the big gray — he stood 16.3 hands — with one of his students, the young Greg Best. By 1987, when Gem Twist was eight, the duo entered the grand-prix ranks. The powerful jumper and his handsome rider quickly won the Grand Prix of Tampa and the Grand Prix of Florida. Chosen to compete in the Pan American Games, they won a silver medal in team competition.

Best earned the title Rookie of the Year with record earnings, and Gem Twist earned his first American Grandprix Association Horse of the Year award. The next year was even better, as Best and Gem Twist won two silver medals — one individual and one team — at the Seoul Olympic Games.

To watch Gem Twist jump was to witness a restrained explosion. He flew over jumps with both joy and desire: His ears were up, eyes bright, front legs tucked perfectly beneath him. By the time he landed, Gem Twist already knew where his rider wanted him next, and he was eager to get there.

So it went for Gem Twist and Best — event after event, year after year, country after country. Not only did Americans love the showy jumper, but so, too, did the international jumping world. Foreign broadcasters nicknamed him "America's great gray." In 1989 Gem Twist earned his second Horse of the Year title, and, the next year, he was named "World's Best Horse" at the World Equestrian Games in Stockholm.

"When Gem entered a ring for any grand prix, and certainly including all of the international events, his neck would go up, his head would go up,

his chest would expand, and he would prance," Golden said. "He galloped with a style that was so demonstrative of a champion and of a very masculine-looking horse. Gem's a Thoroughbred, but he looked like anything but a Thoroughbred because of his muscular look, especially his girth and chest.

"He knew it was an important moment … And because of his color — all white — when he came into the ring, whatever was going on, people would stop … and they would all congregate to watch Gem perform."

In 1992 Gem Twist slipped approaching a fence at the American Gold Cup. Best was thrown and broke his shoulder. A new rider took over — Leslie Burr Howard — and Gem Twist didn't miss a beat. He earned a third Horse of the Year title, a feat still unmatched.

And the victories kept coming. In 1993, however, when Gem Twist suffered an infected suspensory, he headed back to Chado for recuperation.

There, he bonded with Laura Chapot, Mary and Frank's daughter. Although Laura had occasionally ridden Gem Twist during training, she had never competed on him. But when the gray star returned to the show ring in 1995, Laura was aboard. Not surprisingly, Gem Twist, carrying his third rider, continued to win. Fueled by their late-season victory in the $100,000 Autumn Classic, Laura earned Rookie of the Year honors.

The next year Laura and Gem Twist leapt past the competition in the AGA Championships — Gem Twist's third win in the prestigious event — and the Grand Prix of Florida against the largest field in show-jumping history.

But while training in 1997, Gem Twist showed an uncharacteristic lack of enthusiasm for jumping. He had competed at the top level of international competition for a decade. Chapot and Golden decided it was time to retire the eighteen-year-old superstar.

Gem Twist's retirement ceremonies spanned several months at top shows in various states. His final bow occurred November 1, 1997, at the National Horse Show at Madison Square Garden.

Gem Twist headed home. The near-white beauty was ridden regularly and fed his favorite treat — red licorice. When the Chapots headed to Palm Beach for the winter, Gem Twist eagerly climbed into the van. He wanted to remain near the action.

In September 2006 I was honored to visit Gem Twist at the farm where he was bred, foaled, raised, trained, and retired. It was a comfortably warm day, and the sun drifted in and out from behind low, heavy clouds. I drove up to the barn and stepped inside. There, in a washroom, a tremendous gray gelding stood relaxed in cross ties, while three young women provided finishing touches. Gem Twist relished the attention. Although he was twenty-seven, he was alert, curious, stately.

He had recently been laid up with a small filling in his leg, but when he was led outside his stride was unusually long and comfortable. His white tail rippled thickly, and he held his head high. He looked at his world as if he'd never seen such sights before — a passing cat, horses in a paddock, me. He had some melanomas under his tail, as many gray horses do, but he was every inch a king.

I asked Frank Chapot what made Gem Twist great.

"He hit fewer fences than all of the other horses that competed," he replied.

That seemed a humorous answer to this novice, but he continued: "From day one, he didn't like to hit jumps. There's a very delicate balance with jumpers. They have to be brave enough to go down and try, and chicken enough not to want to hit. You put too much chicken in the mixture, they don't go. You put too much bravery in the mixture, they don't care."

The mixture that created Gem Twist was just right.

Michael Golden produced two documentaries about his horse, in which some of the show world's best praised him.

Michael Matz, Hall of Fame rider: "One of the biggest attributes that a horse can have … is the test of time. That horse, from Greg Best to Laura Chapot, has been a winner. It's fun to have a horse like that, that the public can get attached to."

George Morris, Hall of Fame rider, world-renowned hunter and jumper instructor: "Gem Twist is truly the horse of the century, not only in the United States of America, but you could consider him worldwide. I don't think we'll ever have the pleasure of seeing a horse of his greatness again."

Gem Twist with Frank Chapot

Gem Twist's death on November 18, 2006, came as a shock — not because of his age, twenty-seven, but because he looked so grand just two months earlier.

Suffering from a pulled muscle and a deteriorating arthritic condition in his hind end, Gem Twist began having difficulty rising. On November 18 he could not rise, and his veterinarian, Golden, and four or five farm workers tried for several hours to get Gem Twist to his feet. When they couldn't, the decision was made to euthanize him. The immortal jumper was cremated, and his ashes divided between the Chapots and Golden.

Grenzen

1975–2004 CH. M. BY GRENFALL — MY POLY, BY CYCLOTRON

It's all in the family. That was the theme one frosty morning in December 2003 when Moyglare Stud's matriarch, Grenzen, posed with her daughters First Breeze and Touch of Truth for a family portrait. The expression "like mother, like daughter" was never more apt.

And, oh, what a dynasty Grenzen created! The strong-willed chestnut mare is the dam or second dam of four group or grade I winners.

Her first foal, Irish Edition, when coupled with the Moyglare Stud-bred stallion Be My Guest, produced 1990 Belmont Stakes winner Go and Go. Grenzen's son Twilight Agenda, a grade I winner, earned more than $2 million.

Her daughter Market Slide is perhaps the most remarkable of all, producing Melbourne Cup winner Media Puzzle and English Two Thousand Guineas victor Refuse To Bend. Another daughter, Growth Rate, is the dam of group II winner Munaaji.

As Moyglare Stud expressed in a press release upon Grenzen's passing in 2004, "Four Group or Grade One winners on three continents and two hemispheres, including two Classic winners, isn't a bad record for an $11,000 yearling purchase."

Grenzen was born in 1975. Her sire was Grenfall, a major stakes winner sporting the best of Darby Dan blood — by Graustark and out of Primonetta. She was from Grenfall's first full crop (his initial crop numbered only three foals) and would prove his highest earner. Her dam, My Poly, was a winner, yet there was little black type in Grenzen's female line to foreshadow greatness.

Grenzen did not exactly turn heads at the 1976 Keeneland fall yearling sale, where she sold for $11,000. She was a medium-sized chestnut filly with bright eyes and — despite straight hind legs — her overall look was attractive and athletic.

She turned heads soon enough, however. Racing primarily at Santa Anita Park, she won eight races and tied a track record (six furlongs in 1:07⅗). Her biggest wins were the grade II Santa Susana Stakes and Santa Monica and Santa Maria handicaps; and the grade III Las Palmas Handicap and Santa Ynez and Pasadena stakes. She finished second in the grade I Kentucky Oaks, grade II Oak Leaf Stakes, and grade III Ashland and Anoakia stakes.

When Grenzen retired, Walter Haefner, a Swiss industrialist and owner of Moyglare Stud Farm, acquired her breeding rights. Although Moyglare Stud is in County Kildare, Ireland, Grenzen was boarded at Lee Eaton's beautiful Eaton Farms in Kentucky. There, she was bred to the best. Again, she delivered.

I met Grenzen on that December morning when the grass was a carpet of frost. Pensioned since 1998, the twenty-eight-year-old mare was still well muscled and solid of build. She was not tall, yet she had a haughty air, holding her head high. A star flashed between large, blazing eyes as she pawed at the ground. She posed politely, if impatiently, for portraits. She clearly did not enjoy this intrusion.

The farm employees then brought out two of her daughters: First Breeze, a five-year-old Woodman mare, and Touch of Truth, a seven-year-old Storm Cat mare and the dam of multiple stakes winner Society Hostess. They stood together and touched noses to exchange notes on the situation, their eyes wide and manner nervous. They, too, obviously preferred being left alone.

The family resemblance was striking, as both daughters displayed similar stars, unusually bright eyes, and chestnut coats like their mother's. In addition, all three were strong willed and independent. I was taken by a sudden urge to snap a generational photo. After all, few recent broodmares in the world had produced more important female lines than Grenzen.

Grenzen, left, with daughters First Breeze, center, and Touch of Truth

The grooms readily agreed to the photo even though they seemed a bit uncomfortable with the logistics. The mares fussed, and the grooms anxiously eyed them as they brought them closer together. Then suddenly — momentarily at least — the mares decided that posing as a family would probably not hurt them. They stared my way, unmoving, as the camera clicked.

While Grenzen died the next year at age twenty-nine, her bloodlines carry on. Her female descendants make up nearly a quarter of Moyglare Stud's broodmare band.

Touch of Truth, left, with First Breeze; Grenzen, right

Highland Bud

1985 B. G. BY NORTHERN BABY — FLEUR D'OR, BY EXCLUSIVE NATIVE

Theirs was a love story.

THE INTRODUCTION

Betsy Wells first met Highland Bud when the four-year-old arrived from England in 1989. Betsy was Jonathan Sheppard's foreman and an exercise rider, a uniquely generous woman with an equally generous smile. Bud was a brilliant bay with a blaze, three white socks, a "hot" attitude, and a distinctly Northern Dancer look.

Sheppard, a Hall of Fame trainer who specialized in steeplechase horses, had a group of talented employees. A young Graham Motion worked for him, as did other now-familiar racing personalities such as Sanna Neilson Hendriks, Jonathan Smart, Tom Finn, Sherry Fenwick, and Todd Wyatt.

The staff was close-knit, and they gave each other nicknames. Betsy was "Betty," Wyatt was "Young Timer," and Motion was "Bun" — short for "Honey Bun." On occasion, Sheppard would thank Betsy for a job well done by saying, "Good job, Betty." The others picked up on it, kidding Betsy good naturedly: "Good job, Betty."

Everyone at the barn seemed to have a personal "big horse" or two. For Motion, it was Flatterer. For Finn, it was Statesmanship and Storm Cat. For Betsy, it was Highland Bud.

Bred in America, the handsome bay was sold as a yearling to Sheikh Mohammed for $47,000. He raced in England and Ireland, winning on the flat and over hurdles. Sheppard recalled that Bud was a fairly good horse but not quite top class. When he was offered in the Doncaster sale, Sheppard bought him for $170,000 for Margaret and Jesse Henley. At the time, Sheppard said, it was believed to be the highest price ever paid for a National Hunt horse at public auction.

Bud took awhile to adjust to his new surroundings.

"Betsy kind of took him under her wing and made him a special project, as she liked to do," Sheppard said. "She was a pretty smart horsewoman, and she could sense who might be the good ones."

One day during a workout in company, with Betsy aboard, Bud finally got it. He was suddenly competitive and keenly interested. That sealed it for Betsy.

"He had me snowballed after that work," she said. "I just adored him. Conformation-wise, he was a stunning horse, and he had that beautiful rich bay color and the flashy bits like Northern Baby. Plus, he was a terrific mover. To me, it was a perfect package."

Bud and Betsy led Sheppard's morning sets, with Bud's blazed face showing the way. Betsy was in love, and as she did with everyone in her life, she gave her heart completely.

She was rewarded in the 1989 Breeders' Cup Steeplechase when Bud galloped home ten lengths clear. He capped his season with a fourteen-length Colonial Cup victory, and Bud won the 1989 Eclipse Award as steeplechase champion.

Despite a series of health issues that hindered Bud for the next couple of years, he garnered a second Breeders' Cup win in 1992 — on Betsy's birthday, no less.

"There's no greater feeling than being on a horse like Bud and being able to connect with him," Betsy said. "It was very, very special to me."

The Separation

For Betsy, however, the story turned bittersweet. Despite her love for Bud, she went to work for her friend Sanna Neilson, who had left Sheppard to train on her own. Bud continued racing in 1993, finishing second to the rising star, Lonesome Glory, in the Breeders' Cup. And then, in the Colonial Cup, Bud suffered a career-ending injury.

Attempts to turn him into a show jumper and foxhunter failed as Bud's high-strung personality wouldn't allow it. The handsome bay gelding was eventually turned out at Karen and Johnny Gray's farm in Tennessee.

Meanwhile, Betsy faced challenges of her own. In 1996 she was diagnosed with breast cancer and, in 2002, ovarian cancer. Her life became a series of doctors' appointments, surgeries, and chemotherapy and radiation treatments.

The racing community rallied around her as friends organized auctions and fund-raisers, raising tens of thousands of dollars. Some even shaved their heads in support, including steeplechase jockeys Matt McCarron, Roger Horgan, Gus Brown, and Chip Miller. Trainer Jack Fisher promised Horgan that if he won aboard one of his horses, then he would shave his head, too. The horse won, and Fisher kept his word. Fisher's wife and mother-in-law, who owned the horse, also donated a percentage of the winning purse.

Through it all, Betsy remained the same selfless, generous person she had always been. The last Christmas card she would send showed her barefooted with short-cropped hair, dancing with her sister Annie, who also has had cancer, and smiling exuberantly. It read: "Live Love Dance with joy into the New Year."

And through it all, Betsy never forgot Bud. She called to check on him at his Tennessee farm, fearing every year that he would die.

The Reunion

In the spring of 2005, Betsy underwent a surgery that yielded a discouraging prognosis. Her doctor recommended that she find an attainable goal — something to aspire to. She decided she wanted to ride Bud again.

She shared her dream with dear friend Sherry Fenwick.

"At that point," Sherry said, "we became like the Fenwick Make-A-Wish Foundation."

Betsy called the Grays and asked whether they'd part with Bud, and they readily agreed. They shipped him part way, and Todd Wyatt, assistant to Tom Voss and Betsy's longtime friend, sent one of the Voss' vans to transport Bud the rest of the way. Sherry and her husband, Charlie, gave Bud a home at their idyllic Maryland farm, about a half-hour from Betsy's home in Pennsylvania. Although Betsy was in the hospital the day Bud arrived, Sherry provided a play-by-play via telephone.

As he had been sixteen years earlier when he arrived from England, the twenty-year-old Bud was wary at first. He wasn't used to being in a stall, and his eyes burned. But he soon adapted and began clamoring for his dinner like his barn mates.

Once out of the hospital, Betsy, no longer as strong as when she galloped the fiery gelding for Sheppard, tentatively climbed aboard.

"I got on Bud, and I was just like rubbery noodles," she said. "I rode him out in this little paddock. We both needed just to ride around … to get our confidence."

Eventually, they trekked into the farm's open fields and spent happy days riding with Sherry. By late summer, however, Betsy became too weak to ride. It was then that we met.

The Portrait

One sunny morning at Saratoga, I spoke with Anita Motion, wife of Graham, trainer and former Sheppard employee, and asked whether she knew any old steeplechasers who might make good stories. She related the tale of Betsy and Bud. I had long known of Betsy — of her unusual kindness and her recent struggles — due to her vast circle of friends. One of those friends, in 1992, had asked me for a photo of Bud and Betsy. They gave it to Betsy, and she, in turn, sent me one of Bud's shoes. I had not forgotten that kind gesture.

Several days later Anita called me with the news that Betsy had received a grim prognosis.

Highland Bud and Betsy, before his 1992 Breeders' Cup Steeplechase win at Belmont, and, right, at the Fenwicks' farm in September 2005

I called Betsy and asked if I could visit, and she graciously said yes. I flew down a few days later, arriving early at the farm. No one was in the barn, so I strolled down the shed row to the end stall. There, in semi-darkness, glowed Highland Bud's distinctive blaze. He shuffled forward, eyeing me with curiosity.

I eyed him back with greater curiosity. From the crown of his halter, a fake

foretop dangled comically off the side of his head. It seems Bud had recently banged his forehead and lost his foretop, gaining about twenty stitches in the process. M.J. Kierwan, a friend who worked for Jack Fisher, had fashioned a toupee from a clump of Bud's thick tail. She wanted Bud to look his best for his portrait with Betsy. M.J. and Sherry had cleaned the barn immaculately for the same reason.

Betsy arrived and wrapped her thin arms around me, treating me as if I were a long-lost friend. While her body was weak and her steps tenuous, her smile was brilliant and her voice strong. She was beautiful, with dancing eyes, manicured nails, and a flowered lavender sleeveless dress.

Sherry and Betsy's sister Corky accompanied her as Betsy's border terrier, Taylor, scampered around cheerily. First, we removed Bud's toupee. He was decidedly lively, and when Sherry put his bridle on, he tossed his head and his eyes widened. We felt the surge of power.

That didn't bode well for Betsy, whose strength was no match for him. Still, she held the reins for several minutes as Bud buffeted her about, repeatedly pushing her with his head. We replaced his bridle with a halter, and Sherry led him outdoors where he could graze. Bud lowered his head and settled in peacefully. Betsy reclaimed the lead shank, relieved that Bud had calmed down.

Eventually, Betsy and I sat down in a tack room to talk. Her words were honest and heartfelt and she offered no self-pity. Although she could no longer ride Bud, she visited regularly.

"I give him a pat and bring him some carrots," she said. "I go into the stall and give him a hug, when he's accepting. He does have a bit of an attitude, but it's OK.

"It's been a godsend to have him and to be able to ride him because riding to me is like coming home."

We passed the afternoon talking about friendships, horses, life, and cancer. She spoke of her family, including her father, who once served in the cavalry, and her mother, who died of breast cancer at age fifty-eight. She spoke about her sisters Corky, who worked with horses, and Annie, who won a Pulitzer Prize for photography.

And Betsy spoke of her mortality.

"You try to think, 'What have I done in my lifetime? Have I done enough?' And really, in the end of the day, it is all about your friends and your family. If you can leave this earth saying that people can say nice things about you … I think that's very important.

"So, I think I've accomplished a nice thing, in a quiet way, with my friends. I'm not going to be the headline news, but it is very lovely. I don't think I could ask for anything more."

The day before my visit, the Fenwicks threw a party for Betsy, one of several gatherings when her friends came to share in her spirit. Knowing of her love for Bud, they even dragged him out for a group photo.

It was happy affair, and Betsy made certain there was no sadness by keeping her spirits up. Only once did she cry. That was when Graham Motion, a.k.a. "Bun" — who was there when she first met Bud, and who was there through-out Betsy's ordeal with cancer — wrapped an arm around her and said: "Good job, Betty."

❧

Betsy died the morning of February 13, 2006, less than a year after being reunited with Bud. She was fifty-five. She was right about her passing. It was not headline news. But her spirit lives on through her countless friends.

Highland Bud will live out his days with the Fenwicks. They have a new addition at the farm — a miniature donkey they've named Highland Betty.

Irish Actress

1987 DK. B/BR. M. BY SEATTLE SONG — DIANETTE, BY THORN

Irish Actress stood nuzzling her damp, newborn baby as it swayed on rickety legs. Mama, whose face carries an unusual star, an upside-down teardrop, seemingly always produces foals with white on their faces. This foal was no exception — a bay filly with a star.

She was Irish Actress' tenth registered foal, and the twenty-year-old raven beauty knew the routine. In the stall's shrouded light at Mill Creek Farm in upstate New York, a timeless scene played out.

Sniff, lick, lick, push the standing foal toward the flank, teach it where the milk is, teach it, teach it, lick, nicker, nicker, push a little harder …

"Don't worry," said farm owner Anne Morgan, stroking the mare's warm neck. "Daddy will be here soon with lots of carrots."

Daddy is part-owner Mike Alvaro. He and his friend Seamus Crotty purchased Irish Actress in 2002. Since then, the mare's human family has grown.

Mike is a lifelong racing fan who lives in Saratoga Springs, New York, and works for a cerebral palsy advocacy group. How he and Seamus came to buy Irish Actress is a tale born of an Irish pub, Dutch vodka, and an American dream.

"I realized I wasn't ever going to have a million bucks to go buy a horse … ," Mike began, laughing before he could get the story out.

He decided to fulfill his dream through breeding. He had read a lot about it, and one day he and Seamus were talking: "Wouldn't it be great if we just had a horse?"

They considered the Keeneland sales, but their wallets screamed Timonium. Mike perused a catalog of the Maryland auction and spotted Irish Actress' name. He remembered her well.

Irish Actress was a beloved race mare in the early 1990s for owner Austin Delaney and trainer Leo O'Brien. She and her so-called sister, Irish Linnet (who was not related but also ran for Delaney and O'Brien), raced for years. Irish Actress won three stakes (Yaddo and Kingston stakes, Mount Vernon Handicap) and finished second or third in ten others. Over six years she won eleven of fifty-four races, placed or showed in eighteen more, and earned $571,525.

She shared her top achievement with her "sister." In 1991 Irish Actress and Irish Linnet won split divisions of the Yaddo Stakes at Saratoga. That afternoon, Irish eyes most certainly smiled.

Three years later Irish Actress was bred to Storm Cat — and she raced five times as well. The pregnant mare went out a winner in July, taking the Mount Vernon.

Her Storm Cat filly, born in February 1995, never raced, and neither did her next two foals. The two after that each raced once, but neither won. Finally, in 2000, she produced a winner. Gaily Revolver, sent to Japan as a yearling, won four of thirty-seven starts and earned $674,920 (based upon Japan's inflated purse structure).

When Irish Actress entered the Timonium ring in December 2002, she was in foal to Tomorrows Cat, a son of Storm Cat. That night, Mike and Seamus settled in at a Saratoga pub, The Parting Glass, while a friend, Neal Galvin, attended the sale.

"We didn't have credit at the sale because we didn't know what we were doing," Mike said, still laughing. "We were sitting there drinking Ketel One, and by the time the bottle was gone, we owned Irish Actress."

They paid $10,000. (Eight years earlier, in foal to Storm Cat, Irish Actress had sold for $235,000.) Now, Mike and Seamus owned not only a mare but also a very pregnant mare, and they had no place for her. The next day Seamus

Irish Actress, on March 23, 2007, with her newborn Officer filly

pulled into a local Thoroughbred farm and inquired about rates. Irish Actress was on her way to Mill Creek.

Her 2003 Tomorrows Cat filly, Bella Attrice, looked nearly identical to her mother: gorgeous face, wide between the eyes, strong jaw, large star, unusually soft mane, enchanting eyes. "The first baby comes and it's like our kid," Mike said. "We're all out there; Patty [Seamus' wife] is taking pictures; we're calling people and sending cigars. We're having a blast."

Irish Actress didn't produce a foal the next year, but in 2005 she delivered a leggy, strong Royal Anthem colt — bay with a large star. Named Hymnself, the colt was bred by Hamtech Stable (Seamus' new business name) and Mike Alvaro.

The next year's Orientate colt was bred by Hamtech LLC, Breeding Bliss LLC (Mike's moniker), and a new player, Just Jackie Stable, et al. The "et al." consisted of his friend Danny Sauer and Danny's wife, Dawn, and daughter Jackie.

And who are the breeders of Irish Actress' 2007 foal, by Officer?

Said Mike: "Me, Seamus — Hamtech, Just Jackie … oh, and Tony and Denise Foster, and Larry and Marbie Kollath. They're old friends from college."

When Mike, Seamus, Patty, and "et al." visit Irish Actress — and they visit often — they bring carrots … lots of carrots. Her foals, too, have learned that visitors equal carrots. Bella Attrice, now racing, dances sideways at the track to get her treats. And Irish Actress' Orientate yearling sheds his halter in the paddock but readily approaches visitors with carrots.

Although keeping the participants straight can be complicated, Mike and partners now own two additional mares. He hopes others join in so they can buy more and sell or race the offspring.

"Broodmares are just the best because you get to see the babies," Mike said. "And you can get someone like Irish Actress. She's such a sweet, sweet mare … If you grew up as I did, Saratoga is a special place — magical. So when I saw Irish Actress' name [in the catalog] … and I know she had lost some of the luster. But the fact that she did win at Saratoga — they're always a diamond. It's just somebody that shines forever for you."

And now, Mike, Seamus, et al. can toast their 2007 arrival — a bay filly with a star — and the grand old lady, sweet Irish Actress. The occasion surely calls for another bottle of Ketel One — and a whole bunch more carrots.

Kattegat's Pride

1979 GR. M. BY NORTH SEA — PILGRIM'S PRIDE, BY FIRST LANDING

It reads like a classic tale from the pen of C.W. Anderson:

Couple buys beautiful farm. Couple buys first mare at auction. Mare's first foal, a filly, becomes major winner. Filly goes on to be a broodmare, producing another major winner.

Well, the story of Kattegat's Pride isn't quite that fairy tale, but it is close. She did not produce a major winner, but her only daughter did.

The tale begins when Stephen Quick, a builder and real estate developer, and his wife, Susan, purchased the expansive, rolling St. Omer's Farm in Forest Hill, Maryland, in 1976. They converted the fertile property into a beautiful breeding farm.

Although they had owned a show horse, the first Thoroughbred they bought was Pilgrim's Pride, whom they purchased at Timonium in February 1978 for $5,400. She was thirteen. The Quicks sent her to Sagamore Farm to the Nearctic stallion North Sea.

The result was Kattegat's Pride, a gray filly who went on to win ten stakes: the grade III Gallorette Handicap; the Jennings, Geisha, Anne Arundel, Nellie Morse, Conniver, What a Summer, and All Brandy handicaps; and the Silver Ice and Alma North stakes. She earned $511,812 for her efforts.

"My husband said, 'This is easy,' " Sue Quick told *The Maryland Horse* in 2004. "But as you know, it might happen to you once, but … "

Kattegat's Pride took awhile to find her stride. She broke her maiden in her third start and won her first stakes in her fifteenth. Yet, after that, she carried as much as 127 pounds in victories from six furlongs to 1⅛ miles.

She occasionally ventured out of state — as far as Santa Anita, Keeneland, and Hollywood Park — but she generally stayed in Maryland. Seventeen of her nineteen victories came in her home state. The locals loved her.

Kattegat's Pride was crowned champion Maryland-bred three-year-old filly of 1982 and the champion older female in 1983 and 1984.

From October 12, 1982, through February 19, 1983, she won seven straight races, including five stakes. By the time she retired in 1985, she'd raced fifty-four times, winning nineteen and finishing second or third twelve times.

Sue Quick's favorite victory was the 1983 Jennings Handicap.

"In those days, everybody at the racetrack knew Kattegat's Pride," Quick said. "I don't care if they were a $1,000 bettor or a $2 bettor. She was there for so long. We'd come into the track, and people would say, 'There are the people who own Kattegat's Pride.'

"That day, it was [against] colts. The people at the track said, 'The gray mare isn't going to do it today.' She did — [with a] post position of eleven, in a field of eleven. At the head of the stretch, she just found the gear … and said 'see you later, buddies,' and there she went."

As a broodmare, however, the gray mare didn't move so fast. She produced only four foals, and the first two, a colt and a filly, came in the first two years. The Quicks sold the colt for $25,000 and kept the filly, Kattebuck. The years passed and Kattegat's Pride did not get in foal. The Quicks eventually sent her to Tom Bowman, a veterinarian who specialized in reproductive work.

He got two more foals, both colts, out of the mare.

Three of her foals won, but it was her only daughter who continued the Quicks' fairy tale. Kattebuck's fifth foal, Silmaril — born almost twenty years after Kattegat's Pride's first stakes victory — picked up the torch. And did she run with it.

Now six, Silmaril has won thirteen races for the Quicks and their partner,

Christopher Feifarek, including the grade III Pimlico Breeders' Cup Distaff, Maryland Million Oaks, Maryland Million Distaff, Geisha Handicap, and the What a Summer, Northview Stallion Station, Jameela, and Conniver stakes. She was still racing in 2007.

Silmaril's shining moment, thus far, was the 2005 Pimlico Distaff. She was given little chance of beating the reigning Eclipse champion filly, Ashado. Yet Silmaril came to Ashado late and, in front of the hometown crowd, drove past to win by three-quarters of a length.

The twenty-eight-year-old Kattegat's Pride, a sweet-faced mare with a contented manner, whose coat is nearly white with age, resides in a paddock with three fellow pensioners, including a half sister named Miss Puritan. A year or two ago the Quicks tried to keep Kattegat's Pride inside during the winter, but she was miserable. She wouldn't even eat.

She's happy outside, and that's the way the Quicks intend to keep her.

The Luck of Irish Acres

Bucksplasher & Molly's Colleen

Bucksplasher and Molly's Colleen are forever linked. The aging duo, who reside at Noel Hickey's woodsy Irish Acres Farm near Ocala, Florida, produced five foals together. Two were minor winners, one raced once but did not win, one was never named, and the other was the champion Buck's Boy.

Hickey, a sharp and articulate Irish native, was already well known by the time Buck's Boy took his first wobbly steps at Irish Acres. Bettors respected Hickey for his high win percentage and success racing "off the farm." In 1991 he set a record for win percentage on turf by capturing forty-nine of one hundred races on the grass at Arlington. He bred, owned, and trained Lady Shirl, the only Illinois-bred distaffer to win a grade I race (the Flower Bowl in 1991).

Hickey's motto? "Never let a two-year-old work in :21 and change."

Buck's Boy, whom Hickey bred and trained, was an example of his patient and attentive handling. Hickey sold the bay gelding after the three-year-old broke his maiden in his second start. Buck's Boy raced six times at three and won two stakes at four. At five he won six stakes, including the championship-clinching Breeders' Cup Turf. That earned Hickey another distinction: first person to breed and train a Breeders' Cup winner. Buck's Boy placed in two stakes at six, and at seven he added one more grade II win. He retired with sixteen wins in thirty starts, nine stakes victories, and earnings of $2,750,148.

It all started with a gentle homebred mare named Molly's Colleen and a lively chestnut stallion named Bucksplasher.

Molly's Colleen was bred in Ontario by Irish Acres Farm, and her dam, Irish Molly, was bred in Hickey's name. Hickey had purchased Irish Molly's dam, an Irish-bred mare, Cambalee, privately.

Molly's Colleen raced for Hickey three seasons, winning two of twelve races and earning $17,380. While not a great racehorse, Molly was an exceptional broodmare. She had ten named foals, and, of the nine to race, seven were winners. Besides Buck's Boy, Z. Bengal Tiger placed in two stakes, set a course record at Gulfstream Park, and earned $227,487. Beau Sierra competed seven seasons, won or placed in thirty of sixty-three starts, and bankrolled $326,900.

As for Bucksplasher, Hickey acquired him twenty-five years ago for stud duty. He had won five races and finished third in the Gotham Stakes, Whirlaway Stakes, and City of Baltimore Handicap. Yet breeders were probably drawn to him initially because he was gorgeous — inside and out.

Inside, his bloodlines were top shelf. His sire, Buckpasser, was world renowned. His dam, Victoria Star, by Northern Dancer, was a half sibling to stakes winners Nuclear Pulse and Solartic, a close relative to Storm Bird, and the daughter of Canadian Oaks' winner Solometeor. Victoria Star also produced four black-type performers.

Outside, Bucksplasher is muscle-bound with a brilliant burnt-sienna coat. He is absolutely "Wow!" Listed at 15.3 hands, he sports a Northern Dancer look with the added touches of a long blaze, white lip, and two stockings, including a hind one extending above his hock.

Bucksplasher was a popular sire throughout his career, siring stakes winners with regularity. His first foals were born in 1985, and twenty years later his final crop — four named foals — was born.

He sired thirty-one stakes winners, including nine that won graded events. Buck's Boy was his best. Since retirement, Bucksplasher has had one responsibility at Hickey's farm: Be happy. The same can be said for Molly's Colleen, whose final foal was born four years ago.

I'd long considered visiting Bucksplasher, simply because of his stunning look so evident in photos. When I saw him that warm morning in February 2006, he looked even more impressive in person: bright, flashy, and unusually youthful.

Molly's Colleen (1982 dk. b/br. m. by Verbatim—Irish Molly, by George Royal)

The twenty-nine-year-old stallion pranced all the way from the barn to his paddock as the morning sun illuminated his golden copper coat and white markings. Inside his enclosure he jogged lightly — nearly floating — from corner to corner. His head was low as he sniffed for new scents and reclaimed the plot as his own.

He jogged up to investigate the camera, wandered away, and then returned for a second look. His curiosity was childlike and quietly charming.

Bucksplasher (1977 ch. h. by Buckpasser—Victoria Star, by Northern Dancer)

Molly's Colleen, on the other hand, looked her age. She's a dear and seemed willing to do whatever we asked. Her eyes appeared wistful, perhaps due to her deep temples. Her ears were long, and her nose was solid and square. A star perched unusually high over her eyes, nearly at the base of her foretop.

While she was registered dark bay or brown, Molly appeared bay — maybe the result of her refined winter coat. Her paddock mate is another extraordinary mare, Cherry Flare, the dam of grade I winner Take D' Tour.

And so it came to be that Bucksplasher, thirty, and Molly's Colleen, twenty-five, pass their days a few paddocks apart at the lush Irish Acres. They keep an eye on the resident broodmares and foals as well as the young horses heading to and from Hickey's spacious training track. The parents of Buck's Boy have earned their place in the sun.

Lucky Spell

1971–2005 B. M. BY LUCKY MEL—INCANTATION, BY PRINCE BLESSED

The bay mare was one of the first horses Richard Eamer bought, in 1982, and by the time she died in 2005, she was his only mare. She was not only an excellent racehorse but also a top producer — and the second dam of one of racing's most important stallions. She was Lucky Spell, and her luck spanned a spell of thirty-four-years.

When her trainer, Henry Moreno, was asked what he best remembered about Lucky Spell, he answered immediately: "She was very sound, and we ran her often."

Sixty-nine times over five seasons, in fact. The California-bred won twelve races and finished second or third nineteen times. An earner of $253,655, she was the first stakes winner for both her owners, Walt Burris and Lynn Wilder, and her breeder, Mike Schloessman. What's more, she was her owners' entire stable.

Early on she raced twice in claiming events — once against the boys. She easily won both but wasn't claimed. Her connections didn't risk that again.

Lucky Spell won the grade III Las Palmas Handicap on turf and the grade III Princess Stakes on dirt. She won the Las Flores Handicap and the Linita and Time To Leave stakes. She ran second or third in ten other stakes and competed against some of racing's toughest distaffers. Her stablemate, the world-class Tizna, was one of the top mares Lucky Spell defeated.

In Lucky Spell's second career, she was of stakes quality, too. Her second foal, a Bold Bidder filly named Merlins Charm, won an English group III. Her fourth, a Caro filly named Goldspell, won two stakes and earned $186,010.

The year Goldspell was born, 1982, Lucky Spell was eleven and again in foal to Caro. She was offered at the Keeneland November sale. Eamer, founder of a chain of health facilities called National Medical Enterprises and owner of a young breeding and racing operation named Mandysland Farm, bought her for $700,000.

The next spring Lucky Spell delivered a gray filly named Trolley Song. Trolley Song would grow up to produce the multiple grade I winner Unbridled's Song, also bred by Eamer. One of the country's premier stallions, Unbridled's Song commands a $200,000 stud fee at Taylor Made Farm.

Lucky Spell produced her final foal in 1993 when she was twenty-two. By then, Eamer had dispersed most of his horses. By 1994 he'd sold his Kentucky property, and he would eventually sell his lush, green farm near Santa Ynez, California, as well. That property, rich with a vast variety of trees, flowers, and spacious paddocks, was renamed Magali Farms.

But Eamer did not sell Lucky Spell. Magali agreed to let him keep the old mare there. She was a sprightly thirty-three when I visited in 2004.

Laura Cotter, Eamer's longtime farm manager and a youthful blonde, energetic woman, was waiting. I knew her through D. Wayne Lukas, for whom she had worked for many years. She served as spokeswoman for Eamer, who is seventy-nine and lives in California.

Lucky Spell looked fantastic. The Magali crew had done its best to tone down her thick winter coat. I know it's not fair to photograph old horses in winter, because their coats occasionally grow to llama proportions. But sometimes that's the only opportunity I have. Lucky Spell's face was so beautiful — refined, bright-eyed, sweet — that it clashed with her body's winter woollies.

Although she'd had her bath long before my arrival, her thick coat had refused to dry. When I first saw her, she looked like an idling racecar in a pit stop, as three people rubbed briskly on her coat with towels.

When they finally gave up, Lucky Spell danced like a high-schooler at the

prom. She was a delight — cheery and downright cute. Her handlers were proud to show her off, and Cotter gently sang her praises. How many mares are stakes winners, stakes producers, and the second dam of a major stallion? All her life, Lucky Spell has brought luck to those around her.

She was one of Eamer's first mares, and, Cotter said, "she was one of his first loves as a broodmare."

Despite Eamer's being a hugely successful businessman, he has a soft spot for his animals, Cotter said. For Christmas, she's given him T-shirts and sweatshirts that feature his dogs or Lucky Spell. One T-shirt featured a headshot of Lucky Spell and the words: "The Old Girl."

"He always wore them, too," Cotter said.

Of Lucky Spell, she said: "If you go to the pasture, she's the first one to come up to see what you're doing, what you want. She loves attention. She's been a baby-sitter for a lot of foals, and if we had a flighty mare, we'd put her in with her to hang out with — like a goat at the racetrack.

"She takes care of herself. That's why she's lived so long."

And her handlers took care of her as well. Lucky Spell's diet included the popular nutritional supplement Platinum Performance, made for horses, humans, and other animals. Cotter takes it herself.

Lucky Spell lived one more year after my visit. The beloved mare died of heart failure on October 4, 2005, at the age of thirty-four.

"She'd been going out during the day and coming in at night," Cotter said. "I'd go visit her, and she loved carrots right up to the end. She went out that morning, and they brought her in, and … she died during the night."

Lucky Spell's body was cremated and her remains encased in a shellacked box, topped with a small brass nameplate engraved with her name and years of birth and death. Cotter keeps the box for Eamer in her Santa Ynez office. It's "maybe six inches wide and tall, ten inches long, and really heavy," she said.

"Mr. Eamer always wanted to make sure that, with everything, Lucky Spell was taken care of," Cotter said. "She had a lot of TLC."

Mary's Fantasy

1973–2006 B. M. BY OLYMPIAN KING—FANTASY DREAM, BY EVERETT JR.

Mary's Fantasy's back swayed deeply, like a couch whose cushions had lost their springs. Yet for Mary, thirty-two when I visited in 2005, it was not primarily age related.

"She was born with a swayback," trainer Bob Holthus recalled. "She started out that way."

Holthus, along with Olen Sledge, bred and raced Mary's Fantasy, and her swayback apparently didn't slow her down. Strictly a sprinter and easy to train, Mary won eight of thirty-six starts, the grade III Mermaid Stakes and the American Stakes, and earned $82,093. That was a tidy sum in the 1970s.

Nor did her swayback curtail her place in the American record books. She is tied for the honor of the oldest broodmare ever to produce a stakes winner. She was twenty-six when her stakes-winning son, Perfect Fantasy, was born. Two years later a mare named Fantasy Miss matched that extraordinary feat.

Holthus knows Mary's family well. He not only trained Mary's Fantasy but also her dam, a 1965 model named Fantasy Dream. He, or his son Paul, also trained all of Mary's racing offspring early in their careers. Nine of Mary's twelve registered foals raced and eight won, including a second stakes winner, Fantastic Light, and two stakes-placed runners.

Mary's record setter, Perfect Fantasy, won the 2002 Rainbow Stakes for Holthus at his winter base, Oaklawn Park. Perfect Fantasy was claimed soon thereafter and spent years running primarily in claiming events.

He was Mary's final foal, and her days at Holthus' Kilkerry Farm near Hot Springs, Arkansas, were peaceful.

Mary was a bright bay with a kind, thoughtful eye, a large star and stripe, and one sock. Her legs became increasingly sore with age, making blacksmith care difficult, but she still managed to get around. She was one of the oldest Thoroughbreds in the country.

Farm manager Carl Chapman was fond of the geriatric lass. He has worked at Kilkerry so long — since 1969 — that he remembered Mary as a youngster. In 2005, he said: "She's easy to work with, all of the time. She always was. She's a fixture here."

Holthus agreed: "You know it's going to come to an end pretty soon, but as long as she's healthy, we'll keep her around."

As autumn 2006 approached, Mary's Fantasy's health failed. At the advanced age of thirty-three, the gentle, record-setting mare passed away. She was buried on the farm.

"She was losing weight, and we couldn't get weight back on her," Chapman said. "She was just old."

Tom Voss and Mickey Free

Mickey Free

1983 B. G. BY ROCK TALK — BUPERSROSE, BY BUPERS

Tom Voss and Mickey Free were a Saratoga mainstay for many years. The duo — trainer Tom with a stern expression and cigarette in hand, and his pony Mickey, a former steeplechase champion with a willing, quiet step — led fractious racehorses to and from their morning exercise.

Tom was not the only rider the gentle horse toted about.

"Mickey had a very large fan club of children in all his years at Saratoga," said owner Mimi Voss. "Everybody brought their children to go for rides on him: bloodstock agents, trainers, valets, racing secretaries, Saratoga store owners."

I learned that Tom's pony was Mickey Free — whom I remembered from his racing days — in 2000, when the duo led multiple grade I winner John's Call around.

I occasionally chased them back to the barn where, after training, Tom let Mickey into a round pen and the gelding leaped about before quickly settling down. When Mickey was returned to his stall before feed time, the stall-door webbing did not need to be in place. He stayed in that stall and waited, his hungry eyes peering hopefully down the shed row for his meal.

Nowadays, Mickey Free, twenty-four, is a pasture ornament at Mimi and Tom's historic Atlanta Hall Farm in Monkton, Maryland. A medium-sized, attractive bay with a kindly face, Mickey — named for an immortal Indian scout — was born in 1983. Bred and owned by Mimi, he is the son of top Maryland sire Rock Talk and the mare Bupersrose.

Mimi acquired the mare from B. Frank Christmas in 1977. Before retiring to Atlanta Hall as a broodmare, Bupersrose raced seventy-one times from ages two through seven, winning seven races and placing in an additional nineteen.

Despite possessing a small broodmare band — the largest it has numbered is seven — Mimi is a successful breeder. She remembers Bupersrose fondly.

"She was fabulous," Mimi said. "She produced some glorious horses for me. She was really a wonderful, wonderful broodmare."

Tom agreed. "Everything out of that mare could run, just about."

In addition to her first foal, Mickey Free, who certainly could run (and jump), Bupersrose produced stakes winners Menemsha and Teb's Bend. Her daughter Fractious, also a winner, is the mother of Mimi's popular stakes-placed mare Rowdy, as well as the 2006 Gladstone Hurdle Stakes winner, Jimmie Echo.

Mickey Free is the type of horse that trainers love: willing, kind, competitive. Tom Voss is the type of trainer that bettors love: lifelong horseman, attentive to detail, a brilliant mind. They were a formidable team.

Mickey Free faced excellent competition during a thirty-six-race career, including such jump specialists as Inlander, Statesmanship, and Summer Colony. The bay gelding held his own, winning six races and finishing second or third nine times.

His greatest moment came in April 1988 when, as a five-year-old, he sailed to a neck victory in the $100,000 Atlanta Cup Steeplechase. That year he was named the Maryland-bred champion steeplechaser.

"He's the kind of horse we liked so much we hated to run him, as something might happen to him," Tom said. "He was just sort of a sweet horse."

Not long after winning the Atlanta Cup, Mickey suffered a bad reaction to an injection. His neck swelled up, and he never breathed quite right in the face of competition again. At age six, a comparatively young age for a steeplechaser, Mickey Free was retired.

Yet his was not a true retirement, as Mickey remained active with both Tom and the Vosses' daughter, Elizabeth.

"After his racing career he was a wonderful foxhunter," Mimi said. "When Elizabeth was thirteen and she hunted him for the first time, he upset her a little bit. She was used to telling her ponies when they were going to take off and do all the stuff in the hunting field. Mickey was so competitive that he took charge and told her what he was going to do."

Mickey soon settled down a bit, however, and he and Elizabeth shared many foxhunts. Elizabeth also occasionally climbed aboard the aging horse at Saratoga when Tom was training young steeplechase prospects in the Oklahoma track infield. Mickey led the way over the schooling jumps, showing the youngsters they weren't as frightening as they appeared. Even at twenty, Mickey sometimes displayed his spirit by kicking up his heels during those morning sessions.

At age twenty-one, however, the beloved bay gelding — who had visited Saratoga for eighteen straight seasons as a racehorse or pony — did not return. It was time for a true retirement. Tom had found a worthy replacement — John's Call.

Mickey Free now spends his nights in the barn and his days in a paddock with a pony companion.

"We had him for a while as a babysitter because he's very gentle. But he foundered after a while because he was eating all of their food," Mimi laughed.

"He's so adorable."

Still proud of her gentle, food-loving friend, Mimi often brings him carrots — in moderation.

Miesque

1984 B. M. BY NUREYEV — PASADOBLE, BY PROVE OUT

When Miesque obliterated her opponents in the 1987 Breeders' Cup Mile, Americans learned what Europeans already knew: Miesque was one of the world's all-time great milers. She won pulling away, her ears flicking, in course-record time.

When the bay filly returned to America the following year and again drew away from an international cast — with her ears forward — we swooned. She was the "once-in-a-lifetime" racehorse.

And when, as a broodmare, Miesque produced five stakes winners, including one of the world's most important stallions, she became a once-in-a-lifetime broodmare, too — more than anyone could hope for.

Miesque's owner, Stavros Niarchos, was so blessed through the pairing of two of his own: Nureyev, a Northern Dancer colt Niarchos bought as a yearling for $1.3 million in 1978, and Pasadoble, a Prove Out filly he bought for $45,000 in 1980. He had raced both. Nureyev was a French champion miler, whom Niarchos later sold for stud duty. Pasadoble, initially a pacemaker for the brilliant but ill-fated River Lady, won two stakes.

Miesque, a bay filly with a small star high on her forehead, was born at Niarchos' Spring Oak Farm near Lexington on March 14, 1984. The breeder was Flaxman Holdings Limited.

The renowned François Boutin trained her in France, as he had Nureyev. While Miesque was not tall, she quickly grew in reputation. At two she won three of four races including two group Is. One was against colts.

At three she joined the list of all-time great milers. She won six of eight starts, including five group or grade Is at some of the world's premier tracks — Longchamp, Newmarket, and Deauville. Charts of her wins read "handily," "going away," "easily."

And so she came to the United States in November 1987 and dusted an international lineup in the Breeders' Cup Mile. Bettors had a pretty good idea she'd be good as she was the close second favorite at 3.60-1. But they couldn't guess she'd set a new course record, 1:32⅖. She won by 3½ lengths under regular rider Freddy Head. The chart read: "Drew away under a hand ride after taking over … "

Racing again at four, the lovely filly won three of four starts — all group or grade Is. Her only loss, by a head, was to a top Nureyev colt named Soviet Star. When Miesque returned for the 1988 Breeders' Cup Mile, few doubted her. As part of an entry with Blushing John, she went off at 2-1. She ran like 1-2, pulling away to a four-length victory over another solid lineup.

Boutin, whose storied career spanned more than three decades, was understandably proud of his runner. "She is undoubtedly the most consistent filly I've ever trained," he said.

Even rival trainers acknowledged her prowess.

Trainer Charlie Whittingham said, "Miesque is always awesome in her races."

Said D. Wayne Lukas: "When they get that good it's scary — almost freaky."

Miesque thus became the first two-time winner of a Breeders' Cup race. Those impressive wins — her only starts in America — earned her Eclipse Awards for champion turf female both seasons.

The rest of the world also showered her with honors: French two-year-old filly champion, champion three-year-old filly in England and France, two-time champion miler in France, champion miler in England, champion older female in France, and Europe's highweight older female at seven to 9½ furlongs.

And so Miesque, her resume stacked with world-class accolades, settled in for her second career.

The Niarchos family has had countless international successes — Aldebaran, Denon, Six Perfections, Domedriver, Bago, Denebola, Divine Proportions, Aviance, Chimes of Freedom, Spinning World, and more — yet perhaps none is as beloved as Miesque. Her contribution to their family, and to all of racing, did not end with her last race.

How talented was she as a producer? Her first foal, a Mr. Prospector colt named Kingmambo, born in 1990, won three group Is and earned $733,139 before entering stud at Lane's End Farm. He is now one of the world's most successful stallions with a last-listed stud fee — before going private — of $300,000.

Miesque next produced a Private Account filly named East of the Moon, who went on to be highweighted in both France and Europe. She won three

group Is and earned more than $700,000. As a coveted broodmare, she produced four stakes performers before being tragically killed by lightning in July 2006.

Miesque's third foal meant her third stakes winner. Miesque's Son, a Mr. Prospector colt, won a group III, placed in group Is, and earned $134,323. He entered stud at Three Chimneys Farm and was eventually moved to France. In 2006, his son Miesque's Approval won the turf championship.

Number four for the beloved miler? The filly Moon Is Up, by Woodman, won a stakes and placed in two others, including a group event. She is now a producer.

Miesque's fifth foal was her first not to win a stakes. Monevassia, by Mr. Prospector, made up for it by producing European champion two-year-old filly and French highweight Rumplestiltskin, who won two group Is.

It took Miesque five attempts before she produced her next stakes winner, although her 1998 daughter, Inventing Paradise, was stakes placed. In 2000, Miesque produced a handsome A.P. Indy colt named Mingun. He won two stakes, including the group III Meld Stakes, and earned $208,818. He is now a Lane's End stallion.

Miesque's final foals, a 2004 Storm Cat filly and a 2005 A.P. Indy colt, have yet to race.

Interestingly, Miesque's dam, Pasadoble, is also the second dam of European champion Six Perfections. Sporting the Niarchos colors, she, too, beat the males in the Breeders' Cup Mile.

While Miesque always looked terrific in victory — happy, eager, driven — that does not compare with how she looks in retirement in Central Kentucky. She is a classic beauty. Her bay coat is rich reddish-brown, her eyes interested and brilliant, and her body fit and well balanced. Miesque poses like the champion she is, her famous small star lighting her contented face.

Miesque, opposite, with her occasional pasture mate Aviance, who is dam/second dam of champions and/or group I winners Chimes of Freedom, Denon, Spinning World, Good Journey, and Aldebaran.

She watches human passersby with hawk-like interest. Perhaps, just perhaps, it is because so many people offer Miesque her favorite treat: sugar cubes.

When Miesque was in training, she not only enjoyed sugar cubes but also a more unusual treat. Boutin kept large drums of honey for his equine sweetheart. He poured it on her food, and she dove in with gusto.

Sugar cubes are easier, however, and the farm staff keeps a tin on hand for their resident queen. After a quantity of the energy treat, Miesque can be downright frisky on her way back to the paddock.

I might never photograph a faster, more consistent race filly and producer again, and I can't expect to see another like her during my lifetime. I shall always feel honored to have spent time with this one.

Miswaki

The groom led Miswaki from his stall into the yard between the stud barns at Walmac International in Lexington, Kentucky. Miswaki seemed content on this warm May day, but his slowed step reflected his age. His knees were no longer straight, his worldy eyes seemed tired, and his skin showed through his thinning chestnut coat in spots.

He posed dutifully at this beautifully landscaped showplace. He was not easy to impress, and his ears rarely flicked forward for long. With all he'd seen in more than a quarter century, I guess one awed photographer wasn't overly exciting. It's not as if I'd brought a mare with me.

And as the famed stallion disappeared back into his barn, melancholy swept over me. It was the first time I had seen him, and I knew it would be the last. Miswaki died later that year.

"Miswaki was the last of the big three who put Walmac on the map," said Walmac president emeritus John T.L. Jones Jr. "First Alleged, then Nureyev, and now Miswaki have passed on. We were certainly fortunate to have one like him and can only hope to have another one as good some day in the future."

Miswaki was born in Florida twenty-six years earlier, a son of Mr. Prospector out of the wonderfully named Buckpasser mare Hopespringseternal. The thick chestnut colt raced in England, France, and the United States. His biggest victory was the group I Prix de la Salamandre at Longchamp, and in America he captured Belmont's Charles Hatton Stakes. He retired to Walmac at the end of 1981 with six wins in thirteen starts.

Boasting a highly marketable pedigree, a powerful body, and a group I win, Miswaki was well received from the start. And had his only accomplishment been siring 1991 Horse of the Year Black Tie Affair, who earned more than $3.3 million, his career would have been a success.

Yet Miswaki sired top-notch runners for more than two decades. They ran on dirt and turf, in sprints and classics. And in the fashion of Walmac's other immortal stallions, Alleged and Nureyev, Miswaki's foals were coveted worldwide. Among his offspring were high-weighted horses in the United Arab Emirates, Italy, France, Ireland, and Germany.

His daughter Urban Sea won what many consider the world's most important race, the Prix de l'Arc de Triomphe, and she has become one of the world's most important broodmares. She has produced ten foals thus far, including seven to race. All have earned black type, including two group I winners, a group II winner, two group III winners, and an additional stakes winner.

Between Urban Sea's accomplishments and those of his other daughters, Miswaki has become a very influential broodmare sire as well. Among the horses Miswaki's daughters have produced is the European champion Daylami.

By the time I met the aged Miswaki that peaceful day in May, his breeding career was over. When none of the six mares he bred in 2004 conceived, he was pensioned, his legacy already secure.

When age became too much of a burden and he could not rise in his stall, Miswaki was euthanized on December 17, 2004. He was laid to rest near Alleged and Nureyev.

Monique Rene

1978–2003 CH. M. BY PRINCE OF ASCOT — PARTY DATE, BY SPEEDY FRANK

While racing fans around the country may not recognize her name, Monique Rene is a legend in Louisiana.

The brilliant chestnut speedster won twenty-nine of forty-five races — all but four in the Pelican State — and earned $456,250. From 1981 to 1984, she blazed home first in fifteen stakes, including ones with such rich regional names as the Pan Zareta Handicap (twice), Sugarland Stakes (twice), Mardi Gras Handicap, and the Chou Croute, Southern Maid, and Creole State stakes. She was favored in thirty-nine of her starts.

John Franks, the well-known Louisiana businessman and four-time Eclipse Award-winning owner, bought the fleet filly in 1982 when her career was well underway, and she rewarded him with stakes win after stakes win. Inducted into the Fair Grounds Racing Hall of Fame in 1999, she excelled in her second career as well.

She produced eleven foals, including Prince of the Mt., a grade III winner and earner of nearly $400,000 who stands at stud in Louisiana. Monique Rene's daughters also showed their class. Kissin Rene is the dam of stakes winner True Kiss, and Walk Away Rene produced stakes winner Catch My Fancy. Ronique produced grade II stakes winner Kiss a Native, who earned $1,109,022 and was named Canadian champion three-year-old colt. And Clever Monique, who has produced an extraordinary fifteen consecutive foals, is the dam of Yes It's True, a grade I-winning millionaire who stands at Three Chimneys in Kentucky.

I visited Monique Rene in March 2003 at Franks Farms Southland Division in Ocala, Florida, where she was spending another lazy day with a contented group of broodmares. The mares were spread out along a long fence line, relishing the cooling shade provided by several trees. Among them were Rexonette, Slide Out Front, Sophisticated Sam, Twosies Answer, and Monique Rene's daughter Lively Rene.

Monique and Twosie were clearly buddies. Monique was a thick, plain chestnut with a compact stance and short mane. Twosie, dam of Breeders' Cup Juvenile winner Answer Lively, was a leggy dark bay with a high head and a long sun-bleached mane. She looked like an equine model while Monique, at age twenty-five, seemed like a child's chunky red pony. It took imagination to picture her winning fifteen stakes.

A stark series of white numbers ran up Monique's neck, a reminder of long-ago race-fixing scandals that had come to Franks' attention. To protect his horses, each was branded with sequential numbers, the first two indicating the foaling year. Monique Rene, born in 1978, was 78037.

My time passed pleasantly with the mares, who all seemed to enjoy the company. They were all happy to stay close and receive some attention. It was a good day.

But how quickly things change. By 2005 most of the mares had died, and Franks was gone as well. In addition, the vast farm had been sold to developers.

Yet Will Johnson, the farm manager, would not forget Monique Rene.

"You could lead her with a shoelace, she was so nice," Johnson said. "I foaled her daughters, and her daughters' daughters, and her daughters' daughters' daughters."

Johnson also had the unenviable task of euthanizing Monique Rene in late 2003 when the mare was suffering from ailments in both front feet. Monique Rene was buried in an unmarked plot near Alta's Lady, another of Franks' favorites. "It was my favorite spot on the farm," Johnson said, "way in back, where it was very peaceful and very quiet."

Monique Rene's death generated no press release, and few felt the loss. But the gentle mare, the legend, remains forever ingrained in Louisiana racing lore.

North Of Eden (IRE)

1983 B. M. BY NORTHFIELDS—TREE OF KNOWLEDGE (IRE), BY SASSAFRAS (FR)

Arthur Appleton's Bridlewood Farm bought North Of Eden from Bertram Firestone in 1992 for $125,000. At the time, the mare's second foal, Paradise Creek, had started twice, showing promise by breaking his maiden and finishing fourth in a stakes. Yet North Of Eden was merely a promising broodmare with a stellar pedigree and less-than-stellar race record.

Today, she's priceless.

Still a resident at the Ocala, Florida, farm, North Of Eden has produced three grade I winners as well as the dam of group I winner David Junior. In 2001 she was named Florida Broodmare of the Year.

Paradise Creek eventually won an Eclipse Award as 1994 champion turf male. In his career he won four grade Is: Arlington Million, Manhattan Handicap, Hollywood Derby, and Washington, D.C., International. He set a course record in the Manhattan, running the 1¼ miles in 1:57.59. He earned $3,401,416.

Wild Event, North Of Eden's 1993 foal, won the grade I Early Times Turf Classic and several other graded stakes, earning nearly a million dollars. And Forbidden Apple, North Of Eden's 1995 foal, won the grade I Manhattan Handicap, two other graded stakes, and earned $1,680,640. He stands at Bridlewood.

What's more, North Of Eden's 1991 colt, I'm Very Irish, won a minor stakes and finished second or third in two graded stakes.

While winless in her seven starts, North Of Eden possessed the pedigree to be an exceptional broodmare. Her dam, the Sassafras mare Tree of Knowledge, produced the turf champion Theatrical and Japan's extraordi-nary Taiki Blizzard, earner of more than $5.5 million. North Of Eden's second dam, Sensibility, produced group III winner Beyond the Lake and Lake Champlain, a stakes winner who placed in the group I Irish One Thousand Guineas. Pange, North Of Eden's third dam, produced 1964 Prix de l'Arc de Triomphe winner and Italian champion Prince Royal II.

George Isaacs, Bridlewood's general manager for more than a decade, is a lifelong horseman. He began his career at Stanley Petter's Hurricane Hall Stud and has worked at Gainesway Farm, Allen Paulson's Brookside South, and other farms. He speaks of North Of Eden with reverence.

"She doesn't have a mean bone in her body," he said. "She lets you come into her stall and be around her and her foal all you want. She just loves being a mom, the best I've ever been around.

"She is what I'd describe as a perfect conduit mare. She will absolutely pass on all of the characteristics of the stallion that you breed her to, but throw in all of the perfect nurturing parts of the equation that you would want from the mother. She always throws a level-headed, easygoing foal, but they all have the heart of a champion."

Bridlewood hopes to continue reproducing that magic, and several of North Of Eden's daughters enrich their broodmare band. Thirteen-year-old Paradise River produced multiple group I winner David Junior, an English highweight in both 2005 and 2006, and the farm plans to retain her 2006 Stormy Atlantic filly.

Eden's Causeway, four, is in foal to Mr. Greeley, and North Of Eden's two-year-old Stormy Atlantic filly, Storminthegarden, is "absolutely breathtaking," Isaacs said.

North Of Eden was to be bred to Halo's Image in 2007. The longtime respected sire, who stands at Bridlewood, is by Halo and out of a Valid Appeal mare. Both are foundation-type sires for broodmares.

North Of Eden is a lovely rich bay, medium-sized at 15.3 hands. Her long, thick face is highlighted by gentle, trusting eyes. Her back is a bit long for her sire line, but that might be due, Isaacs noted, to the number of foals she has produced. She is powerfully built and carries an unmistakable air of dignity.

I was fortunate to spend time with her in her expansive paddock one warm winter afternoon. An accomplished paddock buddy, Jolie Jolie, dam of grade I winner Jolie's Halo, grazed nearby.

North Of Eden, heavy with foal, wandered up to be rubbed but eventually meandered away to browse in the browning grass. She occasionally lifted her head to stare, for long moments, into the distance. When breezes swept through her long tail, she was a C.W. Anderson painting: the classic broodmare.

It's funny how the mind drifts on such days, in the presence of horses and silence and vast spaces. North Of Eden was mesmerizing, and as I watched her graze, I pondered the intangible nature of greatness.

Northview's Gray Ghosts

Two Punch & Waquoit

The 600 guests formed a circle outside the tent where they had dined on crab cakes and availed themselves of the open bar. Tom Bowman, part-owner of Northview Stallion Station and master of ceremonies at its 2006 stallion show, took the microphone and informed the crowd that Northview's old "gray ghosts" would not be paraded into the circle that year.

It wasn't due to their health, Bowman explained. But because they were aging and their accomplishments were so well known, there was no point in stirring them up and risking injury. Two Punch, especially, as anyone who visited him knew, could still put on quite a show.

The two stallions deserved this special consideration. Both gray, twenty-four, and out of Grey Dawn II mares, Two Punch and Waquoit were members of Northview's inaugural stallion roster in 1989. Northview's rosters have reigned supreme since — not just in the state, but north of Florida and east of Kentucky.

When Maryland's Windfields Farm — revered ground as the home of Northern Dancer — closed in 1988, Bowman, Richard Golden, and Allaire du Pont stepped up to form Northview Stallion Station. As its Web site states, the "founders took on an urgent mission: Ensuring that the Chesapeake City, MD, area would continue as a center of world-class Thoroughbred breeding."

They purchased Windfields and launched their own breeding operation with four stallions: Caveat and Smarten, who both already had runners, and Two Punch and Waquoit. Northview's success was immediate.

Two Punch had begun his stallion career two years earlier at Windfields, and Waquoit was entering stud after a multiple grade I-winning racing career.

At the track, Two Punch was dark gray with dapples and dark points. He raced eight times over two seasons and won half of his starts. He captured the Bachelor Stakes at Oaklawn Park and finished third in Gulfstream's Swale Stakes.

At stud, Two Punch attracted breeders with his sharp looks, fine race record, and coveted pedigree. He was by Mr. Prospector and out of Heavenly Cause, the champion two-year-old filly of 1980. Heavenly Cause was out of the stakes winner Lady Dulcinea, whose dam, Shy Dancer, also produced the additional stakes winners Champagne Charlie, Shy Dawn, and Petite Rouge.

Two Punch's foals came out running. Of the thirty named foals in his initial crop, twenty-nine raced and won. He also sired stakes winners — several in each crop for well over a decade.

Two Punch's stud fee eventually reached $25,000, the highest in the region. He has sired forty-seven stakes winners, including seven graded stakes winners. His best, Smoke Glacken, won an Eclipse Award as top sprinter and earned more than $750,000. He's now a successful sire at Gainesway Farm in Kentucky.

Waquoit, meanwhile, perhaps initially attracted breeders more for his racing exploits than his bloodlines. His pedigree was very good — by Relaunch and out of Grey Parlo — but his dam was no Heavenly Cause and his sire no Mr. Prospector.

Waquoit raced for four seasons, winning thirteen stakes, nineteen of thirty starts, and earning $2,225,360. He broke his maiden at age two and soon won the six-furlong Cape Cod Stakes. But, eventually, the tremendously versatile runner also won the grade I Jockey Club Gold Cup and two runnings of the grade I Brooklyn Handicap — each at the classic 1½-mile distance.

*Waquoit (1983 gr. h. by Relaunch—Grey Parlo, by *Grey Dawn II)*

Two Punch (1983 ro. h. by Mr. Prospector—Heavenly Cause, by *Grey Dawn II)

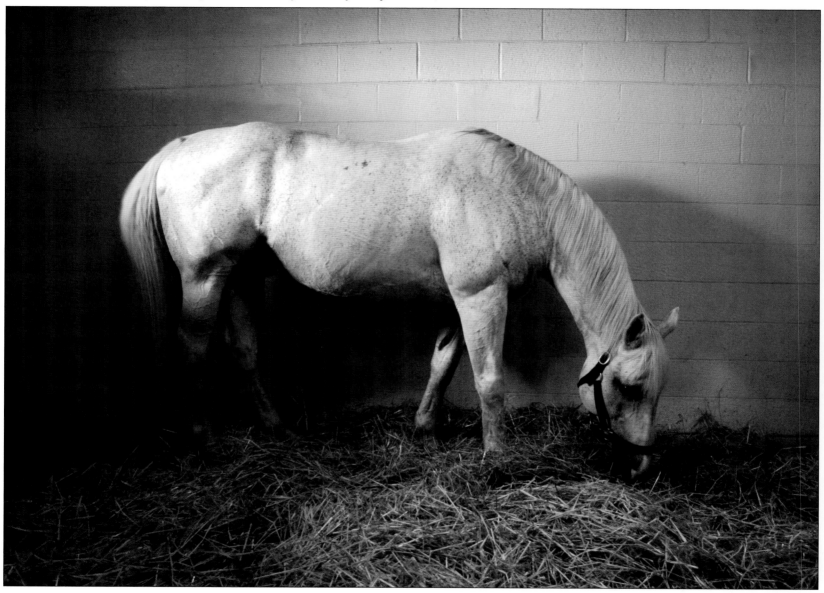

Waquoit, like Two Punch, got off to a strong start at stud. His first crop of fifty-one named foals included six stakes winners. The next year he sired five. To date, he has sired thirty stakes winners, including five graded stakes winners.

His best, so far, was Halo America. From Waquoit's first crop, the popular gray distaffer won fifteen races, including the grade I Apple Blossom Handicap and eight other stakes, and earned $1,460,992.

As the years have passed, Two Punch and Waquoit's once dark, dappled coats have lightened markedly. They're now nearly white.

Two Punch resides in the front stallion barn with younger stallions such as Not For Love and Domestic Dispute. His paddock is closest to the barn. Thick-bodied with seeking eyes and a strong jaw, he enjoys a rivalry with a stallion in an adjacent paddock. He can occasionally be heard pounding on his fence boards with his hoof to show he's still king.

He is one of my favorite models due to his beauty and his worldly, authoritative aura. When being led for photos — or when "in the circle" at previous stallion shows — he often reared in a stunning display of power.

When I once entered his stall for portraits, Two Punch eyed me with curiosity before quietly returning to his hay. While he seemed content to have a visitor, he did not find me worthy of closer inspection.

Waquoit, meanwhile, often peers out his window in the second barn, and his paddock is not as prominent as Two Punch's. Although his age shows and his step isn't quite straight, he is still a classically handsome, long-bodied stallion.

While he is generally relaxed and good to work with, he is strong natured. When I've gotten too close — such as photographing him in his stall — he's approached to remind me that the stall is his. No sweet, coddling visits with this senior.

While both of these beloved sires deserved to skip the 2006 stallion show, it's only fitting that Bowman began by mentioning them. Northview's "gray ghosts," there since the beginning, have earned that honor.

Two Punch in 2004

Olé

1986 B. H. BY DANZIG — PRINCESS ROONEY, BY VERBATIM

Henry Moreno had seen many oddities during his forty-year training career, but he could not believe his eyes that late October afternoon at Santa Anita.

He had watched his horse, Olé, trail in a maiden race and then make a strong outside move entering the stretch. Olé engaged the leader, but, in a flash, the horse inside ducked out and slammed him. The impact nearly knocked Olé off his feet. He lurched to his knees, and his jockey sailed over his head. While righting himself, Olé stepped on the reins. They snapped.

Moreno had been relieved after the race to see just a bit of blood on the horse's mouth. Olé had bitten his tongue, he thought.

But when the trainer returned to the barn, he was shocked by what he saw: Olé recovering from surgery. The colt had broken his jaw on both sides. Moreno's veterinarian had laid the horse out in a stall, anesthetized him, and wired the jaw. By the time Moreno arrived, Olé was already on his feet.

As soon as he got back into his own stall, Olé began munching hay, and he promptly gobbled up some grain tossed into his feed tub.

"He never missed a bite of oats," Moreno said eighteen years later, laughing. "I couldn't believe it. I just couldn't believe it."

Moreno walked the three-year-old colt for three days. Then, with a hackamore bit, Olé readily returned to galloping. Two weeks after surgery he was racing again.

That toughness would serve Olé well.

Olé's dam, Princess Rooney, was one of the best race mares of recent times — the definition of a tough campaigner. The handsome gray won seventeen of twenty-one races and the 1984 Eclipse Award for champion handicap mare. She earned her place in racing's Hall of Fame.

When Princess Rooney sold at Keeneland in 1985 — in foal to Danzig — the bidding was awe inspiring. When the gavel finally fell, Texas businessman George Aubin had secured the pregnant Princess Rooney for $5.5 million. It was a record price for a Keeneland broodmare.

The precious cargo she was carrying, Olé, was born March 15, 1986. The next year the handsome, kind-eyed, and beautifully conformed yearling entered the Keeneland auction ring. Bidding reached $2.9 million but failed to meet the reserve. Aubin turned down an offer of $3 million immediately afterward, Moreno said.

Aubin kept Olé, and the colt soon entered Moreno's California barn.

A lifelong horseman, Moreno trained his first winner in 1950 and, with the exception of a twenty-seven-month stint in the service, has trained horses ever since. He's an old-time, highly respected horseman, and among the world-class horses he's trained are Sangue, Tizna, and Bastonera.

Olé, however, simply was not of stakes caliber. The race in which he broke his jaw, in October of his three-year-old season, was his eighth as a maiden. Three starts later he finally entered the winner's circle.

But five starts later, in a Santa Anita allowance race on March 10, 1990, Olé was in second place making a solid move when he suffered a severely fractured sesamoid. Not only was his racing career over, but the injury was life threatening.

"He had a beautiful attitude, and he had good temperament for a stallion," Moreno said. "He had great potential."

Olé underwent surgery, and pins were inserted into his ankle. Complications soon set in, however, when his body rejected the pins.

"His leg was straight, but his foot went, not completely sideways, but pretty much so," Moreno said. "The vet wanted to rebreak it and straighten it out, and I said no. He'd rejected the pins already, and I didn't want to put him through it again.

"He was in his stall for a year. I paid all the vet bills and brought him home."

Moreno assumed ownership of Olé, and the young stallion entered stud for 1991 at Flag Is Up Farms with a $2,500 fee. He soon moved to Mira Loma Thoroughbred Farm in Mira Loma, California, where he resided for more than a decade.

Olé limped and his left front leg was terribly unsightly, yet he appeared comfortable. And, although he had only a small paddock to keep him from overextending himself, he could still gallop a bit. His attitude remained positive, he ate well, and he loved the ladies.

He had fourteen foals in his first crop, including the stakes winner No Explanation, who earned nearly $400,000. By the late 1990s Olé was breeding more than twenty mares annually. A 1999 arrival, Debonair Joe, won the grade I Malibu Stakes and two other added-money events. By early 2007, that popular gelding, still racing, had earned $571,876.

Olé's runners average a respectable $40,662. Moreno, however, believes Olé could have done better.

"I train horses for a living, and I'm probably not the best hustler for broodmares," he said. "He's done pretty well, considering that the mares we've got here in California weren't blue hens."

When Mira Loma closed in 2005, Olé moved to Harrison Farms. In early 2007, he left California for the land of enchantment, New Mexico. He stands at the Square D Training Stable near Albuquerque.

LaRae and Gary Sumpter, longtime friends of Moreno, have entered an agreement with him to share Olé and a band of mares. They're looking out for the twenty-one-year-old stallion, as is Square D owner Dominic Duree.

"Dominic said, 'I'm putting a goat in. They're real cheap these days. The goat only costs seventy-five dollars, so don't worry about the goat. This old horse needs company,' " LaRae said. "He smothers it just like he's the mother, and they eat together. It's just a real neat deal."

Olé has a sizable box-stall that opens into his private pen. The sandy soil — the farm's near the Rio Grande — provides comfort to the aging stallion's feet. A young stud colt in an adjacent stall keeps him company, and he's got Wilma the goat.

"He's just a real rugged old horse," LaRae said. "He's going to be around forever, I know. He's like some people; he has a high tolerance for pain and a great gut to survive."

Our Mims Retirement Haven

The mares resembled a gathering of the Red Hat Society that bitter January afternoon. On a faraway hill, behind bare-branched trees and brown brush, the ladies were bedecked in brilliant-green, royal-blue, and rich-purple plaid blankets. Some dozed while others grazed on muted grass.

Some boasted excellent race records while others boasted first-rate broodmare careers. Some boasted neither. Yet regardless of background, the aged ladies at Our Mims Retirement Haven share one thing: They're all loved.

Jeanne Mirabito owns and runs the spacious Paris, Kentucky, farm, whose motto is: "Specializing in restoring health and spirit in aged mares." A lifelong horsewoman, Jeanne got the idea while tending to Our Mims, the 1977 champion three-year-old filly. Jeanne acquired her in 2000 with the help of the Thoroughbred adoption organization ReRun. Our Mims' owner was happy to be relieved of the old horse, while Jeanne was thrilled to provide her a home.

She and her husband, Pete, set about converting an old tobacco barn into one fit for horses. A carpenter built the first stall, a neighbor added more, and Jeanne constructed the rest: nine roomy stalls in all. She named the farm Ahwenasa — Cherokee for "my home."

Our Mims wanted for nothing. Receiving the finest senior feed and regular veterinary and blacksmith care, the old mare blossomed, and Jeanne's life was forever changed. She fashioned a plan to fill the stalls with other unwanted, older mares.

When Our Mims died in December 2003, Jeanne was crushed and almost abandoned her plan. But when she heard that Our Mims' younger sister, Sugar and Spice, needed a home, she opened her heart again and let Sugar in.

Sugar's arrival emboldened Jeanne to create the retirement haven in May 2004. Along with Sugar and Spice, Hope of Glory, the 1974 Alcibiades Stakes winner, was an original resident.

Despite Jeanne's loving care, neither Sugar nor Hope lasted long. Sugar died in September 2004 at age twenty-seven, and Hope, thirty-two, followed the next month. Sugar went home to Calumet Farm, and Hope was buried at Ahwenasa.

Forced into the realization that her farm would occasionally be a hospice, Jeanne continued undeterred. She acquired five impressive pensioners in November 2004:

• EXACTLY SO, winner of the grade II Gallorette Handicap, stakes-placed in France, and dam of French group I winner Exactly Sharp.

• JAMRA, a full sister to leading sire Clever Trick.

• IZA VALENTINE, 1985 California Broodmare of the Year and dam of grade I winner Fran's Valentine.

• TABA, Argentina's 1975 champion two-year-old filly and dam of champion Turkoman.

• MY TURBULENT MISS, dam of grade I winner Prized and grade II victor Exploit.

Some of those ladies didn't last long either, despite Jeanne's attentive watch. Yet others carried on, and another mare, Timeless Sue, second dam of thirteen-time stakes winner Bourbon Belle, soon joined the group.

Word spread about the farm, and soon Jeanne couldn't accept all the mares offered. She did her best to place those she could not keep. Still they came,

Jamra (1981 gr. m. by Icecapade—Kankakee Miss, by Better Bee)

Irvina (1976 b. m. by Turn to Reason—Chalvedele, by First Fiddle)

one after another, the senior mares and even a gelding and spare pony or two. Most arrived without pension plans.

Enter Cheryl Bellucci. She and her husband, John, met Jeanne at a ReRun function in 2000. They visited the farm, and Cheryl was overwhelmed by both Jeanne's love for Our Mims and her desire to create a haven for older mares.

Cheryl offered to help Jeanne, and when Our Mims died, Cheryl raised the funds for the memorial stone. She was so successful that she asked to help out with more fund-raising and soon held the title of director of fund-raising and promotion.

While she assists in many other areas — from applying for non-profit status to helping acquire mares — Cheryl works tirelessly toward raising money. She solicits donations and sells such items as halters, photographs, and horseshoes, often on eBay and through Cafe Press. Still, she can raise only a fraction of what is needed to run the farm — and keep the mares in blankets.

The neighbors help, too. Alicia Brown, a high school student, asked to

Left: Iza Valentine (1976 b. m. by Bicker—Countess Market, by Count of Honor); middle: Hana Bride (1982 b. m. by Coastal—Sue Me Not, by Verbatim); right: Smokies Love (1977 ch. m. by Levant—Smokey's Sister, by Nahr Love)

work with the horses to gain experience for her agriculture class. Soon, her whole family was pitching in: her father as a general mechanic, electrician, and carpenter; her mother, who raffled handmade quilts to buy materials for a water line to the barn; and her sister and three brothers, who helped with stall cleaning and mare grooming.

The equine elders now number nine with stall space — eight mares and one gelding — and two ponies with barn dibs. In winter they are let out each morning and kept in at night. They enjoy meals custom created according to their likes and needs. Jeanne makes certain each horse is comfortable before heading to her own house for supper. Her current roster:

• Iza Valentine, born on Valentine's Day 1976, is a gorgeous reigning queen. The near-black mare is a sweetheart, but she does not like cats and chases them from her stall. She suffered a mild stroke in August 2006 and bowed a tendon later in the year. While she is now slower, she is still comfortable.

• Hana Bride was slaughter bound when saved by Washington state's Columbia Basin Equine Rescue, and through the assistance of the Exceller Fund, she was eventually routed to the retirement haven. Jeanne says she's "just plain paranoid." Hana occasionally starts hollering when the horses head in for dinner, and Jeanne swears the old mare sees imaginary monsters. Inevitably, the whole group gets riled up and bolts back into the field.

• Hana's best friend, Alabama Nana, won several stakes including the grade III First Flight Handicap for trainer D. Wayne Lukas. She seems to remember from whence she came, and she prefers things efficient and tidy. If her stall is clean and she's not fussed with too long, then Nana is happy.

• Smokies Love is about as laid back as a horse can be. She and the barn's only gelding, a Quarter Horse named Barhopper, are sponsored by their owner.

• Irvina arrived in early 2006. She was thirty and depressed. Now? She's often first in line to eat, her eyes are bright, and she delights in the game "I can open any gate with my teeth … Watch!"

• Jamra frets if kept indoors too long, and she's learned Irvina's charming trick of opening her door latch. This old gray mare can be a handful.

• Timeless Sue looks much younger than her twenty-eight years. She's good to work with — willing and cooperative — but Jeanne knows to ask rather than to push her to do things.

• Princess Royale is indeed royalty. The Australian gray is by one of that country's greatest stallions, Bletchingly, and out of its champion three-year-old filly Rom's Stiletto. Princess set an all-time Australasian record for a filly when she sold for $600,000. Still, she ended up in Indiana, where a vet purchased her for $400 before she was donated to the retirement haven.

❧

In a far corner of a large field near the elder barn, the earth slowly settles on nearly indistinguishable plots where past residents have been laid to rest. Jeanne

Top left: Princess Royale (AUS) (1985 gr. m. by Bletchingly—Rom's Stiletto, by Sharp Edge); above: Alabama Nana (IRE) (1981 ch. m. by Thatching—Image Intensifier, by Dancer's Image); left: Timeless Sue (1979 ch. m. by Timeless Moment—Strella, by Reflected Glory)

a home, Jeanne felt she needed a break.

Jeanne's neighbors were helping to remove Hero's body from her stall when young Lloyd, then four, asked which horse would move in next. Jeanne explained that she was too heartbroken to take in another right away.

Lloyd persisted. How long would it take for Jeanne's heart to feel better? Jeanne could not respond or her tears would flow. She recalls Lloyd's next words. He, too, was near tears, and his voice was a whisper: "But where will all the ladies go? Who will love them?"

Jeanne pulled out her cell phone and called Irvina's owner.

✧

Irvina lasted for more than a year at Jeanne's, but she succumbed May 4, 2007, at age thirty-one. She was buried on the farm. Days later, Jeanne took in twenty-five-year-old Little Miss Porter.

knows where each horse is buried and hopes one day to buy memorial markers.

The deaths don't get any easier for her. When a mare named Hero's Hurrah, died in January 2006, Jeanne was, again, crushed. She was still mourning the death of the mare Misty on New Year's Eve, and several other mares had died in 2005. Irvina had not yet moved in, and while Jeanne knew the old mare needed

The Patchen Wilkes' Whites

White Beauty was a phenom. When she was born milky white — at odds then considered three-million-to-one — no one believed she was a Thoroughbred. Even Herman Goodpaster, her breeder and then-farm manager at Patchen Wilkes Farm in Lexington, Kentucky, considered the possibility that a white stallion had jumped a fence to court his mare.

After The Jockey Club's careful scrutiny, however, her heritage was confirmed. Born May 7, 1963, by a chestnut stallion and out of a bay mare, White Beauty was, indeed, a Thoroughbred.

She truly was a horse of a different color — the first Thoroughbred registered "white" by The Jockey Club. And she was a sensation. She not only raced, winning twice, but also spawned an alabaster dynasty.

Goodpaster bred four of the first six registered white Thoroughbreds in America: White Beauty, Beauty 'n Motion (born 1975, out of White Beauty), Precious Beauty (1981, out of White Beauty's daughter World O'Beauty), and Late 'n White (1985, also out of World O'Beauty).

By the time businessman Warren Rosenthal bought Patchen Wilkes in 1981, Goodpaster and his white horses had moved on. Rosenthal and his farm manager, Barry Ezrine, kept in touch with Goodpaster, and Rosenthal mentioned that he would love to have white horses on the farm again.

"Warren had always wanted a white horse here," Ezrine said. "One of the first horses we bought was a white pony that he bought for his grandkids to ride. It had to be white … He's always been one to preserve the history of the farm."

One day Goodpaster said to Ezrine: "Does your boss still want one of those white horses? I've got a mare out at Judy Fuson's place right over there on the other side of the interstate."

Yes, Ezrine said, Rosenthal did. Goodpaster's mare Precious Beauty, a

Patchen Beauty and The White Fox

Precious Beauty (1981 wh. m. by Jatulla—World O'Beauty, by Reverse)

granddaughter of White Beauty, was being used to produce racing Paint horses. But her foals had been coming out white and, as such, could not be registered as Paints.

"We went over with Warren and a friend of his, and Precious Beauty had a beautiful white foal, with blue eyes, by her side," Ezrine recalled. "They said we could have her after they weaned the foal."

And so Precious Beauty moved to Patchen Wilkes Farm in 1990.

"It was just kind of preserving the history of the farm," Ezrine said. "We never really thought about breeding white horses, but after we got a white mare we decided we might as well try to breed her."

Precious Beauty's first registered foals were chestnut and bay, but the third time proved the charm. Patchen Beauty, a snow-white filly by the gray Hatchet Man, was born in 1995. Her birth received so much publicity and attention — including via the rapidly expanding Internet — that she became the most popular white Thoroughbred since White Beauty.

Precious Beauty eventually produced seven named Thoroughbred foals, but only Patchen Beauty was white. Sadly, Precious Beauty was kicked in late December 1999 while in foal to Boone's Mill. On January 4, 2000, some three months before her due date, she slipped her foal — a white filly.

In early 2004, when she was twenty-three, Precious Beauty's hind end began giving out. The old white mare was euthanized in her paddock on May 21, 2004, and buried in the front yard of the main house. A gravestone marks the spot.

Then it was her white daughter's turn to carry on the Patchen Wilkes' tradition. Patchen Beauty won two races and earned $54,268. More importantly, she has produced three white beauties of her own:

• The White Fox (2002), a colt by Storm Cat's half brother Pioneering, is a freshman stallion at Hopewell Farm.

• Spot of Beauty (2004), a filly by Skip Away, has won at Beulah Park.

• Patchen Prince (2005), a colt by Pioneering, is a two-year-old in training at Turfway Park.

The media wrote much about the Goodpaster-bred White Beauty and Precious Beauty as well as Patchen Beauty. But what became of the other two white Thoroughbreds Goodpaster bred: Beauty 'n Motion and Late 'n White?

Goodpaster kept them at a farm not far from Patchen Wilkes. He was getting older and knew he needed to find another home for them. Ezrine agreed to take the white mares to Patchen Wilkes even though he knew they were nearly wild. They lived in a field with another horse.

"There were three horses out there together, and they were like herd animals," Ezrine said. "You couldn't separate them. I went out every day and tried to get them in the barn to put halters on them. They'd start climbing the walls."

He eventually got them to accept the halters, and then, after tranquilizing them, vanned them to Patchen Wilkes. "The two white horses, we still could not separate them," Ezrine said. "They would go nuts. The old white mare was swaybacked and was the meanest, most cantankerous mare I'd ever been around. She'd bite you. Her name was Beauty 'n Motion — and she was just dead mean."

He chuckled when he said her name, and he didn't seem too heartbroken when he added: "She finally foundered and died."

The other white mare — a half sister to Precious Beauty — wasn't even registered. Ezrine called The Jockey Club to see whether it was possible to register a sixteen-year-old. It was, and she was named, appropriately, Late 'n White. She became a Patchen Wilkes' lawn ornament.

Nowadays, Late 'n White is quite tractable. She's twenty-two and resides with several other pensioned standouts: Close Comfort, the second dam of champion Mubtaker; Gazayil, Mubtaker's dam; and Ring Dancer, the dam of three stakes winners, including Cefis.

Rosenthal is marketing his white horses. The White Fox is featured on www.thewhitefox.com, which offers a White Fox children's book and T-shirts. And fans eagerly await The White Fox's foals as well.

At Patchen Wilkes, time is taking its toll. The area around it is being built up as Winchester Road, just outside of New Circle Road, has proved to be a commercial windfall. Rosenthal has sold some of his property and plans to sell more. A housing development called Patchen Wilkes, on land that was once part of the farm, sports a large, white model of a horse at its entrance.

For now, Late 'n White grazes in peace, and Patchen Beauty passes her days in a spacious paddock near the main office. Their brilliant ivory coats dot the farm's green landscape and hark back to that fateful day in 1963 when White Beauty was born.

Late 'n White (1985 wh. m. by Triomphe—World O'Beauty, by Reverse)

Left to right: Personal Ensign and Gus Koch, My Flag and Seth Hancock, Storm Flag Flying and Charles Koch

Personal Ensign

1984 b. m. by Private Account — Grecian Banner, by Hoist the Flag

Personal Ensign's story is about family. And so, on September 26, 2006, that historic family connection was recorded in a photograph when Personal Ensign was posed with her daughter My Flag, and My Flag's daughter Storm Flag Flying. They represented three consecutive female generations to win a Breeders' Cup race — an accomplishment not only unparalleled but also unlikely to happen again.

ↄ৲

Personal Ensign was bred by Ogden Phipps and born at Claiborne Farm near Paris, Kentucky. For generations Claiborne has raised first-class horses in its own name and for longtime clients. No other client, perhaps, has such a long and deep-rooted association with Claiborne as the Phipps family.

Personal Ensign was by the Phippses' young sire Private Account. A grade I winner, Private Account was out of one of the Phipps' best race mares and producers, Numbered Account. Numbered Account was a daughter of the Phippses' immortal Buckpasser.

Personal Ensign's dam, Grecian Banner, was a Phipps-bred, too, who also produced the Phippses' grade I winner Personal Flag. He and Personal Ensign won grade Is in 1987 and 1988.

Grecian Banner was named Kentucky Broodmare of the Year in 1988 but, sadly, she died that year of peritonitis with farm manager Gus Koch at her side.

When Shug McGaughey began training Personal Ensign, he had just started working for the Phipps family. After she broke her maiden in her first start at two, in late September 1986, McGaughey brought her right back in the grade I Frizette Stakes. She won.

McGaughey and the Phippses were certain Personal Ensign was extraordinary, but before she could prove that in the Breeders' Cup, she fractured her left rear pastern in a morning workout. Five screws were inserted.

"Before that, we thought she was very special," said Ogden "Dinny" Phipps, Ogden Phipps' son, "and I think special not only because she was immensely talented, but she also was smart enough to really take care of herself after that injury and the recuperation period. That was not an easy injury."

She returned to racing about a year later and won four races at three, capping her comeback season with a win in the grade I Beldame Stakes.

At four Personal Ensign went from the kind of horse you talk about for a few years to one you remember for a lifetime. She remained undefeated while winning seven consecutive races, six of which were grade Is. She beat two top male handicap horses, Gulch and King's Swan, in the Whitney Handicap, and in the Maskette Stakes she wore down Kentucky Derby winner Winning Colors.

Next came the Breeders' Cup Distaff. And on a cold, dark, and rainy afternoon at Churchill Downs, the long-faced, angular filly joined the immortals.

Early in the race, under Randy Romero, she was seemingly beaten on a track she disliked. Yet Personal Ensign slowly began gaining on the freewheeling leader, Winning Colors. While victory seemed impossible, she somehow nipped the Derby winner at the wire. Many believe it is the greatest effort by a modern Thoroughbred.

That was Personal Ensign's final race, and it kept her perfect: thirteen consecutive victories and the first champion to retire undefeated since Colin in 1908. She was ranked the forty-eighth best American racehorse in the twentieth century.

was vanned home to Claiborne Farm. Koch remembers that, too.

"We brought her in here, and she was high strung," Koch said. "A lot of good race mares are. She was tough. The blacksmith couldn't get her shoes off at first. I'd go in there every day with a man named Jim Robert Willoughby, and we would pick her feet up in the stall and work with her, and then we got her out in the hallway where we could pick her feet up. And then she calmed down enough for the blacksmith."

Some mares like that might prove to be more trouble than they're worth, but there was no chance of that happening with Personal Ensign.

"Her first foal was just outstanding," Koch said. "We knew she was a great race mare, but then we realized she was going to be great on the farm, too. And of course, as we say, the rest is history."

Personal Ensign's first foal was grade I winner Miner's Mark, and her second, Our Emblem, finished second or third in eight graded stakes and sired War Emblem, winner of the 2002 Kentucky Derby. Her fourth foal, a long-faced chestnut filly by the Phippses' Easy Goer, was named My Flag. She won the Breeders' Cup Juvenile Fillies, three other grade I stakes, and earned more than $1.5 million.

Personal Ensign's fifth foal, Proud and True, finished third in a graded stakes, and her sixth, Traditionally, won the grade I Oaklawn Handicap. Her eighth, Salute, placed and showed in graded stakes.

"I was at Churchill Downs when she won the Breeders' Cup," said Koch, Claiborne's manager. "Winning Colors had beat us in the Derby [Claiborne's Forty Niner was second], so we were able to turn the tables a little bit. What an awesome feeling that was. This was a Phipps horse, of course, but it was all in the family."

Personal Ensign, with her perfect record and earnings of $1,679,880,

All told, eight of her eleven foals raced, and one is a two-year-old of 2007. Her eight runners all won, and three of those won grade Is.

"She overcame more adversity than any other broodmare I've ever been around," Koch said. "Her intestinal fortitude is off the charts. I'm sure she had that desire at the racetrack, and that made her a champion. She went through a problem — peritonitis after foaling one year — that would have killed a lesser horse. She just refused to cave in to it. She showed all of us — the vet, people on the farm here."

The remarkable achievements haven't ended with Personal Ensign. Her daughter My Flag produced Storm Flag Flying, who carried on the family tradition by winning the Breeders' Cup Juvenile Fillies. Storm Flag Flying was crowned champion two-year-old filly of 2002.

And so it came to be that the Claiborne group gathered that warm September morning to pay tribute to Personal Ensign and to family. Dinny Phipps' daughter, Daisy, arranged the portrait of Personal Ensign with My Flag and Storm Flag Flying as a gift to her parents. Koch held Personal Ensign, farm owner Seth Hancock held My Flag, and Koch's son, assistant manager Charles Koch, held Storm Flag Flying.

The priceless mares were led behind their barn, and it didn't take long to place them for the photo: oldest, middle, youngest. Although the mares gave no indication of recognizing one another, they cooperated as if they understood the significance of the moment.

So, too, did the staff. Just after the formal portrait was taken, workers appeared from seemingly nowhere, quietly stepping in to hold the mares or take photos of their own They were young, old, male, female. Some held small cameras or picture phones. All were respectful — reverent, even. The mares stood patiently.

Koch paid tribute to all the people who came out to see the famous mares together.

"We have families here who have been here for two or three generations for the Hancocks," Koch said. "Those men back there, like Billy Purcell, have been here for forty years. Two of his sons were back there, and both of them were born on the farm. They're both foremen now. Charles [Koch] was back there, and he was about six or seven when we moved here.

"People tend to come to Claiborne and stay. Actually, they still look at me funny because I've only been here twenty-eight years, and they grew up here."

Later that morning Personal Ensign was taken to a field on another part of the farm. There, she began her retirement years with fellow pensioners Narrate, Arabian Dancer, and Korveya.

Later, Koch said that Personal Ensign was adapting well.

"The old mares out there are having a good life. They get along great. And she's mellowed a little — maybe," he chuckled.

"She knows she's special and wants to be left alone. "She deserves it."

Personal Flag rekindled different memories in different people. Shug McGaughey said he was a "puppy" to train, and Kate Feron of Akindale Farm, where Personal Flag entered stud, said he was no problem. By the time he stood at Prestonwood Farm years later, however, he was so threatening that grooms — two at a time — carried wooden bats when leading him to his paddock.

Bred by Ogden Phipps — a product of Phipps' Private Account and Grecian Banner — Personal Flag was born in 1983. The next year Grecian Banner produced a full sister to Personal Flag named Personal Ensign.

Ogden "Dinny" Phipps, son of Ogden Phipps, described Personal Flag as "a great big horse, and he had the same sort of big head Personal Ensign had."

"He was easy to train," said McGaughey, the Hall of Fame trainer. "He was just kind of a big old, clunky Private Account kind of horse."

Personal Flag entered the 1986 Belmont Stakes on a three-race win streak. On a sloppy track he finished fourth.

The Haskell also came up sloppy, and he finished second to the slop-loving Wise Times. And the Travers? Sloppy.

"I thought maybe he was the best that day," McGaughey said. "He got stopped about the eighth pole, and [Jorge Velasquez] had to take him up and take him really wide."

Personal Flag finished fourth, but Broad Brush, a top horse known for his occasionally errant ways, had angled into him. Personal Flag was elevated to third.

His first grade I win, in the Widener Handicap at Hialeah late the next year, got lost in the furor over a two-year-old Kentucky Derby prospect. In the race after the Widener, Seeking the Gold broke his maiden in his first start, and

that's all the reporters wanted to ask McGaughey about — not Personal Flag.

Personal Flag was also overshadowed by his younger sister. The same day Personal Flag won the grade I Suburban Handicap at Belmont — July 4, 1988 — Personal Ensign won Monmouth's Molly Pitcher Handicap. (Two days earlier Seeking the Gold had won the Dwyer. It was a memorable Fourth of July weekend for the Phippses.)

And the same afternoon Personal Ensign retired undefeated after her heart-stopping victory in the Breeders' Cup Distaff, Personal Flag's career ended when he lumbered home sixth in the Classic.

Personal Flag, who won four graded stakes, eight of twenty-four races, and $1,258,924, headed to Akindale Farm in New York for stud duty. The plain-headed, 17-hand stallion proved an immediate success. Initially, he was tractable as well.

"Personal Flag was fine at Akindale," said Feron, the manager. "Girls handled him. Sometimes he would run away from the gate with his shank — never anything worse than that."

Personal Flag moved to nearby Sugar Maple Farm and then, as his foals gained national prominence, to Kentucky's Prestonwood Farm. Prestonwood also shipped him to the Southern Hemisphere for breeding. Along the way, Personal Flag got so tough that he was sometimes walked by two grooms, armed with bats.

Enter Joe McMahon, owner of McMahon of Saratoga Thoroughbreds in New York. He was looking for a new stallion, and he settled on Personal Flag. Sally Jenkins recounted the tale in her book, *Funny Cide*:

"Joe was in need of a new stallion, he said, and Prestonwood was looking to get rid of a problem horse. He proposed a deal: He would take the horse and see what they could do with him, in exchange for a controlling interest in him. [Rich] Decker, intrigued, agreed to the deal. He would ship the horse to the McMahons and resyndicate him in New York."

Personal Flag, overseas at the time, moved again. When McMahon picked him up at the quarantine facility, he was ready for anything.

The horses had been released except for Personal Flag. Workers had kept the horse until last, and when McMahon was allowed to take him, it was late at night.

"Joe walked down to Personal Flag's stall," Jenkins wrote. "Leaning on the walls outside the stall were two wooden clubs. A handler gave the clubs to Joe. 'There he is,' he said, and stepped back. Joe realized that the barn crew was still hanging around. Joe got the feeling they wanted to see if Personal Flag was going to draw blood."

Personal Flag disappointed them. He did not try to savage McMahon, and he quickly settled in at their farm. He was strong willed, but they learned to get along with him. Some days, for instance, Personal Flag did not want to go to his paddock.

"He would just give you his look," McMahon said. "When he showed you the whites of his eyes, we'd just say, 'OK, he doesn't want to go out today.' We'd put him back in his stall. The trick with this horse was not to force him because if you fought him, he would fight with you.

"But he opened doors for us."

Because of the McMahons' affiliation

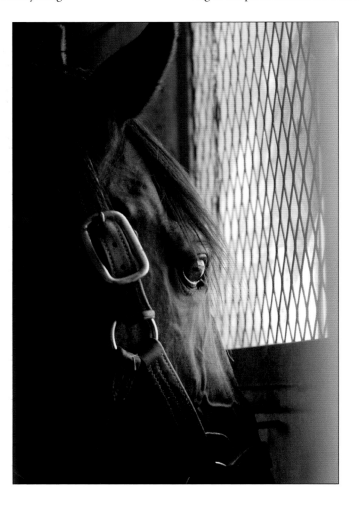

with Prestonwood, they boarded a mare named Belle's Good Cide. On April 20, 2000, she foaled a Distorted Humor colt named Funny Cide. He, and subsequent dealings with Prestonwood, changed the McMahons' lives forever.

Personal Flag seemed at peace in his old age. He was often dirty from rolling in his paddock and his mane was often long and unkempt. Workers only fussed with him when necessary, and they muzzled him for breeding sessions. His final crop came in 2004, after which he was pensioned due to declining fertility.

Personal Flag died the following summer at twenty-two. At the time of his death, he'd sired 279 winners from 522 starters, in the dual hemispheres, and his progeny had earned $31,910,353. His top earner, Say Florida Sandy, won nineteen stakes and earned more than $2 million.

The oversized stallion — the puppy, the rogue, the grade I winner, the popular sire — was buried near the stallion barn.

"We loved him, we got along with him, and we hated to see him die," McMahon said. "He was the best thing that ever happened to us."

I will always remember Personal Flag gazing, motionless, from his stall window for long moments. I'd watch him, always reminded of the Hans-Heinrich Isenbart saying:

A strange stillness dwells in the eye of the horse, a composure that appears to regard the world from a measured distance. It is a gaze from the depths of a dream.

Pirate's Bounty

1975–2006 DK. B/BR. H. BY HOIST THE FLAG—BAD SEED, BY STEVWARD

When Pirate's Bounty entered stud for the 1981 season, Martin Wygod, owner of River Edge Farm, told his farm manager Russell Drake to be selective with the mares. Drake didn't think that would be a problem.

The near-black stallion was sired by Hoist the Flag and out of a stakes-winning Stevward mare, but his race record wasn't stellar and he had soundness issues. In addition, the California stallion ranks were rich with sire power at the time. Wygod priced Pirate's Bounty at $4,000.

Drake recalled his conversation with Wygod.

Drake: "I don't think you have to worry about me being too selective because I don't think anyone will breed to him at that price."

Wygod: "Well, how many mares do I have?"

Drake: "You have about fifty or sixty."

Wygod: "Well, just breed all of mine."

Drake: "By the time you find out four or five years down the road if you can get a runner, you're going to eat a lot of hay."

Wygod: "I can afford the hay. You just breed them."

Drake did, and while the horses ate the hay, he ate crow. Pirate's Bounty became one of California's all-time leading sires. Eventually commanding a stud fee of $10,000, he sired sixty-three stakes winners — including two grade I winners. His progeny earnings topped $31.9 million. He was California's leading sire three times. And the ladies — Wygod's and others — lined up to visit him.

Wygod bred Pirate's Bounty, who was born in Kentucky. His sire was world-renowned, and his dam, Bad Seed, was anything but a bad seed. She won seven races, including the Golden Poppy Handicap at Golden Gate Fields. Her dam, Rich and Rare II, was an English champion two-year-old filly.

Bad Seed produced just one stakes winner — Pirate's Bounty — yet she appears in the pedigrees of grade I stakes winner Key Phrase and other stakes winners such as Yankee Gentleman, Maximize, Palmerton, Kresgeville, and Half Ours. The last named, a grade II winner who is still racing, was sold for $6.1 million at Keeneland in November 2006 to dissolve a partnership.

Pirate's Bounty did not race until he was four, and a knee injury plagued him throughout his career. He raced competitively in the East, never finishing off the board in seven starts (three wins, two seconds, two thirds). All the races were at Aqueduct, except one, the $30,000 Millburn Stakes at the Meadowlands. Pirate's Bounty won that by 1½ lengths.

But after transferring to California early in his five-year-old season, Pirate's Bounty won only one of eight. And off he went to Wygod's farm in Buellton, California.

The beautiful 170-acre farm, not far from the Pacific Ocean, had begun operations in 1976 and would become one of California's finest. By the time Pirate's Bounty arrived for the 1981 season, Pass the Glass and Bold Hitter were established farm stallions.

Yet the new arrival would soon claim the River Edge throne. And what a reign he had.

His first crop included California Derby (grade II) winner Hajji's Treasure, Anoakia Stakes (grade III) winner Wayward Pirate, multiple stakes winner Woman in Space, and stakes winners Studious One, Big Bounty, and Pirate's Regatta.

His grade I winners were Wygod-bred fillies of 1991 that captured their big races in 1995 at Hollywood Park. Pirate's Revenge won the Milady Handicap, and Private Persuasion the Vanity Invitational Handicap. And Pirate's Bounty's richest offspring, the eight-time stakes winner Feverish ($908,983), was also a filly bred by Wygod.

Wygod's faith was more than justified.

And Drake, despite his early doubts, grew tremendously fond of Pirate's Bounty.

"He was a real straightforward horse," Drake said. "Most stallions are going to take advantage of you when they can. If he was going to bite you, he'd look right at you, and he didn't wait until you turned your back. He was honest."

And in the breeding shed?

"Of all the stallions I've been around in my lifetime," Drake said, "he was one of the best to breed. He was a terrific kind of romancer."

His romancing resulted in nineteen crops, but after the 1999 breeding season his reign came to end. He got just two mares in foal and was pensioned.

Pirate's Bounty lived out his days on the farm he helped make successful, near broodmares carrying his bloodlines and farm workers who revered him. Although Pirate's Bounty grew rickety and slim, his fire continued to smolder. He was let out daily and enjoyed grazing in the California sunshine.

At the age of thirty-one, however, his fire dimmed. In August 2006, Pirate's Bounty was euthanized and laid to rest on the farm. A marker notes the spot where he lies.

"That one horse, he probably did us more good than any horse we'll ever have," Drake said. "He treated River Edge Farm very, very, very well."

Drake laughed gently and said: "I'm kind of sorry, looking back, that I doubted his ability."

Precisionist

1981–2006 CH. H. BY CROZIER — EXCELLENTLY, BY *FORLI

Fate led me to Precisionist that September day in 2006. I was in the Lexington area for one day and had an hour to spare before heading to the airport. I called the folks at Old Friends, where Precisionist had recently settled in. I had no idea that Precisionist was sick — let alone that he would die the following afternoon.

THE EARLY DAYS:

Precisionist was born in Florida, bred by the famed horseman Fred Hooper. His sire and dam — Crozier, the 1963 Santa Anita Handicap winner, and Excellently, by Forli and out of a multiple stakes producing mare — were Hooper homebreds.

While training at Hooper's nine-hundred-acre-plus farm near Ocala, the youthful Precisionist had good and bad days. He tossed his exercise rider one morning and ran into the back of a parked car. The tailgate and tailpipe were broken, but Precisionist was unscathed. Another morning he easily out-breezed a workmate, and Hooper and Robert Williams, farm manager, clocked him in a blistering :34.

"We thought we had something then," Williams said.

THE RACING YEARS: 1983–1986

Precisionist won twenty of forty-six starts during his career, including seventeen stakes, six of which were grade Is. He sprinted and ran classic distances, won on dirt and turf, and earned nearly $3.5 million.

Yet Precisionist was initially nervous and unratable. Jay Hovdey of *Daily Racing Form* called the two-year-old "a wild-eyed firebrand."

Over time, Precisionist matured under Ross Fenstermaker's training (he trained Precisionist for most of the colt's career). Their regime included frequent paddock schoolings and leisurely mornings.

The Hooper colorbearer won three of five starts at two, and at three he won five of twelve — including the grade I Swaps by ten lengths.

At four, Precisionist won four of nine and swept the three-race Strub series, a feat previously accomplished by just four horses: Hillsdale, Round Table, Ancient Title, and Spectacular Bid. Precisionist won the seven-furlong Malibu, the nine-furlong San Fernando, and the ten-furlong Charles H. Strub. He also clinched the sprint championship by winning the Breeders' Cup Sprint.

Yet some believed he deserved more, including *Blood-Horse* editor Kent Hollingsworth:

"For champion handicapper and Horse of the Year, we would nominate champion sprinter Precisionist, an older horse no 3-year-old beat this year, which gave five to eight pounds to Greinton six times … which could go head and head and win at 1¼ miles, win at 1⅛ miles, win at a mile in 1:32⅖ — and come back in his first start in 19 weeks to win a sprint championship in 1:08⅗." Instead, Horse of the Year honors went to Spend a Buck.

Precisionist ranked first on *The Blood-Horse* Free Handicap for Older Males of 1985. That honor earned him *The Blood-Horse* cover, and it earned me my first photo to appear in the magazine.

At five, Precisionist won the grade I Californian and Woodward, and the grade II San Pasqual and San Bernardino. In the 1986 Breeders' Cup Classic, however, he finished third, and although he beat Lady's Secret both times they met, she was crowned Horse of the Year.

THE STUD YEARS: 1987–1988

While training in early 1987, Precisionist fractured his cannon bone, and he headed to Florida's Bridlewood Farm for stud duty. But he didn't stay long.

Only one mare bred to him that year got in foal, and Hooper brought his beloved horse home.

"I still believe in him," Hooper said. "It's not unusual for a horse to be a shy breeder his first season at stud."

Precisionist's problem, however, wasn't being a shy breeder. As an ominous footnote, Precisionist's lone foal born in 1988 died soon after birth.

Precisionist headed back to the track.

The Racing Year: 1988

Precisionist returned triumphantly at seven, despite literally stumbling at the start. In his first race he tripped out of the gate, tossed his regular rider, Chris McCarron, and finished first — by himself.

He won three of ten starts, including a graded stakes, and set a Del Mar mile record, 1:33⅕, that still stands. He returned to Hooper's farm to stand stud in 1989, but his problems continued.

The Stud Years, part two – or "what to do"? 1989–1996

Hooper continued standing Precisionist at stud, but mares simply weren't conceiving. "Precisionist's sperm has been analyzed more times than Ben Johnson's urine," *The Blood-Horse* reported in 1994. "Last year, Hooper sent Precisionist to … New Bolton Center for four months, hoping to solve the riddle. Hooper even sent up eight mares from Florida … The scientific conclusion: 'His semen wasn't contacting the egg in the mares,' Hooper said. 'I spent $44,000 and got no results. I've done all I know how to do.' "

Hooper even put Precisionist briefly back in training in 1991.

Overall, Precisionist sired four named foals. All four made it to the races, and two were winners.

The Ellison Years: 1996–2006

Siobhan Ellison was working on her doctorate in molecular biology when she decided she'd like to study Precisionist. She contacted Hooper to see if

he'd send the struggling stallion to her, and Hooper acquiesced. In 1996 he shipped Precisionist to Ellison's nearby woodsy, sheltered farm.

For the most part, Precisionist lived there for a decade as Ellison studied the aging champion. She concluded that his sperm lacked a particular protein that would enable it to attach to a mare's egg.

Hooper visited regularly.

"He'd pull right up to the paddock in his car, jump out, and Precisionist would come right over to him," Ellison told *The Florida Horse*. "He'd always bring a five-pound bag of carrots, and Precisionist would eat every one of them."

In summer 2000, the *Thoroughbred Times* interviewed then 102-year-old Hooper. Ever optimistic, he said: "We've gottten some good news lately … It seems that some vets have developed a new serum that has helped another stallion with similar problems to Precisionist's. After they inject the serum into the mare, this other stallion's been able to get them in foal. I hope it can work with Precisionist, too."

But on August 4, 2000, Precisionist lost his devoted owner — and biggest fan — when Hooper died. His dreams for Precisionist went unfulfilled.

Nonetheless, Precisionist seemed content, sharing his lush paddock with an aged mini-mule named Mary Margaret. A run-in shed with a fan provided relief from summer's heat. They often slept side by side.

On average, one Precisionist fan visited monthly. I visited twice, in 1998 and 2003. The second time, Precisionist was days away from being inducted into the Hall of Fame. He seemed relaxed, youthful, powerful … and he loved his Mary Margaret.

Mary Margaret, a tiny gray darling with sad eyes, showed her age. Precisionist had retained his slim look although his back swayed a bit. He jogged for the camera, cantered, and reared slightly, befitting a champion.

Old Friends, 2006

In June 2006 came the announcement that Precisionist, twenty-five, was moving to Old Friends Equine near Lexington.

"The heat gets to him," Ellison told the *Daily Racing Form*. "Every year it was getting tougher and tougher to keep him comfortable."

Mary Margaret stayed behind because of her age, but Old Friends' accessibility and fan-friendly policy provided Precisionist an expanded fan base. Countless people visited the Hall of Famer — even Chris McCarron.

Precisionist with Michael Blowen on September 26, 2006

But those carefree days did not last long as Precisionist was soon diagnosed with tumors in his soft palate and nasal passages. The cancer was persistent and spreading, and Precisionist's breathing became labored. He was sent to the Hagyard Equine Medical Institute several times, but nothing worked.

And so, on September 26, I visited Precisionist one last time. Michael Blowen, founder of Old Friends, and several farm volunteers were tending to the slim chestnut stallion in a small paddock, stroking him and wiping blood from his nostrils. A tracheotomy the day before had eased his breathing, but when they led him into the yard he was clearly uncomfortable.

Back in his stall, he shuffled slowly to a large window and peered out. His look was wistful, as if he understood.

That evening Blowen brought Precisionist carrots. The horse looked at the carrots, then at Blowen, then at the carrots, before turning to stare out the window. Blowen spent the night in the barn.

Precisionist was euthanized the next day and buried on the farm. National Public Radio's *All Things Considered* broadcast a touching eulogy.

The Old Friends' Web site paid tribute:

"Precisionist taught us a lot. Not just about how he liked his stall fluffed and where he liked his neck rubbed but about dignity and, of course, class …

"As great as he was as a race horse, it can't compare with his other qualities — intelligence, patience, stoicism, and bearing. On Wednesday afternoon, his final day, he proved he didn't leave his class on the race track."

Princess Rooney

1980 GR. M. BY VERBATIM — PARRISH PRINCESS, BY DRONE

Princess Rooney's owner, Robert Gentry, told the story: "There wasn't a better race mare in the world when she was running. She's had a lot of hard luck with her babies, though. She's just a black cat."

Princess Rooney was the best of her time, winning a remarkable seventeen of twenty-one starts, including her first ten for trainer Frank Gomez and her last five for trainer Neil Drysdale. The elegant gray lady, so competitive she was a handful to train, won ten stakes, including five grade Is: Breeders' Cup Distaff, Kentucky Oaks, Vanity Handicap, Spinster Stakes, and Frizette Stakes. A $38,000 yearling purchase, she earned $1,343,339. She was the 1984 champion handicap mare and, seven years later, was inducted into racing's Hall of Fame.

In her career finale, the 1984 Breeders' Cup Distaff, Princess Rooney romped by seven lengths. Her time for the mile and a quarter, 2:02⅖, was a full second faster than Wild Again's for the Breeders' Cup Classic later that day. The performance earned her that week's *Blood-Horse* cover girl honors.

The next year she sold at the Keeneland November breeding stock sale, in foal to Danzig, for $5.5 million. (The resulting foal, Olé, is featured in this book.) It was a record price for a broodmare at Keeneland.

Ten years later, brothers Robert and Bruce Gentry purchased Princess Rooney, this time in foal to

Deputy Minister, for $130,000. She resides at Gentry Farm in Lexington, Kentucky.

Her breeding career has been anything but a romp, and her record reflects thirteen cases of "barren," "slipped," "no report," or "foal died." She has eight registered foals, including a three-year-old named House of Words. (House of Words has raced twice through April 2007, including a fifth-place finish at Keeneland in his second start). Seven of Princess Rooney's foals have raced, and five have won.

Her daughter Lady in Waiting, a stakes-placed runner, is dam of the multiple stakes winner Kid Grindstone. And her daughters Rose Tiara and Rooneys Princess, who also both reside on the Gentry farm, have each produced a stakes-placed runner. But there are, so far, no shades of Princess Rooney.

With her roles of racehorse and broodmare behind her, twenty-seven-year-old Princess Rooney is still vital. The royal gray mare, her coat flecked with dark spots and her white eyelashes accentuating contented, trusting eyes, has new responsibilities.

"She has a pretty important job on the place," said Bud Downs, a farm manager. "She's turned out with some yearlings, and she keeps them safe.

"She's very comfortable here. She's in good flesh and looks great. She seems very happy and full of life."

Proper Reality

1985 DK. B/BR. H. BY IN REALITY — PROPER PRINCESS, BY NODOUBLE

The majestic stallion surveys his kingdom at Bob Holthus' Kilkerry Farm in Royal, Arkansas. His large, proud eyes burn with power, and his dark bay coat gleams. When he gallops across his paddock, he appears much younger than his twenty-two years. Holthus, who trained Proper Reality, is now providing the old stallion a home.

The son of In Reality was bred and raced by James and Juanita Winn. He was broken at Kilkerry, not far from Oaklawn, where Holthus is the all-time winningest trainer. Holthus was honored with inclusion in the Arkansas Walk of Fame in Hot Springs in 1999 and, three years later, at Oaklawn Park for fifty years of winning races there. The track's Web site calls him "an Oaklawn legend."

"You could do about anything you wanted with him," Holthus said of Proper Reality. "You could work him a half in :50 or a half in :47. Whatever you wanted him to do, he was willing to do it."

The colt flashed promise at two, breaking his maiden by fifteen lengths at Louisiana Downs. But his shins flared up, and he was sent back to the farm where his shins were pinfired. He returned to Oaklawn four months later, winning an allowance and the Southwest Stakes and finishing fourth in the Rebel Stakes. When he captured the Arkansas Derby, he confirmed for youthful jockey Jerry Bailey, who rode Proper Reality in all but one of his nineteen races, that he was a Kentucky Derby contender.

"I was going into the Kentucky Derby with a legitimate chance," Bailey wrote in his biography, *Against the Odds*. "After being on two starters who were not nearly good enough, every bone in my body told me Proper Reality and I could get the job done."

Winning Colors led at every pole that day, and though Bailey tried to catch the filly, Proper Reality flattened out in the lane and finished fourth.

Yet he had an excuse: The colt had suffered a saucer fracture of the left front cannon bone. The fracture was slight, however, and he kept training for the $500,000 Illinois Derby in June.

"He trained pretty good on it," Holthus said, "and then he won the Illinois Derby. He was far out in the middle of the racetrack."

Proper Reality underwent surgery and headed back to Kilkerry for recuperation. He returned the following February and won two of four stakes. He shipped east and finished second in the Pimlico Special before heading to Belmont Park for the Metropolitan Handicap.

The powerhouse Phipps entry of Dancing Spree and Seeking the Gold was favored. Seeking the Gold, Pat Day up, usually ran close to the lead and Dancing Spree, ridden by Angel Cordero Jr., was a closer. Various horses held the lead early on, yet, as they entered the long homestretch, a battle between Seeking the Gold and Dancing Spree began in earnest.

Bailey sat back and waited.

"The reputations of rough-and-tumble Cordero and the unflappable Day already were made," Bailey wrote in *Against the Odds*. "They were bound for the history books. This furious three-horse fight for the wire was my chance to show the world that Jerry Bailey could ride a little bit, too."

In a thrillingly close three-horse finish, Bailey pushed Proper Reality to a scant nose victory. While Proper Reality would win again, that dramatic Met Mile was his crowning achievement. In October that year, an X-ray revealed the earlier fracture had reappeared, and four-year-old Proper Reality was retired.

After years at stud at Claiborne Farm and then in Oklahoma and Texas, he came back to Kilkerry. He's still breeding — he sired three foals in 2006 — but mainly he oversees the day's events from his spacious paddock. He's a farm favorite who, according to farm manager Carl Chapman, is easy to handle and throws correct babies. When he spots mares and their foals in nearby paddocks, he puffs up, arches his neck, and gallops their way in an awesome display of power. And he enjoys watching the horses in training, too.

"He plays with all the babies we're breaking on the racetrack," Chapman said. "He runs down there, plays with them — scares the devil out of them."

Bailey acknowledges that he was usually not sentimental about his horses. Yet, of Proper Reality's Metropolitan Handicap, he wrote: "It was no mean feat to outride Cordero and Day to the wire, and yet the will and courage of Proper Reality had helped me accomplish that.

"I cannot say he was the best horse in the country in 1989. I am sure he fought harder than anyone else."

Puchilingui

1984 RO. H. BY NATIVE ROYALTY — CAROLINAWAY, BY NEEDLES

Colored Thoroughbreds are a wonder to me — perhaps because they're so beautiful. And none is more wondrous than Puchilingui. I'd marveled at his photo in the stallion directories for years and had long wanted to visit him in Michigan. One cold morning in January 2007, I wound my way up Double Tree Paint Farm's long, snowy driveway. On both sides were paddocks dotted with multicolored horses, most descended from Puchilingui.

Smack dab in the middle of the driveway, staring at me, stood an elderly paint-colored mare. I got out of the car and gently guided the sweet lass to the side. Closer to the barn I passed another free-range mare.

The barn was ordinary from the outside — not fancy but stout, offering shelter from Michigan winters. Inside, a radio played country music.

There were seven Puchilinguis in the barn, and the big horse himself. He glowed in his stall, and, to his left, his near-white son, the stallion Chet DT, peered out. In a corner stall was a spotted yearling, and down the way were other brightly marked horses —Thoroughbreds and a Thoroughbred–Quarter Horse mix.

They were a visual wonderland.

Puchilingui has been a mixed blessing for his owner, Jerry Tyler.

The horse is unique — and astonishingly beautiful. Tyler has fielded large offers for him, and Puchilingui has become a foundation sire. However, Puchilingui's appearance has caused problems throughout the horse's life, some even resulting in litigation.

Either way, Tyler's life has been far more colorful for having him.

It all began in Florida in 1984, when Puchilingui was born at Farnsworth Farms. His dam, Carolinaway, who produced a minor stakes winner named Act Away, was bay. So was his sire, Native Royalty. And his grandsires, Raise a Native and Needles, were chestnut and bay, respectively. Yet the foal was spotted — flat out pinto looking. He was white with big brown and chestnut spots, a multicolored tail, black-tipped ears, and black spots between his hind legs.

"When that foal was born, it was a shocker. I never saw a horse marked that way — with so much white," Marion Lewis, longtime farm manager, told *Daily Racing Form*. "He was really pretty. He had chestnut, bay, and white coloring, just like a rainbow."

Foal-identification photos were sent to The Jockey Club, and a Jockey Club representative soon investigated. The foal underwent "extensive blood-typing and parentage verification," said registrar Edward "Buddy" Bishop. Everything checked out. The spotted wonder was, indeed, a Thoroughbred.

Even the most astute students of Thoroughbred color could remember few spotted Thoroughbreds in history. *Daily Racing Form* later wrote: "The color of Puchilingui is the unresolved mystery. Foaled before the heyday of blood-typing, which began universally with all foals of 1987, Puchilingui is clearly a colorful animal, but most horsemen would steer away from using him as a sire because, according to geneticists, a thoroughbred of this color just can't exist."

It's been discovered since that the coloration derives from the "sabino" gene. What causes it to appear suddenly, in such flamboyant style, is still uncertain. But once it does, it's highly reproducible.

Despite the "steer away" pronouncement in the *Daily Racing Form*, reproduce the color is exactly what Tyler wanted to do. In January 1989 he bought Puchilingui — whose name is a South American Indian term for the town

Puchilingui offspring, left to right: Jinx (dark bay mare), Punz (gray/roan mare), and Chet DT (gray/roan horse)

clown or town crier — after he'd raced six times in 1987 and 1988 in South Florida. Puchilingui didn't turn heads except for his flashy appearance. He lost five races by an average of thirty lengths, finishing no better than seventh. In his only victory, a Calder six-furlong sprint, his odds were the lowest of his career: 25-1.

"I talked to the jockey who won his race," Tyler said. "They wanted to break his maiden, and he said, 'Yeah, I whupped that sucker from wire to wire.' … Puchilingui was lazy. He went like thunder for the first quarter mile, and then he was done."

Yet Puchilingui boasted excellent conformation, a solid pedigree, and lots of "bling." Tyler and his wife, Nancy, tried promoting him nationally as both a Thoroughbred and Paint sire. That didn't go well.

At one farm, mares bred to him weren't reported, so the Tylers moved him. At another farm, a man changed Puchilingui's registration papers into his own name. Tyler had to go to court four times, spending $64,000, he said, to prove the horse was his. The Tylers brought Puchilingui home.

The Jockey Club and American Paint Horse Association didn't make things easy, either. Puchilingui was initially registered incorrectly as chestnut, despite having black in his mane and tail (his base color was bay). Tyler bred a chestnut Quarter Horse mare to Puchilingui, and they produced a bay foal. As two chestnuts cannot produce a bay, the foal's registration was denied.

Tyler appealed to The Jockey Club, and Puchilingui's registration was eventually changed to roan. Roans can produce any color, so both registries were satisfied. It apparently didn't matter that the "roan" description was as inaccurate as chestnut.

The Jockey Club also did not care to record horses as white. Despite several of Puchilingui's offspring being white, they weren't registered that way. In addition, the spots on Puchilingui's foals occasionally faded to white, forcing the Tylers to take pictures very early so foals could be registered with the American Paint Horse Association.

That's just a taste of the confusing and hotly debated world of colored horses. As for Puchilingui, he has resided at the Tylers' Double Tree Paint Farm for more than a decade now. He's twenty-three. His daily routine?

"He pretty much stays in his stall," Tyler said. "If I let him out, if it's muddy or dirty, he rolls and he rolls and he rolls — and he rolls. I'm putting one of my round pens back up, and he'll get out two or three times a week. If you leave him out more than fifteen or twenty minutes, he gets so sweaty. I bring him back in and have to put a blanket on him, even in winter."

The Tylers have been married forty-five years, and their lives are colored and patterned. Jerry was, by trade, a diemaker. Over the past forty years he has acquired a beautiful collection of boulders called plaid stones and pudding stones. Plaid stones are granite with mixed colors, and pudding stones are white quartz marked with red jasper spots. Nancy creates beautifully patterned, colored quilts of heirloom quality.

They acquired their first horse — a pony — soon after buying the farm in 1971. The horses quickly added up. Jerry entered the horse-show world.

For my photo session with Puchilingui, Jerry pulled out several beautiful halters — remnants from his showing days, including some adorned in silver and gold. I chose silver, and Jerry led Puchilingui outside.

The stallion seemed joyous — dancing, jogging, and rearing. Jerry, a natural horseman and a youthful sixty-six, held on comfortably. Puchilingui, even as he circled, paid close attention to Jerry. Years ago Jerry free-longed the stallion: He taught him to exercise in an arena — even over jumps — without a longe line. The stallion learned to watch Jerry's every command.

"He's really good natured," Nancy said. "He jumps around like that when Jerry takes him out. Most people are put off by that, intimidated by it. But it doesn't bother Jerry because he's not being aggressive. He's just being him."

Soon we were sitting around the kitchen table as Jerry sifted through old articles and photos of Puchilingui and his offspring. There was the near-white Polly D T at a show, and Select Snow Squaw, also near-white, winning a race.

There were photos of Puchilingui from the first day Jerry saw him in Florida, and snapshots of several of his beautifully spotted foals. Not all are registered with The Jockey Club.

"The main reason is they give you a real rough time with the markings," Jerry said. "They may send the papers back two or three times; the description isn't good enough. The Jockey Club has given me fits over the years. I'll bet they've spent $50,000 in legal fees [because of me]. They don't give me such a hard time anymore."

Puchilingui is a prolific color producer and a foundation sire for Paint Thoroughbreds — horses dual-registered with The Jockey Club and the American Paint Horse Association. As colored Thorough-

bred breeding programs grow in popularity, his offspring are prized. Nowadays, in large part due to Puchilingui, quite a few registered Thoroughbreds have spots.

Puchilingui had thirty foals registered with the American Paint Horse Association through 2006 (not all are full Thoroughbreds). He had forty-two registered Thoroughbred foals; three won races. Those numbers, of course, don't reflect Puchilingui's total production because not all his foals were registered and many foals were never intended to race. Still, he has not bred as many mares as he could have.

"I advertised his stud fee at $12,500," Jerry said. "That was the biggest mistake I made. I should have started him at $750 to get a lot of babies out there. He's standing for $1,200 now."

Jerry produced an old *Blood-Horse* ad featuring Puchilingui and a photo of the spotted Puchilingui breaking his maiden at Calder. Then Jerry came across a small piece of paper containing a name, address, and phone number. He looked at it for a moment as if placing it in his memory.

"This guy here, this horse broker out of Canada, he offered me $225,000 for Puchi," Jerry said. "He had a buyer in Ireland that wanted to stand him as a party [spotted] horse."

"You've kept the card," I replied.

He smiled, tucking it away. "Yes," he said. "I've still got the horse, too."

Quick Call

1984 B. G. BY QUACK—SADIE MAE, BY SADAIR

Quick Call grazed on long, dry grass, seemingly oblivious to the icy wind that ruffled his furry coat. He was tethered by a lead shank to a quiet gentleman who moved with him as he grazed. The man was tethered to the farm by an obligation to society. If all went to plan, he would be paroled in April 2008.

Quick Call is most associated with his sheer speed and a partiality for Saratoga Race Course. Yet his days, and those of his fellow Thoroughbred Retirement Foundation retirees, are considerably slower and quieter at the Wallkill Correctional Facility in Wallkill, New York.

❧

Chris Clayton was a freelance exercise rider when trainer Sid Watters asked whether she'd exercise Quick Call. Clayton had recently given up a career as a jockey. Her sister Marjorie, married to Angel Cordero Jr., was an exercise rider and jockey, and her other sister, Barbara, galloped horses and later became a veterinarian.

Clayton was a slim beauty, with straight, light hair, sharp features, powerful muscles, and a wild streak. It was no accident that Watters called on her.

"He said he had a trouble horse that he wanted me to gallop for him. Nobody could stay on him," she said. "So I said, 'Oh, OK, you know me — kamikaze pilot.' So I started galloping him, and we got along really well.

"I galloped him for five years. He was very difficult to gallop; he was really strong, and he was such a brat. But other than that he was such a mellow guy."

Clayton loved the challenge.

"I think he's the smartest horse I've ever been around in my life," she said. "He dropped me nine times over five years. You'd never know when it was going to happen, but you'd just all of a sudden be on the ground, and you didn't even know what happened. He would just stand there with his head down like, 'What are you doing down there on the ground?'

"I'd go to reach for him, and my hand would be like two inches from the reins, and that's when he would cut. He did it every single time. It was so funny."

Quick Call occasionally had a temper, and despite appearing sleepy in the starting gate — head down, body calm — he was a live wire. He inevitably broke on or near the lead. Once, when George Martens climbed aboard for a minor stakes, Watters warned him not to "wake the horse up" behind the gate. Nevertheless, Martens smacked Quick Call as they loaded.

"Quick Call took one step out of the gate and dropped George," Clayton chuckled. "That was the only race he ever did that, and George said, 'You were right. It was my fault.'"

From June 1986 through June 1992, Quick Call raced eighty-six times. That was no small deed, as Watters gave him winters off. Quick Call spent the season turned out in a sixty-acre field with other horses at Mike Smithwick's farm in Hyde, Maryland.

Quick Call won Belmont's grade II Tom Fool Stakes and two runnings of Saratoga's grade II Forego Handicap. The sprint specialist won sixteen races and placed or showed in twenty-seven others. His consistency earned him a devoted fan base — and $807,817.

Opposite: Quick Call and Robert Crump in December 2006

Although he savored a good sprint, he won at up to 1¹⁄₁₆ miles — on turf or dirt, muddy, good, sloppy, or fast. He could motor six furlongs in 1:08⅘ and seven in 1:21 flat.

Saratoga was clearly his August place to be. He won nine of his first fourteen Spa appearances — from 1986 until 1990 — and twice ran second. When he raced unsuccessfully upon his upstate return at age seven, in 1991, fans forgave him.

By then, the gelding clearly was descending the ladder, and late that year he was transferred to trainer Jimmy Croll in Florida. Quick Call raced over the winter for the first time. It was also the first time he was entered in claiming races.

By June 1992, the grade II Saratoga winner, now eight, could be claimed for $14,000. Unhappy to see Quick Call like that, Watters contacted the owner, who offered to give Quick Call to Watters. Watters called on Clayton, again, this time to ask whether she wanted the horse.

"I said, of course, yes!" Clayton said.

And Quick Call became the first horse she ever owned. She sent Quick Call straight to Smithwick's farm in Maryland. While it was a trek from Aqueduct or Belmont — nearly three hours — Clayton visited Quick Call regularly. She rode him in the sixty-acre field.

"There were little jumps, and there were streams and all sorts of things," Clayton said. "It was such a great thing. I was so lucky to have that for him."

Those happy days lasted until necessity forced a change. Clayton and her husband moved, and circumstances dictated she make the difficult decision to give Quick Call up in late 2001.

She had heard about the Thoroughbred Retirement Foundation (TRF) program at the Wallkill Correctional Facility, where inmates tend to retired Thoroughbreds. Among the benefits the program offers prisoners are chances to develop horse-related skills, work outside, take on responsibility, and earn a little money.

After visiting the prison, Clayton decided it would be a suitable home for Quick Call. He was healthy and sound, with few needs. Equine friends and a watchful eye were what Quick Call needed most. There, he found both.

On the day of my visit in December 2006, I was escorted the short distance from the prison to the expansive and beautiful farm. Quick Call was grazing contentedly as a prisoner gently held his lead shank in a gloved hand. His other hand grasped a currycomb that he rubbed along Quick Call's furry neck and shoulder.

This was Robert Crump, a youthful forty-five and serving a sentence for attempted robbery. He freely admitted taking the wrong path in life, but now, he said, by learning about horses, perhaps the right path had found him.

He had grown up on his grandparents' farm in North Carolina with horses, dogs, chickens, and cows. He helped tend to them but never cared to learn about them. In the late 1960s, he and his mother moved to Yonkers, New York. Horses entered his life again at Wallkill, when he started working with the TRF retirees — and enjoying it — from the unknown claimer to the stakes-winning Quick Call.

"It's fun for me because there are a lot of things I've been taught that I never knew," the quiet-spoken Crump said. "I've acquired a whole new compassion concerning animals."

Asked whether he might work with horses when he's released, he said without hesitation: "Yes, indeed. I'd love to."

Clayton and Quick Call were reunited at a TRF fund-raiser at Saratoga in summer 2006. Excited by the visit to his old haunt and the festivities, Quick Call dragged his handlers all over the place. But when they gave Clayton the lead shank, Quick Call calmed down. Clayton spent hours with him that day.

When she led him back to the barn where he was staying, Clayton realized that, oddly enough, it was the same barn where he'd been stabled fifteen years earlier. The smart old gelding hadn't forgotten, either. As Clayton led him past his old stall, he stopped and tried to go in.

Clayton misses her rides on Quick Call, but she's happy about his living at Wallkill.

"It's wonderful. It's such a perfect fit. It helps everybody," she said. "These people really learn compassion. If you can love an animal, there's something really good in you."

Raise the Standard & Solar Slew

The mares did not resemble each other and their pedigrees, while superlative, were dissimilar. Their legacies are in vast contrast, too. One produced a generation of talented runners, broodmares, and sires, while the other produced one horse of immortal stature.

Yet Raise the Standard and Solar Slew were friends during their twilight years, grazing side by side at Kentucky's Brookdale Farm. They are buried near each other as well.

Raise the Standard was meant to be a superb producer. She was by Hoist the Flag and out of Natalma and, thus, a half sister to Northern Dancer. Her produce printout numbers eleven pages, loaded with black type and familiar names: the champions Machiavellian, Coup de Genie, Denebola, Way Of Light, and Bago; the group I winners Exit to Nowhere, Bluemamba, Orpen, and fourteen other stakes winners.

Most descend from Raise the Standard's first offspring, Coup de Folie. She is deceased, but several of her daughters, including Denebola and Moonlight's Box, carry on the family bloodlines.

The majority of Raise the

Raise the Standard

Solar Slew

Standard's foals were bred by Windfields Farm or E.P. Taylor, the breeder of Northern Dancer. Yet she had difficulties as she aged, and for five straight years, 1994 through 1998, she did not produce a live foal. Her 1999 arrival, a Forest Wildcat filly named Nutcase, was bred by Brookdale's Fred Seitz and, in 2002, she had one more foal for Seitz, a filly named Highest Standard.

Solar Slew, Raise the Standard's pasturemate, was by Seattle Slew and out of Gold Sun. Gold Sun won eleven races in Argentina, including a group I, and Gold Sun's dam, Jungle Queen, was a winner and produced five stakes winners. While Solar Slew raced, she did not win. But she, too, had every right to be a good broodmare.

Her second foal was Mulca, a Puerto Rican champion. Yet it was the fourth of her eleven foals that gained her immortality. He was Cigar.

One of the greatest racehorses of modern times, Cigar was a two-time Horse of the Year. He was also twice champion older horse and he reeled off a record-tying sixteen straight victories. He earned $9,999,815 to become America's all-time leading earner, and won nineteen races — including eleven grade Is. He captured the Breeders' Cup Classic in 1995, capping an undefeated season, and won the inaugural Dubai World Cup in 1996.

Allen Paulson purchased Solar Slew as a two-year-old for $510,000. After her lack of success, he sold her for $20,000, but when Cigar won his first stakes race, Paulson bought her back for $150,000.

After Paulson's death, Solar Slew, in foal to Deputy Minister, was sold at the 2000 Keeneland November breeding stock sale. Brookdale Farm purchased the mare and kept the resulting foal, a filly named Arcadiana, who was bred in the names of Fred Seitz, Ted Folkerth, and Marvin Delfiner. Arcadiana has produced three foals.

Solar Slew produced no more foals, being barren in 2002 and aborting in 2003. Powerfully built and rounded, she carried her head unusually high. Her right eye was missing. Brookdale purchased her that way. Raise the Standard, in old age, kept

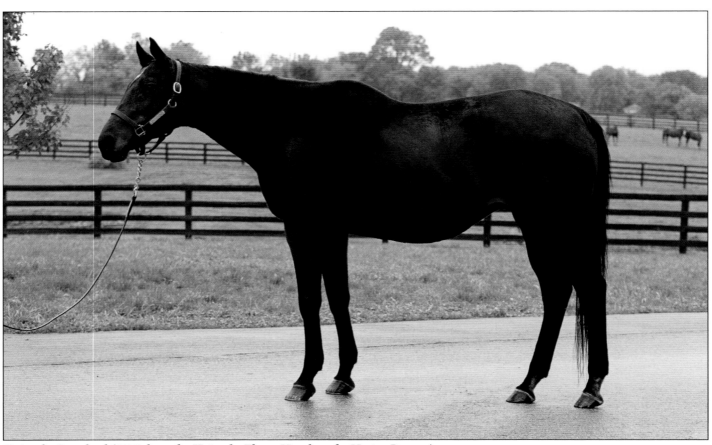

Raise the Standard (1978 b. m. by Hoist the Flag—Natalma, by Native Dancer)

her head low, and she sported a classic, long-bodied look. She had trusting eyes. Both were good to work with, but Raise the Standard was a gem.

Solar Slew and Raise the Standard died in 2004, when Solar Slew was twenty-two and Raise the Standard twenty-six. Their bodies were laid to rest behind the Brookdale stallion barn, near such outstanding mares and stallions as Brown Berry, Ballade, and Deputy Minister.

Raise the Standard's seemingly countless top-class descendants — sires, broodmares, and current runners — carry on her legacy. For Solar Slew, however, it's a different story. Other than champions Cigar and Mulca, only one other black-type winner, grade III victor Laura's Lucky Boy, appears in her two-page produce printout. Mulca died at four, and Cigar proved infertile.

Yet for those who saw him race, Cigar is legacy enough.

Solar Slew (1982 dk.b/br. m. by Seattle Slew—Gold Sun [ARG] by Solazo)

Secrettame

1978–2006 CH. M. BY SECRETARIAT — TAMERETT, BY TIM TAM

When the famed veterinarian William O. Reed and his wife Audrey sold their longtime property, Mare Haven Farm, Secrettame was part of the deal. After all, the twenty-six-year-old mare was as much a fixture as anything else on the property.

Mare Haven was an expansive, charming farm on Old Frankfort Pike in Lexington, Kentucky. For decades, magazine ads promoted the farm and its stallions. One, showing the strong, light gray Native Charger galloping across his paddock, was familiar to anyone with a *Blood-Horse* or *Thorough-bred Record* subscription.

Reed was an internationally respected equine surgeon, best known for the difficult operation he performed on Ruffian in 1975. Among his other patients were Hoist the Flag, Tim Tam, Damascus, Dr. Fager, and Conquistador Cielo. His longevity was established by the fact that the first famous horse he operated on was Stymie, in 1948.

Reed was also a respected Thoroughbred owner and breeder. He bred the 1980 English champion miler, Known Fact; two-time filly classic winner Goodbye Halo; multiple group winner and sire Lion Cavern; and the grade I winner and influential sire Gone West.

All but one came from the same taproot. Known Fact was produced from the Reeds' foundation broodmare, Tamerett, while Gone West and Lion Cavern came from Tamerett's daughter, Secrettame.

Tamerett was a winner whose bloodlines featured some black-type performers, yet nothing could foretell that she would become such an illustrious producer. In addition to Known Fact and Secrettame for Reed, she also produced multiple grade I winner and successful sire Tentam; grade II winner Terete; and stakes winner Tamtent for previous owner, Gedney Farm. Her daughter Taminette produced grade I winner Tappiano and the

successful sire A. P Jet.

Secrettame was a sheer beauty who bore more than a passing resemblance to her sire, Secretariat. She had his same three white stockings and a blaze down her face. Her coat was the same red chestnut, and her body was sculpted muscle. She also carried a distinct air of aloofness — a haughty air that emphasized her queenly status.

Secrettame was bred by Mare Haven and sold as a yearling for $400,000 to an agent for Villa Blanca Farm. She began racing at three with three straight wins and a narrow loss in a stakes, yet a fractured pastern bone then sidelined the promising filly. Reed placed three screws in the bone, and the filly returned to the races more than a year later, in October 1982. She won her first race back and finished fourth in a stakes. However, her owner was cutting back on his Thoroughbred holdings, and Secrettame was sold at the Fasig-Tipton fall mixed sale.

Reed bought the four-year-old Secrettame back for $1.15 million, and she raced the rest of her career under Audrey Reed's name. Secrettame's final tally was six wins — including the Shirley Jones Handicap — and a second in ten starts, with earnings of $101,598. Then, she headed home to Mare Haven.

Secrettame's first foal was Gone West. The Mr. Prospector colt won six of seventeen starts, including the grade I Dwyer Stakes and grade II Gotham and Withers stakes, and earned $682,251. But it was as a sire that he made his lasting mark. Among his offspring are the champions Speightstown and Zafonic, two-time Breeders' Cup Mile winner Da Hoss, Breeders' Cup Turf winner Johar, and multiple grade I winner Came Home. What's more, in 2005 Gone West was England's leading broodmare sire.

While Gone West would make any broodmare's career, Secrettame produced another important black-type winner: Lion Cavern, a handsome, deep-chestnut Mr. Prospector colt who won three group or graded events and stood at stud. Five of Secrettame's other foals stood at stud, too: Multiengine, Danzatame, Secret Claim, Demidoff, and Krusenstern.

The Reeds were so fond of Secrettame that they summoned the esteemed photographer Tony Leonard to record her foalings. As the years passed, the aging mare occupied a prime spot in the front paddock near the Mare Haven office. There, she could graze, and ignore farm visitors, and the farm staff could view the precious chestnut mare.

However, on August 9, 2000, employee Shane Sands saw something no one ever wants to see. While sitting in the farm office, the *Thoroughbred Times* reported, Sands heard a loud crack of thunder. He looked out the window and saw the top of the broodmare barn, which had been struck by lightning, in flames. He and five other employees ran into the burning structure. Later, Sands was quoted as saying, "the glass was breaking [out of the barn windows] and the horses were [screaming] and didn't want to come out."

All were pulled to safety including Secrettame and her seven-month old Seeking the Gold colt. Later named Lord Ultima, he became a Japanese stakes winner who had earned $773,605 through 2006.

Secrettame delivered her final foal, her fifteenth, in 2003, when she was twenty-five. After that, the queen spent her days relaxing. While she occasionally stopped grazing to acknowledge visitors along the fence line, it was only to check whether they had carrots. Even then, she would sweep one or two into her mouth before sauntering away.

In September 2004, with Dr. Reed critically ill, Mare Haven was sold to an Illinois couple, Susie and Clint Atkins. As part of the deal, the Atkins would provide Secrettame a home for life.

"There is no way I would ever, ever move her," Audrey Reed told *The Blood-Horse* in 2004. "I wish I had a dollar for everyone who has come up to me in the past month and asked if we would breed her [to their stallion] one more time and have another baby out of her. Forget that, it will be a holiday for the rest of her life. She deserves that. She has been so good to us. She is the farm."

Dr. Reed died the next month. The Atkins renamed the property CASA Farm and embarked upon major renovations. Susie grew very fond of their resident geriatric grouch. "I'd go visit her and talk with her regularly because I just liked to let her know we were still around," she said. "But she really liked her privacy. She didn't want to be bothered."

Secrettame insisted upon her privacy until the very end. The morning she colicked she exhibited no signs of distress until the impaction was beyond treatment. Although she was shipped to Rood & Riddle, nothing could be done. She was euthanized the afternoon of March 17, 2006, at the age of twenty-eight.

Her body was returned to Mare Haven, and she was laid to rest near a creek beside her immortal dam, Tamerett. Mrs. Reed purchased headstones for both.

Of Secrettame, Susie Atkins said: "She's got a good view of the foaling barn, plus she's down by the stallions, and she loves to tease them. I can see where she is, and it's like she's looking over the rest of us, too."

Thomasina Caporella was in the Fort Lauderdale airport when the agent, noticing her name on the flight ticket, shouted, "Shocker T.!" That happened often in the mid-1980s when Shocker T., Caporella's lovely chestnut distaffer, won seemingly every race in sight — short, long, on turf, on dirt.

Her husband, Nick, owned Big C Farm in Reddick, Florida, with Nick's brother, Bob, and mother, Jean. It was there that Shocker T. took her first steps March 26, 1982.

Thomasina Caporella had received a breeding to the stallion Nodouble from trainer Bert Sonnier, and she purchased Shocker T.'s dam, Very Lucky, from family friends, the Sessas. Very Lucky was a stakes winner at Monmouth Park and set a track record (five furlongs in :57⅗) .

Shocker T. was leggy and lovely, with a rich copper coat, three stockings, and a sizeable blaze. Her face was dished and unusually feminine, yet she was power in motion. Her name was unusual, too.

One morning when Nick was shaving, Thomasina mentioned that Very Lucky had foaled. She asked what they should name the filly.

"He quickly said, 'Shocker T.,' " Caporella said. "I said, 'How did you come up with that?' He said, 'Every day of my life you shock me.' "

Trainer George Gianos liked what he saw when the two-year-old Shocker T. arrived at his Calder barn in early 1984.

"I rate young horses on the way they move," Gianos told *The Blood-Horse* in 1986. "As a mover, on a scale of one to ten, I rated Shocker T. between nine-and-a-half and ten. She was a little flighty as a baby; she'd duck birds and get startled very easily. She dropped a few boys in the morning. I was always standing at the gap to catch her."

Shocker T. bucked shins, and a saucer fracture of her right shin kept her from racing until age three. But then, racing in Caporella's red, white, and green colors — complete with red shadow roll — she came out winging. She cruised home in her first start, seven furlongs at Hialeah, by nine lengths — in 1:23⅗. Three weeks later she finished second in a six-furlong allowance.

"People couldn't understand why I was upset about her finishing second in 1:09⅕," Gianos said. "I still felt she hadn't really run her race. She wasn't breathing right when she came back. I had her scoped, and she had an entrapped epiglottis."

Shocker T. underwent surgery, and her connections had to wait again. It was worth it.

From June 24 to December 18, 1985, Shocker T. lived up to her name and shocked Calder crowds with eight consecutive victories. Seven were added-money events: Grassland, Coral Gables, My Charmer, Burn's Return, and Sweet Tooth handicaps, and Office Queen and Gloxinia stakes. With regular pilot Gene St. Leon aboard, she won from six furlongs to 1⅛ miles, with an even tally of four wins on turf and four on dirt.

The *Miami Herald* noted, "Shocker T. … became the first horse to win eight successive races at Calder in its 15-year history. No records are available concerning the most consecutive stakes won by any horse at South Florida's thoroughbred tracks in 60 years of racing. But pressbox experts were willing to bet their last two dollars that no other horse had won seven consecutive stakes at all three tracks in one year, much less at just one track."

While her imposts were not staggering that year — the heaviest was 122 — her victories were often facile. She was a natural speedster who often took the lead from the get go, playing "catch me if you can."

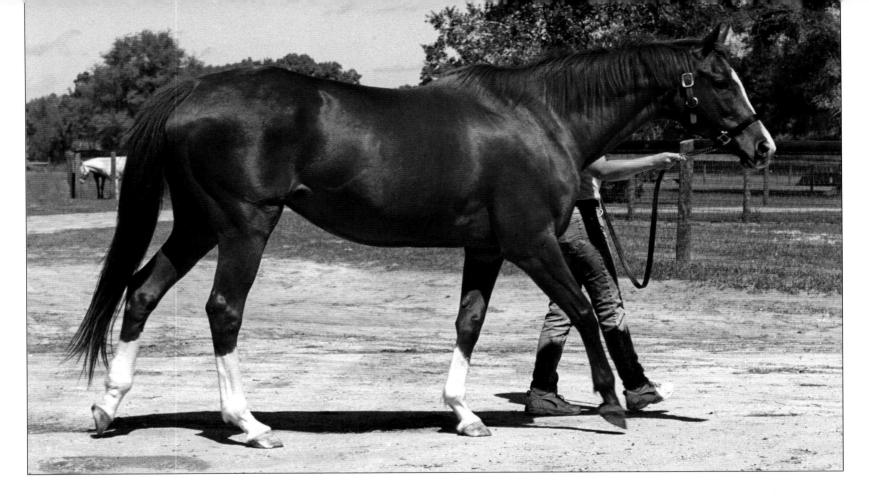

No one could — until the La Prevoyante Handicap on New Year's Day 1986. In her first try at 1½ miles, Shocker T. finished a game second, by three-quarters of a length, to Powder Break.

That year Shocker T.'s connections expanded her horizons. Only two of her eight starts were at Calder, where she won the Meadowbrook Farm Handicap under 127 pounds. She raced twice at Gulfstream and won the grade II Black Helen Handicap at Hialeah.

In July, she shipped to Delaware Park for the $100,000 Delaware Handicap. Gianos worried because early in her career she washed out badly just shipping around Florida, but Shocker T. traveled and raced like a champ. With the Caporellas cheering her on, she showed her heels to the fine Claiborne filly, Endear, and won the prestigious Del Cap by an easy 7½ lengths in 2:02⅕.

Shocker T.'s racing career was "so very special for our entire family," Caporella said. "Nick's parents and brother were able to experience these times not only in Florida but in New York and Delaware. Both our families followed Shocker T. wherever she went."

She then went to Saratoga for the grade II John A. Morris Handicap. Again, the daughter of Very Lucky proved she was world class, winning the 1⅛-mile stakes over a muddy track by 1¼ lengths.

It was there that I finally saw the Calder wonder filly — her beautiful face, her beaming jockey, her ease in victory. Despite the dark and the rain that day, she blazed through the murk like a fog light.

With thirteen victories in seventeen starts, it was on to Belmont Park for the Ruffian Handicap. It was to be her final race.

Her record was such that despite the strong field that included Lady's Secret, Steal a Kiss, and Endear, Shocker T. was 3-1. Yet she finished an uncharacteristic fourth, more than sixteen lengths back. News followed that Shocker T. would be sidelined for several months with a saucer fracture of her left front cannon bone. According to *The Blood-Horse*, she "underwent surgery in which a screw was inserted and two holes drilled in the bone to strengthen the area and make the injury heal faster."

At year's end Caporella's homebred took honors as Florida's champion older female.

While training for a 1988 return, Shocker T. pulled muscles in her back. With thirteen wins and three seconds in eighteen starts — she never finished worse than fourth — Shocker T. was retired.

She lived in Kentucky during most of her breeding career but eventually returned to her Big C home in Florida. She didn't duplicate her on-track success as a broodmare, but that would have been a tall order. Still, seven of her ten registered foals raced, and six won. All were well-bred, sired by the likes of Alydar, Nijinsky II, Danzig, Thunder Gulch, and Deputy Minister.

Faygo was her best. The dark bay Mr. Prospector colt won six of twenty-eight races, earned nearly $120,000, and captured the Meadowlands' Broad Brush Handicap. He stood in Florida until dying in a 2003 barn fire at Meadowbrook of Ocala Jockey Club. He is buried at Big C along with the Caporellas' old campaigner, Darn That Alarm, who also perished in that tragic fire.

Shocker T.'s final foal, a 2003 Yes It's True filly named Circuit Breaker, won two races in 2006 and has added another in 2007. Caporella kept two of Shocker T.'s daughters: Glass Hat and Jr. T.

I visited Shocker T. at Big C when she was twenty-one. To my eyes, she hadn't changed since her racing days. Her body was racy and lean, her eyes sharply attentive, and her face slim. She still looked every part the champion race filly, but the aging lady was not keen about playing model. She stood for just a moment before becoming antsy.

When she was walked, however, she relaxed into a long, open stride. She looked around as if the world were new to her. The day was typical Florida — hot and sticky, with brilliant blue skies and harsh shadows.

"She's a very determined mare," said Dick Wilson, farm manager, "but that's what made her so good at the racetrack."

On September 3, 2006, Shocker T.'s determination was rewarded with induction into the Calder Race Course Hall of Fame. Each year, that track holds the Shocker T. Handicap.

Shocker T. shall live out her days at Big C. The farm has a new, state-of-the-art broodmare barn and continued success in breeding horses and selling yearlings.

But Shocker T. will always be special. She was Caporella's first homebred stakes winner. She's the reason Thomasina Caporella was recognized by strangers in airports.

What's it been like breeding and owning such a horse? Said Caporella, simply: "It's the greatest feeling in the world."

Once upon a time, William T. Young's face was not a familiar one at racetracks around the country, and Storm Cat was just another two-year-old with a promising, but uncertain, future.

At the Meadowlands after Storm Cat's victory in the 1985 Young America Stakes, the interviewer twice referred to Young as a Pennsylvania breeder. After all, his Storm Cat was a Pennsylvania-bred, and this was Young's first grade I win.

Ever polite, Young twice replied: "I'm from Lexington, Kentucky."

And of his burgeoning Overbrook Farm, he said: "We have no grandiose plans. I just want to get a good runner now and then. It's just a small operation."

Tiger Woods might as well have said he wanted to play in a couple of golf tournaments. As the racing world knows, Overbrook Farm — even then more than a thousand acres — became a world force. Who could have known then that Young's colt would become the most expensive, and perhaps the most influential, stallion in the world?

Not even the late Young himself, the breeder of Storm Cat, a son of Ashford Stud's first-year sire Storm Bird and the young Secretariat mare Terlingua. Foaled February 27, 1983, at Derry Meeting Farm, the strong-willed colt did not initially inspire Kentucky Derby dreams.

He "wasn't highly regarded as a foal," Young told *The Blood-Horse* in 1985. "He wasn't the handsomest of horses. No problems of note, but he wasn't outstanding in appearance. However, you can't always tell what you have in a horse's first year, and that was the case with this horse. He really developed to the point that we got excited about his prospects."

Early on, Overbrook's Dr. Robert Copelan contacted the consummate trainer, Jonathan Sheppard, and asked whether he might be interested in training the colt. Copelan mentioned Storm Cat's pedigree.

"I'd never even heard of Mr. Young, so I said, well, let's think about it," Sheppard chuckled in 2007. "But I remembered Terlingua very well. She was kind of built downhill with high hindquarters and a neck on her like a greyhound and sort of a low, flat wither. She was remarkably fast. She captured my imagination so much when she was running in California. I thought, what a thrill to be offered to take something out of her."

However, Sheppard soon struggled just to control Storm Cat. By the autumn of the colt's two-year-old season, he had become unusually headstrong, rearing and bolting after pulling up in morning training. Sheppard decided to make Storm Cat pull up next to his pony. The colt soon began biting the pony.

"One day I took a little whip out with me, and when he tried to grab the pony's neck I snapped him on the nose with the whip," Sheppard said. "And that had quite the reverse effect from what I'd intended. 'Oh, you wanna fight? Sure!' He reared up on his hind legs and started trying to box me. So I decided that wasn't a good idea."

Sheppard continued chuckling as he recalled little-known stories about Storm Cat's racing career. Before the Breeders' Cup Juvenile, Storm Cat worked out on Sheppard's beautifully manicured turf field. It was shaped like a figure eight with no poles, and hence, no way to record times.

A *Daily Racing Form* reporter called to ask about the workout, and foreman Betsy Wells answered his questions honestly. The next day's *Form*, Sheppard

recalled, read: "Storm Cat, who's pointing to the Breeders' Cup Juvenile, worked on Jonathan Sheppard's farm in Pennsylvania, but assistant trainer Betsy Wells said she had no idea how far or how fast."

And the night before that Breeders' Cup, Sheppard attended a dinner party. About ten people were there, including fellow Breeders' Cup trainer Neil Drysdale. The host toasted them, wishing them victory. That wouldn't be possible, Sheppard said, because they were in the same race.

"In that case," the host replied, "I hope it's a dead heat."

At the eighth pole, Storm Cat seemed a certain winner, but Tasso, the Drysdale-trainee, bore down upon him in the final stride. They hit the wire in a near dead heat. Sheppard thought he'd won, but the photo, and the juvenile championship, went to Tasso.

Storm Cat soon underwent arthroscopic surgery to remove bone chips in a knee joint. After a longer-than-expected recovery he returned triumphantly October 31, winning a six-furlong race at the Meadowlands in 1:09⅖. It was his final victory. He suffered inflammation in his left foreleg while training and was retired.

Storm Cat entered stud for 1988 at Overbrook — that farm with no grandiose plans — with four wins and three placings in eight starts, and earnings of $570,610. He was well bred but had soundness issues and a slightly offset knee. In addition, his initial stud fee was not cheap: $30,000.

"He was not well liked, and he was overpriced initially," said Overbrook Farm's Ric Waldman in 2007. "When the market tells you that your stallion's overpriced, the stud farm needs to overreact on the reduction to try to stimulate some interest. We didn't overreact … we just nibbled down and never really did grab our customer base until he hit and became successful."

As breeders awaited Storm Cat's runners, the fee dipped annually, to $20,000 in 1991.

"Mr. Young did try to entice people to breed to him during Storm Cat's unproven years," Waldman said. "Largely we took what we could get. But in his fourth year, while the breeding season was still on, the two-year-olds from his first crop started running early. Mr. Young decided to give free seasons to Storm Cat to breeders who had bred to him previously and paid a full stud fee. Some breeders took us up on it. Mr. Young was right. We had all this spare capacity with Storm Cat, and we gained good will and increased a little bit his fourth book of mares. It was smart business."

Storm Cat's horses could flat out run. His first crop featured eight stakes winners and his second, nine. His fee began climbing, to $25,000 in 1992 and $35,000 the next year. For ten of the next eleven years it increased — to an astounding $500,000 in 2002. There it remains, the highest stud fee in the world.

Some stallions ride high on the exploits of one "big horse," but not Storm Cat. His foals win short or long, on dirt or turf, as two-year-olds and older, in this country and overseas.

"When the international market embraced him, that was really like he had arrived," Waldman said. "Then his sons started hitting. That was another threshold that he passed. And then his daughters hit. It's been just a continual positive building process."

He has sired 150 stakes winners, and his foals have earned more than $100,000,000. He has twice led America's general sire list and seven times led the juvenile sire list. His yearlings are coveted. In 2004 Northern Dancer led all stallions in number of million-dollar yearlings with fifty-two. His grandson, Storm Cat, has soared past that with eighty.

Storm Cat's champions or highweights include Giant's Causeway, Storm Flag Flying, Sweet Catomine, Ambitious Cat, One Cool Cat, Black Minnaloushe, Denebola, Mistle Cat, Catrail, Munaaji, and Silken Cat.

He sired the dual classic winner Tabasco Cat, and among his thirty-one grade/group I winners are Cat Thief, Sharp Cat, Bluegrass Cat, Raging Fever, High Yield, Good Reward, Sardula, and Hold That Tiger.

Overbrook's stallion manager Wes Lanter, previously stallion manager at Three Chimneys, where Seattle Slew stood, remembers the first day (January 7, 2000) he worked with Storm Cat.

"I'd had the experience of being with a major horse before, but it was still, well, it's still Storm Cat." Lanter said. "So it was intimidating in its own way."

"The first time I ever hooked onto him he tried me, like 'Who are you?' He acted kind of tough. Once he figured out I knew what I was doing he's been good, pretty much, ever since.

"Even at twenty-four, he's the most highly energetic horse. And being a real handful, sometimes, he can just scare you because he feels so good. I want him to feel good, but sometimes I say, 'Man, would you just slow down and take care of yourself?' "

No matter how valuable a horse is, there's only so much you can do to protect him. But several years ago, when his feet got tender, the farm installed a rubber mat across driveways and a bridge — any place Storm Cat might walk that's not grass. He's let out in his paddock like any other stallion, and when the weather's favorable, he stays out all night. Suffice it to say that the farm staff keeps a close eye on the weather report.

Overbrook limits Storm Cat's bookings because, even with his astronomical fee, breeders line up for his services. In 2007, he was expected to breed about one hundred mares (his biggest book was 122). Let's see, at $500,000 a pop, that's, well, you do the math.

Storm Cat, listed at 16 hands, has taut muscles and sharply keen eyes. His manner is calculated, controlled, sheer power. Technically a dark bay or brown, Storm Cat's sculpted form reflects chestnut, black, brown, and even blue on sunny days. His jowl line is thick, like a Quarter Horse, and his face tapers to a refined nose. His stallion crest is marked.

Both left legs sport high socks, and his head carries a star above the cowlick. Small white hairs trace down his face. A slim white crescent shines be-tween his nostrils. A small trace of white coats his lower lip.

As he heads to the breeding shed, he prances, his eyes widen, and his nostrils flare. He pulls at his groom. He chomps on the lead shank. He bellows.

And in the shed?

"He walks in, he does his job, and they get in foal most of the time," Lanter said.

When he's done, he's usually led back to his paddock, his veins swollen beneath his slick coat. He strides matter-of-factly past a life-sized statue — of him, of course — near the stallion barn. His son, Cat Thief, grazes in a field across from his. Storm Cat settles right back to grazing, just like any other horse.

"There was one time Storm Cat was feeling good," Lanter said. "He goes tearing across his paddock. He's buck-kicking, and he just bucks up and when his front feet go down it's — blam — the ground just goes out from under him, and Storm Cat does a roll. He gets up, he looks around, and he just starts walking, like it's no big deal.

"I immediately got on the phone to Dr. Yocum [Overbrook attending veterinarian and now farm manager]. He was fine, but he took four weeks away from my life with how my heart was beating. It's one of those things horses do every day. It's just something you don't want to see Storm Cat doing."

Of course, Storm Cat is not your everyday horse, even though there was a day, once upon a time, when his breeder might have been from Pennsylvania and thought it'd be enough to get a good runner now and then.

Storm Cat in 1999

Strike Gold

1980–2005 DK. B/BR. H. BY MR. PROSPECTOR—NEWCHANCE LADY,
BY *ROI DAGOBERT

Strike Gold's stallion career waned in his later years. He started off highly touted, spent years at the top-rung Walmac International in Kentucky, and eventually moved to California. There, he shifted from farm to farm. Breeders stopped inquiring about him, and, at age twenty-five, he died far from the spotlight that had shined upon him in his youth.

Trainer Billy Turner remembers. It was January 1983, and the dark bay Mr. Prospector colt stood in his stall after his maiden victory at Gulfstream Park. Tartan Farms' John Nerud stopped by and asked Turner, the colt's trainer, whether Strike Gold might be for sale.

Turner recalls saying: "Well, Mr. Nerud, why would you want to buy him? You just retired Fappiano, and he's by Mr. Prospector."

And he recalls Nerud's response: "Fappiano's just not the type that makes a great sire. This one is."

Said Turner in 2007: "Coming from John Nerud, that made me sit up and think, because he's a brilliant breeder — one of the best we've ever seen … Fappiano turned out to be a really good sire."

Strike Gold did too. But first, Turner had to get him to the races. That took time and patience.

"He just wouldn't stand the training as a two-year-old, so I just fussed with him," Turner said. "I figured he was the best horse I had in the barn at the time. I figured we'd stall around until we found the right opportunity."

The maiden victory that had caught Nerud's attention took place at Gulfstream on January 27, 1983. At 2.20-1 under Eddie Maple, who would ride Strike Gold in all six starts, the colt cruised home four lengths clear. The six-furlong time, 1:09⅘, was the fastest by a three-year-old at the meet.

Strike Gold struck next in February, winning a seven-furlong Gulfstream

allowance in 1:22⅖ at odds of .50-1 (he was odds-on in four of his starts). Again, Strike Gold's time was fastest at the distance for any three-year-old at Gulfstream that season. And then, at Aqueduct, Strike Gold scored an easy win in the grade III Bay Shore Stakes.

Turner immediately dismissed any notion of trying Strike Gold in the Kentucky Derby and kept him sprinting. On May 13, the colt won a six-furlong Aqueduct allowance at odds of 1-10.

Strike Gold headed postward just twice more. In June, over a muddy Belmont oval, he finished fifth, beaten by less than four lengths. And at Saratoga, on July 29, Strike Gold faced his elders for the first — and only — time in a six-furlong allowance.

"He ran every step of the way," Turner said. "Shimatoree was the best older horse going that distance at the time. And it's the classic case of the best three-year-old running against the best four-year-old. The four-year-old wins."

Strike Gold finished second, and the six-furlong time of 1:08⅗ missed the Saratoga mark by three-fifths of a second. It proved his final start.

"He was owned by a syndicate, and we bought him for $165,000 as a yearling," Turner said. "Well, a Florida group came along and offered them $2.5 million, so they sold him. In that period of time, syndication of a Mr. Prospector was a really big deal, and they wanted to get him into the breeding shed, which they did. He turned out to be a good sire."

Strike Gold was medium-sized with a powerful body and the traditionally strong Mr. Prospector head. While Mr. Prospector was only thirteen when Strike Gold won the Bay Shore, he had already sired thirty-three stakes winners, including a Horse of the Year and two other champions.

Strike Gold was initially well received in Florida, yet that state provided a

bred champion two-year-old. He turned out to be Strike Gold's second-leading earner ($476,989), winning fourteen races, including the grade III Nashua Stakes.

Strike Gold's richest offspring, Traces of Gold, a two-time champion older mare in Texas, earned $664,672 and won ten stakes, including three runnings of the Brown Bess Handicap. Arches of Gold, a grade III winner and multiple track record-holder, earned $434,006. Our Gatsby, who ran in the Preakness, earned more than $350,000. And Ray of Gold, Daimon, and Hit the Mahagoney each earned more than $200,000.

Strike Gold was shipped to California in the late 1990s, and, by February 2004, the aging stallion was standing at Marlene and Gary Howard's Hideaway Farms in San Jacinto, California. The lovely property — nestled in a scenic valley — was unusually lush and green despite the season.

Strike Gold didn't look his twenty-four years. He appeared strong and proud, despite his knees not quite straightening. He very much reminded me of his immortal sire.

Sadly, Strike Gold was euthanized in October 2005.

"He was feisty, but not mean. He was just kind of aggressive," Marlene Howard said. "That last year, he wasn't booked to any mares. He started having trouble getting around, probably arthritis. He started losing weight, and even though we had him on Equine Senior, he just wasn't maintaining his weight. It was time."

At the time of his death, Strike Gold had sired twenty-five black-type winners and his progeny had earned approximately $16.5 million. Two of his sons — Make Luck and Wee Thunder — appear on *The Blood-Horse*'s 2007 online *Stallion Register*, and his daughters are producing stakes winners.

Nearly a quarter century after training Strike Gold, Turner still speaks of him fondly.

"Every now and again somebody comes up to me and says, 'So-and-so just won such-and-such, out of a mare by Strike Gold,' " Turner said. "You always like to see them go on and do good things. He was the real McCoy, no doubt about it."

limited market. He was moved to Kentucky's Walmac International for the 1987 season.

He remained there for more than a decade, quietly churning out quality albeit often sprint-oriented runners. Turner, who owned mares and a season to Strike Gold, remained a loyal customer.

Turner's mare Popol Vuh (by Czaravich, whom Turner trained) was bred to Strike Gold and got Popol's Gold. Turner developed him into a New York-

Sugar and Spice

1977–2004 B. M. BY KEY TO THE MINT — SWEET TOOTH, BY ON-AND-ON

The Calumet Farm cemetery was busy that warm September afternoon. A busload of tourists had just visited the graves of the farm's greatest horses including Calumet's stallions Bull Lea, Citation, and Alydar; and its eminent broodmares. One was Sweet Tooth, mother of Alydar, who lay near her first, second, and third dams. And here, too, was Our Mims, Sweet Tooth's champion daughter.

Across from Our Mims' grave, a backhoe idled next to a freshly dug hole. On a day when senses were sharpened by dappled sunlight and the strong, cool scent of newly exposed earth, another of Sweet Tooth's offspring was coming home: Sugar and Spice.

❧

I first saw her in the Saratoga paddock before the 1980 Alabama Stakes. As an impassioned fan of her half brother Alydar — a powerful, strong-faced chestnut — I looked for a family resemblance. Instead, Sugar was a lovely, delicate-faced bay filly with a small star and sweet look. At the hand of an aging, heavy-set groom, the filly stepped gracefully.

She was enchanting.

When I saw her next, it was 2003, and my heart broke. Sugar, who had not had a foal in four years, was at a boarding farm near Lexington, Kentucky, turned out with other old mares. One foot was wrapped with green tape, and she could barely walk.

When I approached, she stretched her neck toward me, and her eyes fluttered shut at the touch of my hand. As she pressed against me, I rubbed her chest and down her sore legs. When I finally left, she limped after me a short way but then stopped and watched me out of sight.

I could not get her out of my mind. I eventually sent an e-mail to Jeanne Mirabito, who had given a home to another old Calumet mare, another Sweet Tooth daughter who had been forgotten: Our Mims. If the owner was willing, I asked Jeanne, might she give Sugar a home?

Jeanne had taken in Our Mims — a strong-willed queen who was the 1977 champion three-year-old filly — after the mare was no longer productive. Her owner was happy not to have to care for Mims, and Jeanne brought her home to her Paris, Kentucky, farm.

Jeanne and Our Mims shared peppermints and adventures for three years,

until the aged mare died in late 2003. Jeanne was devastated. Our Mims had sparked a dream in Jeanne to create a hospice for older, unwanted mares, but that dream seemed to have died with Our Mims.

Then Jeanne had a dream, an actual dream, in which Our Mims asked her to help someone close to her. The next day, she received my e-mail. *Help someone close to her.*

Jeanne contacted Sugar's owner, who agreed to part with the twenty-seven-year-old mare. When Sugar arrived at Jeanne's farm in May 2004, she moved into Our Mims' stall, which was adorned with photos of its former resident.

Sugar had a rash, and hair hung from skin that could not conceal her gaunt frame. Her hooves desperately needed trimming, and one was severely split. As when I had seen her, she struggled to walk. Yet her wistful eyes were still unusually trusting.

This was a far different horse from the dish-faced bay who had won the grade I Mother Goose in 1980 and the grade II Cotillion and Ashland stakes, who had won or placed in nine grade I and II stakes. She had joined Calumet's broodmare band upon retirement, but when the farm's stock was dispersed in 1991, Sugar was sold for $425,000. In 1994 she was sold again, this time for $250,000. In 2004, Jeanne bought her for a dollar.

Jeanne bathed her with special shampoos and served her nourishing, carefully planned meals. X-rays of her pained knee determined she had been the recipient of a hard blow in recent years, possibly a kick. At her former home the other mares could "fight for their supper," but Sugar didn't have the strength to fight back. I had feared that this mare so loving and generous of heart would die in that field, unloved and forgotten; that the knackers would cart the gentle, little bay mare away without even knowing her name.

"Sugar was the sweetest mare I ever met," Jeanne recalled. "She showed gratitude like none I had ever seen before. Every touch was met by a soft caress with her muzzle. Even though she was so much in need of nourishment, she never took a bite of food until she thanked me with the sweetest chortle as she put her head against my chest."

And the spice? Jeanne learned about that one day while eating an apple.

"That old gal became all spice," Jeanne remembered. "She ripped that apple out of my hand in a flash."

From then on, Sugar got an apple a day.

Even though little could be done about her injured knee, her rash healed, she gained weight, and her eyes sparkled. She felt frisky enough to rip all of Our Mims' photos off her stall walls.

In the process she gave something back to Jeanne, emboldening her to create Our Mims Retirement Haven for older mares. Sugar and Spice headlined the press release as its first official resident.

"Our Mims gave me the task. Everything I do is in her honor," Jeanne said. "Sugar and Spice gave me the courage to fulfill that task. What a pair of sisters."

After four months at the haven, on September 13, 2004, Jeanne found Sugar lying in her field. She asked her to follow her into the barn, and the old mare struggled to her feet and obliged. Jeanne called the vet.

"I could tell she was in pain," Jeanne said. "I could see how very tired she was."

Sugar ate some breakfast, limped back outside, and lay down again in discomfort. Jeanne called the vet again and asked him to hurry. While Jeanne and her aunt waited, they rubbed Sugar's legs and fed her apples.

Jeanne had already made arrangements with Calumet Farm for Sugar to be buried there, just as Our Mims had been the year before. Now, Jeanne stroked Sugar's head, telling her she was going home to Calumet.

"Her eyes lit up, and she struggled to raise her head high enough to put it against my chest and gave her special 'thank you' chortle," Jeanne recalled. "My tears fell on her, and she snuggled in for one last hug."

Moments later, the vet arrived.

Sugar's service was simple, attended by just a few of her special friends. I watched as her body was gently laid in the grave and a small bucket was placed near her beautiful face. It was filled with carrots — and many apples.

September's warm sun splashed across her as the backhoe showered down dirt. After such a long life, it didn't take long. In a few minutes, Sugar and Spice was gone.

Sultry Sun & Solar Splendor

Sultry Sun's sons, Solar Splendor and Sultry Song, were like night and day. Solar Splendor, a Majestic Light gelding, was sweet, plain, willing, angular, and slight of build. His coat was a light chestnut. He clearly preferred the turf and was often a front-runner.

Sultry Song, a year younger, was near-black, imposing, with a Roman nose and thick physique. Sultry Song could occasionally test both his exercise rider and groom. The Cox's Ridge colt liked the main track and often came from behind to win.

Both were bred and owned by Live Oak Plantation and trained by Pat Kelly, and each won three grade I stakes. Sultry Song was more popular, perhaps — people love a dark, powerful, grade I dirt performer. As such, I preferred Solar Splendor due to my penchant for the underdog. I first noticed his gentle ways after his first grade I win, the 1991 Man o' War Stakes at Belmont Park. I followed the gelding back to Kelly's barn.

I settled in a fair distance from the barn and sat down, waiting to see whether he might be brought out for a bath. Suddenly, the assistant trainer, whom I'd never met, called over to me: "Hey, want a beer?"

Next thing I knew I was photographing Kelly's beaming family with Solar Splendor, in the afternoon's golden light, for the portrait on their Christmas cards. Solar Splendor was a very willing model.

Several weeks later the barn had even more reason to celebrate. Solar Splendor won his second grade I, the Turf Classic, about an hour after Sultry Song won the grade II Jamaica Handicap.

"They're quite a twosome," Kelly told *The Blood-Horse*. "I've won double-headers before, but never two stakes."

As dusk settled upon Belmont, the celebration continued in Kelly's tack room. Solar Splendor, who was being walked in the shed row, was stopped in the tack room doorway for a photo as revelers raised glasses in his honor. The unusually benevolent gelding looks surprised in the photo — seeming not to share in the revelry.

The next year, 1992, the two sons of Sultry Sun ushered her into a most exclusive club: dam of two grade I winners in one year — in this case, in one afternoon. On September 19, 1992, Solar Splendor won his second Man o' War, and Sultry Song won the Woodward Stakes.

Sultry Song also won the grade I Hollywood Gold Cup and Whitney Handicap that season. Boasting earnings of $1,616,276, he entered stud at Claiborne Farm in Kentucky.

Solar Splendor, the underdog gelding, raced three more seasons. All told, he won eleven of forty-two races. He won six stakes, placed in six others, and earned $1,386,468. Along the way he equaled Belmont's 1⅜-mile course record in 2:12.45. Fans, including me, grew ever fonder of the gentle chestnut.

When he was retired, Solar Splendor headed home to Charlotte Weber's Live Oak Stud near Ocala, Florida. He took up residence a few paddocks away from his dam, Sultry Sun.

The 4,500-acre farm is one of the Sunshine State's most successful — and attractive. Lawn jockeys and handcrafted signs feature the farm's colors of

Solar Splendor (1987 ch. g. by Majestic Light—Sultry Sun, by Buckfinder)

Solar Splendor

white, red, and black. The landscaping is meticulously coordinated, and, appropriately, live oaks provide a green canopy of Southern splendor.

Even before her famous sons had their days in the sun, Sultry Sun had some of her own. She won nine of fourteen races, including the grade II Molly Pitcher Handicap and the Coconut Grove Stakes. In the first, she missed Monmouth's 1 1/16-mile record by three-fifths of a second, running 1:41⅗. In the second, she sped the seven furlongs in 1:22⅕. During her

two-year career, she earned $222,277. In 1984 Sultry Sun was crowned Florida's champion handicap female.

Eventually, due to her grade I-winning sons, she earned the state's Broodmare of the Year award in 1991 and 1992.

Sultry Sun produced sixteen foals, including three graded stakes winners. Her 1995 Mr. Prospector colt, Strategic Mission, won a grade III and is now a successful young sire. Sultry Sun's final foal, El Sultry Sun, is a two-year-old of 2007.

In February 2006, I saw Solar Splendor for the first time in eleven years, and I finally met his famous mother as well.

Solar Splendor's frame had filled out and winter's chill had brought out a thick coat, but there was no mistaking him. His was the same sweet face I had photographed at the Kelly barn years earlier.

He was waiting, all gussied up, in a broodmare barn. He seemed to say, "Phew!" when the groom brought him outside because that's where he was comfortable; he lived outside with several buddies. He stood a few minutes for portraits.

After that, he was released into a small paddock near the barn so I could take additional photos. It took him approximately a second to realize that his chums weren't there. He circled the enclosure, whinnied, looked from corner to corner, and nickered to neighbors in nearby paddocks. *Worry, worry, worry.*

When we finished and he was led toward his own paddock, he jogged next to his handler, tossing his head. *Hurry, hurry, hurry.*

Like Solar Splendor, Sultry Sun was not comfortable trapped in the barn and not overly tickled to stand for photos. Her paddock companion waited nearby, and she reached out to touch his nose several times. She, too, had grown extra fur for the season.

The twenty-six-year-old mare's face was beautifully refined with exotic and enchanting eyes, and she paid keen attention. An unusual star high on her face spread upward in wisps. Her temples were flecked with white, and veins traced along her surprisingly solid jowls. Her sun-bleached mane was tipped in dark rich red.

Seven months later I found myself at the farm again, although this time

Above: Sultry Sun (1980 dk. b/br. m. by Buckfinder—Sunny Dame, by Damascus)

not to photograph Sultry Sun or Solar Splendor. In passing their paddocks, however, I could not resist stopping to take a few photos.

Both had shed their winter coats, and both readily came up to say hello. They spend their days wandering their respective fields with their pals, swishing tails and taste-testing the Florida grass. Little is asked of them.

That day the old mare wasn't even wearing a halter, although a slim neckband revealed her name. I thought that of all the horses at Live Oak, she's the one who needs no identification. Everyone knows this dark beauty. She's Sultry Sun.

Summing

1978 B. H. BY VERBATIM — SUMATRA, BY GROTON

He is the oldest living Belmont Stakes winner.

In 1981, Summing halted Pleasant Colony's Triple Crown bid when he swept victoriously beneath the wire at Belmont Park. Although it wasn't Summing's only stakes win — he also won the Pennsylvania Derby, Hill Prince Stakes, and Pegasus Handicap — it was the one that earned him immortality.

He became a classic winner.

Summing retired in October of his three-year-old season due to an ankle injury, and he was whisked off to stud at the farm where he was raised, Jonabell Farm near Lexington, Kentucky. He was by the popular Speak John sire, Verbatim, and his female line was strong. His stakes-winning dam, Sumatra, also produced multiple graded stakes winner One Sum, grade III stakes winner Twosome, and stakes winner Some For All.

Summing sired two stakes winners from his first crop, and his best runner, Epitome, came two years later. Winner of the Breeders' Cup Juvenile Fillies, Epitome was 1987's champion two-year-old filly.

Despite siring accomplished runners such as Mexican champion filly Brazilian Beat and grade I winner Sumptious, Summing was moved to California for the 1992 season. Nowadays, the twenty-nine-year-old is a contented pensioner at Dinesh Maniar's Getaway Thoroughbred Farms in Romoland. Retired from breeding in 2003, Summing has only two foals in his last crop.

An unusual racy, handsome rich red bay, Summing sports a high star, widely set eyes, and a tapered muzzle. Though difficult at times during his racing career, he is now, generally, a dignified pensioner. Yet he does have his moments.

When we visited in 2004, the farm had him beautifully prepared. Although it was winter, Summing's short coat glowed. He tolerated us for a short time but then reared repeatedly — but gently — to express his annoyance.

When he was let out into his paddock and his halter was removed, Summing galloped gracefully to the far corner and looked back with curiosity. He appeared much younger than his twenty-six years.

His is a proud countenance.

Getaway plans to provide a lifetime home to Summing. According to a farm spokesman, Maniar believes that "Summing is still a grand champion, and he deserves to live like a king."

Tall Glass O'Water

1982 CH. M. BY THIN SLICE — WATER BABY, BY NORTH SEA

Trainer Rick Violette had just won the Yaddo Stakes at Saratoga with a promising filly, Tall Glass O'Water. For her owner Alfred G. Vanderbilt, one of the most important horsemen in the sport's history, it was his first New York stakes win in more than a decade.

So why was Violette frustrated? Because Pat Day got all the press. The jockey had been on a zero-for-thirty-three streak, and the media found that more interesting than the end of Vanderbilt's dry spell.

The next day's headlines varied from the simple, "Day ends winless streak," to the groaner, "Day Ends Drought on Tall Glass O'Water." Day was even quoted: "I guess you could say it's been a long time between drinks of water for me."

But the end of the drought for both Day and Mr. Vanderbilt came at a price. Tall Glass O'Water never raced again.

A lovely, compact chestnut with a star and stripe, she was born in New York in 1982. She was regally bred, although not in the usual sense. Her sire and dam were not the strongest of bluebloods. Yet Vanderbilt, her breeder, certainly was.

Alfred G. Vanderbilt. He was more than a figurehead, more than unapproachable royalty. Vanderbilt was genuine, and grateful fans cheered his horses for generations.

Tall Glass O'Water arrived thirty-two years after the birth of Vanderbilt's most famous racehorse, Native Dancer. Her pedigree traced to the immortal "Gray Ghost of Sagamore" and contained three crosses of Native Dancer's dam, Geisha.

Vanderbilt was famous not only for his Thoroughbreds but also for his foal-naming practices. The filly's sire, Thin Slice, and dam, Water Baby, produced Tall Glass O'Water.

Despite her name, Violette recalled, "As a two-year-old, she was kind of a butterball. She was not that tall and always carried a big belly, but she showed some talent."

She won three of her first five starts and finished second in the other two. The 1985 Yaddo was her first stakes, for state-bred fillies and mares, three-year-olds and up. For the first time she had to race 1⅛ miles, and for the first time she raced in the mud.

Tall Glass O'Water met challengers at every point in the race. She fought them all off, one after another, to win by 1½ lengths. Violette was happy for the filly, but he was even more pleased for Vanderbilt. After all, "Mr. V." was no usual owner.

"He was a bundle of history and aristocracy and worldliness all in one," Violette said. "He kind of jump-started my career. I had a lot of automatic stall space and had good barns at Belmont and Saratoga.

"We used to eat dinner at his house frequently, and we played Trivial Pursuit. We got to meet a lot of very, very significant people through him. The history behind the man is incredible."

Violette's delight turned to disappointment when Tall Glass O'Water turned up with a tendon injury after the race.

"I remember like it was yesterday," Violette said. "I kept it sort of quiet so Mr. Vanderbilt could enjoy the win as long as possible. I didn't tell him for a week or so because he was having so much fun on the backside, hearing, 'Congratulations!' and all ... She was a very, very nice filly, and she would have gone on, I think, to have some fun going against three-year-olds later that fall."

Instead, Tall Glass O'Water went home.

She produced only seven foals, and six were winners. Her sixth and by far her best, a Belong to Me gelding named Ewer All Wet, won six stakes, placed in six others, and earned $435,883.

Her final foal, How Dry I Am, was another witty name in the Vanderbilt repertoire — yet it proved prophetic for Tall Glass O'Water. She had fertility problems and didn't produce another foal.

Three months after Vanderbilt died in November 1999, his horses were dispersed through the Midlantic winter mixed sale at Timonium. Tall Glass O'Water had not had a foal in three years, and she was eighteen, but a Florida breeder bought her for $3,500.

As a tremendous Vanderbilt fan, I tracked down Tall Glass O'Water in 2003. Her owner had tried for three years, unsuccessfully, to get her in foal, and now he didn't know what to do with her. I contacted a friend, who got in touch with Shon Wylie. Shon and her friend Lori Neagle were the co-founders of ReRun, a foundation for the rehabilitation and placement of retired Thoroughbreds. Although Tall Glass O'Water at twenty-one was older than their usual adoptees, they made an exception and worked out an arrangement with her owner.

The chestnut mare eventually ended up at Lori and Jack Neagle's New Hope Farm in Salvisa, Kentucky. It's a happy place specializing in horses with special needs, and the Neagles are tireless. Jack, a carpenter and a former jockey, designed and built the barn with the assistance of another carpenter. And Lori was very happy to stock that barn with horses.

This is where Tall Glass O'Water, whom Lori nicknamed Tally, will live out her days in the company of other pensioners — supported by ReRun or the Exceller Fund, with which Lori is also affiliated.

Another source stepped in to help as well.

Violette, who had not seen Tally for more than twenty years, stopped by the farm in 2006 and spent an hour with his old Yaddo winner. Tally had been diagnosed with Cushing's disease, a common affliction in older horses. Although the medication is tasty (it tastes like bubble gum, and Tally loves it), it's not cheap and must be given daily. Violette made a generous donation to help pay for Tally's care.

These days Tally is still a butterball. She seems content with her equine buddies and is especially fond of Natrone, a Dixieland Band gelding. The two chestnuts, both stout of girth, wander their large field together. Natrone — nicknamed Natie Potatie (and on occasion, Natie Stuffed Potatie) — often wears a muzzle to slow his eating.

Tally, for her part, is a long-time cribber, but Lori only occasionally stifles her efforts with a cribbing strap.

"She hates it, and I feel sorry for her," Lori said. "She is a real sweetie, loves attention, and loves her treats — carrots, peppermints, frosted oatmeal cookies, animal crackers, fortune cookies, and sugar ice cream cones. But

she still has the fire in her that made her a great racehorse. At twenty-five, she can — and will — still compete with Natie and the others running in the field."

When I visited in the summer of 2006, the horses were waiting in the barn. Tall Glass O'Water craned her neck over her stall door, peering toward the lucky gray mare in an adjacent stall. It was a daughter of Exceller named Almata, sponsored by the Exceller Fund, whom Lori was visiting and feeding an oatmeal cookie.

While Tally waited patiently, her ears were pricked, and her eyes hopeful. *Please, please, please bring me a cookie.*

Of course, Lori did.

Lori Neagle with Tally

Terlingua

1976 CH. M. BY SECRETARIAT — CRIMSON SAINT, BY CRIMSON SATAN

D. Wayne Lukas was relatively unknown in the Thoroughbred world when he visited Keeneland's sales yard in 1977 to view the yearling filly. He was a highly successful Quarter Horse trainer, so it was only natural he'd be drawn to the speedy-looking Terlingua.

"I thought about her so many times before going to Keeneland that I knew exactly what she looked like," Lukas told *The Blood-Horse*. "I could see the cross of that large horse [Secretariat] on that mare with all the conformation for speed [Crimson Saint], and I had a picture of her in my mind. I knew exactly what to expect."

The picture looked like this: a muscular, stout, and solid chestnut filly who appeared as if she were built downhill due to her tremendous hind end.

Her sire was Secretariat, and her dam was Crimson Saint, co-holder of the world record for a half-mile (:44⅘). Horseman Tom Gentry had purchased Crimson Saint for $295,000 while she was carrying Terlingua, whom he offered as a yearling.

Lukas bought her for Texas horse owner L.R. French for $275,000. French later sold a half interest to a friend, Barry Beal. Terlingua was named for a Texas region that boasts two annual chili cook-offs, including the World Chili Championships.

The filly was spicy as well. To reduce her heat, Lukas ponied her for hours in the hills of San Luis Rey, California. At first he didn't tell his employees, who worked with both Quarter Horses and Thoroughbreds, that Terlingua was a Thoroughbred. They wouldn't have been able to tell by looking at her.

"She has Secretariat's head and her mother's ears," Lukas told *The Blood-Horse*. "She also has a funny walk. She's so muscular that it gives her rear end a swinging effect when she walks."

Describing Lukas, Edward Bowen wrote in *Thoroughbreds of 1978*: "Lukas, in his early 40s, is an outgoing sort, with an eye for the dramatic, and he felt Terlingua was good enough to forego such things as maiden races and non-winners-of-two."

Terlingua came out running in her first start, the 5½-furlong Nursery Stakes at Hollywood Park. She won in a stakes-record 1:03⅖. Then she captured the grade II Lassie Stakes, running six furlongs in 1:08⅘, the fastest time ever for a two-year-old filly at Hollywood. And just a week later she ran in the grade II Hollywood Juvenile Championship Stakes against the boys. She led from the break and won by 2¼ lengths. The six-furlong time, again, was 1:08⅘. Flying Paster was second.

People compared her to Ruffian, and offers poured in. Lukas' response?

"She's not for sale at any price," he said.

Next, Terlingua took on fillies again in the one-mile grade II Del Mar Debutante. She won by nine lengths at odds of 1-10.

Fans loved her, and not just for her speed. She was from Secretariat's second crop, and fans eagerly awaited his heir-apparent. She had the look — even her face markings resembled her sire's — and the brilliance.

The Blood-Horse's Robert Hebert wrote: "Many believe, as does this reporter, that Terlingua is the finest 2-year-old filly ever to race in the West."

The rest of the country beckoned, and the wonder filly — four for four — traveled to Belmont Park for the grade I Frizette Stakes. Terlingua didn't train well there, Lukas said, and on race day, at 2-5 odds, she struggled home third.

Fans forgave that effort, and she headed to Keeneland for the grade II Alcibiades. She went off at 1-2, but, over a sloppy oval — a surface she was

unfamiliar with — she finished second, beaten by six lengths. It was her final start at two.

Called "the West's sweetheart" — despite her fiery temperament — Terlingua returned in February at Santa Anita, easily winning the grade III Santa Ynez Stakes in a stakes-record 1:21⅕. It was her fourth stakes record in five California appearances. Among the vanquished was the previous year's Eclipse Award winning two-year-old filly It's in the Air.

Lukas entered Terlingua in the Santa Anita Derby against colts, and she finished fifth. Then she lost her edge against fillies. After five consecutive losses, Lukas — saying her issues seemed mental rather than physical — sent her back to the farm.

After a seven-month layoff, she won the Las Flores Handicap in — what else? — stakes-record time (1:08⅖ for six furlongs). A week later she set a stakes mark in the La Brea Stakes (1:20⅘ for seven furlongs). Despite that brilliant return, she lost her final three starts. She was retired after suffering a slab fracture of her right knee during a workout.

Her final record of seven wins (all stakes), four seconds, and one third — in seventeen starts — was extraordinary. She set six stakes records and earned $423,896. But, amazingly, she saved her best for the foaling barn.

William T. Young, a respected Lexington businessman, was just getting started in the horse business when he purchased Terlingua. While he initially owned her in partnership with Ashford Stud, he bought her outright in 1982.

The first Terlingua foal registered solely in Young's name — her second foal — was Storm Cat. By first-year sire Storm Bird, Storm Cat provided Young his first grade I victory. Then, as the racing world knows, he became, arguably, the world's most influential stallion while standing at Young's Overbrook Farm. His stud fee is $500,000.

Terlingua's next foal was Chapel of Dreams, a lovely chestnut filly by Northern Dancer with a face reminiscent of her mom's. She specialized on the turf, won five stakes races, and earned $643,912.

Terlingua's 1990 foal, Wheaton, a colt by Alydar, was a winner who initially stood at stud in Florida and then in Pennsylvania. He died in 2006.

Terlingua's 1993 foal was Pioneering, a Mr. Prospector colt who won two of six starts and then entered stud at Overbrook. He has sired sizeable crops and consistent runners, and his average earnings index is 1.48. His best include the grade I winner Behaving Badly and the Puerto Rican Horse of the Year Triano. His most popular runner, perhaps because of his name, is probably Danthebluegrassman, an earner of $418,044.

Six of Terlingua's eleven foals were winners. Overbrook sold some, but her 2000 foal, the broodmare Final Legacy (by Boston Harbor), and, of course, Storm Cat and Pioneering, reside on the farm. Terlingua lives there, too.

Final Legacy's two-year-old Siphon filly, Ranchy, whom Overbrook sold for $50,000 as a yearling, broke her maiden at Santa Anita on April 11, 2007, by two lengths. That prompted Overbrook's Ric Waldman to say that Final Legacy "might be the one to carry through the genes of her mother."

Terlingua, thirty-one, lives in a large field with an ex-jump mare named Ashley. She can still be spicy. The day I photographed her, several grooms tried their best to maneuver her into an attractive pose — lifting one leg after the other, seesawing her back and forth. She would have none of it. She didn't seem to mind our company, and she didn't raise a fuss, but she was clearly disinterested.

She won. I eventually settled on informal portraits.

"Terlingua can still be a real pill," said Wes Lanter, Overbrook's stallion manager. "We used to use one of her buddies as a mare that we used prior to breeding sessions — a test mare. When we would go get [the test mare], Terlingua would cut her buddy away, like a cutting horse, like 'Oh no, you're not.'"

Terlingua's needs are few, but the Overbrook staff does its best to keep the resident queen happy.

"She lives out 24-7, she has a run-in shed, and she uses it," Waldman said. "She's fed twice a day, and she is fed a senior feed called Prep 14. She's brushed and receives normal care, but it's outside. She's just more content that way. You let a horse like that dictate to you how they want to be treated."

Asked what Terlingua has meant to Overbrook, Waldman paused, as if trying to express the magnitude in words.

"It goes without saying that without Terlingua, there's no Storm Cat. Without Storm Cat, the significance of Overbrook would be a lot less. And not just Overbrook, but the breed, as everyone is seeing with the success of Storm Cat's sons and now his daughters. But in dollars and cents, it's more than you would imagine."

Three Chimneys' Trio

It's been twenty-three years since Wild Again and Slew o' Gold battled down the stretch in the inaugural Breeders' Cup Classic. Wild Again emerged victorious in one of the most thrilling Classics ever. Slew o' Gold, a close third, was elevated to second after the disqualification of Gate Dancer.

And it's been twenty-one years since Capote — named for a mountain in Texas rather than the famed novelist — blazed through a spectacular two-year-old season that culminated in a Breeders' Cup Juvenile score.

Now pensioned at Three Chimneys Farm, Wild Again, Slew o' Gold, and Capote are "living the life of Riley," said stallion manager Sandy Hatfield. "They go out and come up every day, get their grooming, their good eats. They get all the good stuff, and they don't have to work."

Slew o' Gold was the first stallion to stand at Three Chimneys, and he remains farm manager Dan Rosenberg's favorite. A winner of seven grade I stakes, including two Woodwards and two Jockey Club Gold Cups, Slew o' Gold was twice a champion — three-year-old colt in 1983 and handicap horse the following season. An earner of $3.5 million, he was known not just for his keen competitive spirit but also his grand appearance. Slew o' Gold was Bucephalus — neck bowed, dancing, burning eyes — the stuff of thunder and legends.

Wild Again, meanwhile, raced primarily out of the headlines — until the 1984 Breeders' Cup Classic when, at 31-1, the handsome near-black horse held on desperately to defeat a stellar lineup. His owners' faith — Black Chip Stable supplemented him at a cost of $360,000 — paid off in spades as he earned more than $1.3 million.

For Capote, fame came early, as the brilliant dark bay Seattle Slew colt won

Capote (1984 dk. b/br.h. by Seattle Slew—Too Bald, by Bald Eagle)

Slew o' Gold poses near a statue of his sire, Seattle Slew, at Three Chimneys.

In 2001, after seventeen seasons, Slew o' Gold was pensioned. He sired four grade or group I winners in his first crop, but he never again reached those heights. Capote retired in 2003 after siring sixteen crops. His best was Boston Harbor, who, like his father, won the Breeders' Cup Juvenile and two-year-old championship. Wild Again, sire of nineteen crops, was pensioned in 2004. He produced many outstanding horses, including millionaires Wilderness Song, Milwaukee Brew, Wild Rush, and Shine Again.

These days, the spotlight has shifted toward Three Chimneys' young stallions Smarty Jones and Point Given, and the pensioners have moved from the front stallion barn. Yet the three seniors — still remembered by many visitors — reside in quiet dignity at Three Chimneys.

*Above: Wild Again (1980 dk. b/br. h., by Icecapade—Bushel-n-Peck by *Khaled); right: Slew o' Gold (1980 b. h. by Seattle Slew—Alluvial, by Buckpasser)*

three of his first four starts. The D. Wayne Lukas trainee capped his juvenile season with a strong win in the Breeders' Cup, as the 2-1 favorite, and then an Eclipse Award as champion two-year-old. The future seemed his for the asking. But Capote lost his next six starts — including being eased in the Kentucky Derby — and was retired.

Slew o' Gold took up residence at Three Chimneys in 1985 while Capote and Wild Again entered stud at Calumet Farm. In December 1991, they moved to Three Chimneys as part of the Calumet dissolution. There they joined not only Slew o' Gold but also Seattle Slew, who sired both Slew o' Gold and Capote.

Thunder Puddles

1979 CH. H. BY SPEAK JOHN — BIG PUDDLES, BY DELTA JUDGE

Thunder Puddles, a son of Big Puddles, hates getting wet. If it's going to rain, then he wants to be inside. If you don't bring him in, then he makes you pay.

"He goes up to the gate," said Kevin Myers, his longtime groom at Highcliff Farm in upstate New York. "If you don't catch him in time — if he gets wet — he runs around and makes you go get him. You get just as wet as he does."

On the other hand, Thunder Puddles wants his hay moistened.

"He picks up every piece and soaks it in water, or he'll put it on the ledge in his stall and grab that," said Highcliff's Suzie O'Cain. "It's a mess in front of his stall — constantly."

The horse, as everyone who knows him will tell you, has personality. But what does that mean?

For Thunder, in addition to his aversion to rain, it means spending hours digging his straw into a giant mound on which he lies down — and snores. It means keenly watching the daily routine — grooms, stallions, visitors — and scarfing down as many sunflower seeds, the salted variety, as Kevin will allow.

He stomps and "squeals like a pig," O'Cain laughed, when mares visit or stallions stand too near his stall. And if he feels he's been forgotten at feed time, or if he's low on water, then he nickers gently as if summoning a waitress in a restaurant.

When Myers leads him to his paddock, Thunder pins his ears and bucks and bucks — and bucks some more. But he never kicks toward Myers. His handlers trust him completely, understanding that he's a horse with personality.

Thunder Puddles was foaled in New York on March 19, 1979. Thunder's sire was the respected Kentucky stallion Speak John. Speak John, who died the year following Thunder Puddles' birth, sired twenty-four stakes winners, including champion two-year-old filly Talking Picture, the grade I winner Text, and the popular sire Verbatim.

Thunder Puddles was his leading earner. The oversized chestnut colt won all but one of six starts at two, but at three and four he held his own against the big boys — and girls. And while five of his first eight starts were on dirt, the big-striding colt clearly preferred the grass. All of his stakes wins and placings came on turf.

Thunder Puddles, who raced for Herb Schwartz and Robert Boggiano, won the grade II Rutgers and Red Smith handicaps and the state-bred Kingston Stakes and West Point Handicap. He ran second or third in five grade Is, including the Turf Classic, Rothman's International, and Washington, D.C., International. He twice finished second to Horse of the Year All Along.

Boasting seven wins, five seconds, and three thirds in twenty-five starts, Thunder Puddles earned nearly $800,000. He arrived at Highcliff for stud duty on December 2, 1984.

His personality showed right away, and he quickly became a favorite with farm staff and visitors.

"When people would come to see him as a stallion prospect, forget their checking him out," O'Cain said. "He was checking them out. He's really into people. He's easy to humanize."

The first time I photographed the colorful giant, he certainly checked me out. In 1994, when he was fifteen, Thunder Puddles was brought out for a conformation photo. I'd seen pictures of him, but they hadn't prepared me for his magnificence. A full 17 hands, Thunder towered above his handler, but, like the old saying, he could have been led by a thread.

His imperious stare was humbling, and his high-headed, raw, chestnut build reminded me of his most famous ancestor, Man o' War. He was breathtaking.

He was also, by then, sire of a grade I winner. His son Thunder Rumble, also a New York bred, won the Travers Stakes in 1992. The week of the race, a local TV crew visited the farm to film Thunder Puddles, the proud father. The crew set up a video camera inside the paddock.

"Thunder Puddles looked at the camera, he ran away, he bucked, he reared, he whinnied, and came back and looked at the camera like, 'Is that what you wanted?' " O'Cain said. "He's such a ham."

All told, four of his offspring each earned more than $350,000 — excellent for a regional sire. As his largest crop numbered thirty-five — most were considerably smaller than that — the numbers become even more impressive. Thunder Puddles' influence on the New York breeding industry was tremendous.

As he neared twenty, however, his popularity waned, and from 2000 on his foal crops numbered in the single digits. Eventually, Herb Schwartz decided to pension him.

He asked Highcliff what he should do with the old stallion, and Thunder provided the answer. His stallion awards over the years had been placed in an account. Through his offsprings' good deeds, Thunder had financed his own retirement by bankrolling more than $30,000.

Schwartz sent O'Cain a note on July 10, 2003: "Dear Suzie, He is in your hands now. Take good care of him. I'm sure you will."

At twenty-eight, Thunder Puddles lives on his own 401(k), sopping his hay, digging mountains of straw, bucking to his paddock, squealing like a pig, and jonesin' for salted sunflower seeds. He's a one-horse vaudeville show. Just don't leave him out in the rain.

***Thunder Puddles with
Kevin Myers***

Turkoman

1982 DK. B/BR. H. BY ALYDAR—TABA (ARG), BY TABLE PLAY

Turkoman stood tall that January day at Mira Loma Thoroughbred Farm in Mira Loma, California, as if he understood what stallion manager Tony Arroyo was saying about him. Arroyo, seventy in 2004, was a devotee of Calumet Farm. And while he had never visited the famed Kentucky farm, Turkoman, by Calumet's Alydar, brought him close.

"I'm a Calumet fan. I always have been, all of my life," Arroyo said. "I couldn't stand Affirmed because I was an Alydar fan. And I can take you to my house and show you just about every picture of Citation that's ever been taken."

Turning toward the proud stallion standing outside his barn, Arroyo said: "Turkoman's kind and gentle, and not aggressive toward people. He's just a nice horse. More people come to see Turkoman than anybody. Even if they don't come to breed to him, they take his picture anyway."

I took many that day. Like Arroyo, I, too, was a passionate Alydar fan, and Turkoman was one of his finest.

Standing seventeen hands, the unmarked dark bay stallion confirmed Arroyo's words by politely allowing the groom to move him wherever we asked. When he was released into his large paddock, the grand stallion powered his way at a happy gallop — ears forward, eyes focused — to the far end. There, he gazed at broodmares in a nearby paddock. They were beyond Turkoman's reach, but he seemed certain they were his alone.

Sometimes called "Little Calumet" for its finely maintained landscaping and color scheme — white fencing and barns with red trim — Mira Loma was a jewel among California farms. Turkoman made his way there from nearby Circle H Ranch for the 2004 breeding season.

In 2005, however, Mira Loma was sold to developers, and Turkoman was on the move again. Now twenty-five, the aged stallion holds court at E.A. Ranches in Santa Ysabel.

Turkoman was foaled April 11, 1982, in Kentucky, the son of Alydar and Taba, Argentina's champion two-year-old filly of 1975–76. Taba's biggest win was the grade I Premio Polla de Potrancas, that country's equivalent of the One Thousand Guineas. Taba produced thirteen foals to race, and eleven won, but Turkoman was her standout.

Known to bite and tug sternly at exercise riders, he broke his maiden in his only start at two. At three, Turkoman ran competitively in stakes, including runner-up finishes in the grade I Travers and Swaps. He ran an impressive third in the 1985 Breeders' Cup Classic, finishing behind Proud Truth and Gate Dancer, and then won the grade III Affirmed Handicap at Hollywood Park in December.

But it was the next year, at four, when the oversized, late-running Alydar colt finally found his stride.

"I've always felt this could be a great horse, that when he grew into his body we'd have a terror on our hands," Gary Jones, his trainer, told *The Blood-Horse* early that year. "He was six months behind; now he's caught up."

Turkoman won four of eight starts in 1986, including the grade I Widener Handicap and Marlboro Cup. At Hialeah, his 1:08⅕ clocking in the Tallahassee Handicap missed the six-furlong mark by a fifth of a second, and his 1:58⅗ in the Widener shattered the twenty-six-year-old mark for 1¼ miles, set by Bald Eagle, by a full second.

His worst finish that year was a fourth in the Metropolitan Handicap.

In his three other losses he finished second — generally a fast-closing second — to such famed runners as Groovy (seven-furlong Forego Handicap) and Creme Fraiche (1½-mile Jockey Club Gold Cup).

Despite finishing second in the Breeders' Cup Classic to longshot Skywalker, Turkoman won the Eclipse Award as champion older horse. He retired with eight wins, eight seconds, and three thirds in twenty-two starts and earnings of more than $2 million.

Turkoman entered stud at Darby Dan Farm in Lexington, and his first three crops were large — each numbered more than forty foals. His first crop yielded three stakes winners, his second five, and his third featured seven. Yet he slipped from fashion as the years passed, and Turkoman was eventually transferred to California.

Turkoman has sired three grade I winners — Turk Passer (Turf Classic International), Man From Wicklow (Gulfstream Park Breeders' Cup), and Captain Garfio, who won the Derby Nacional in Peru and was named that country's champion three-year-old colt. He also sired Turko's Turn, a lovely chestnut stakes winner who, because she produced Point Given, earned the title of 2001 Kentucky Broodmare of the Year.

Through early 2007, Turkoman sired thirty-two stakes winners, and his daughters had produced thirty-eight more. His runners average a very respectable $48,845. In addition, his sire production index is higher than the national average.

Alydar would be proud.

Twilight Ridge

1983 B. M. BY COX'S RIDGE — WAVING SKY, BY *QUIBU

Michael G. Rutherford, a Texas oilman and horseman, was friends with D. Wayne Lukas back when they raced Quarter Horses in the 1960s. When they started buying Thoroughbreds, both drew upon their Quarter Horse backgrounds and looked for horses with lots of substance.

When Lukas' major client, Eugene Klein, dispersed his bloodstock at the famous Night of the Stars mixed sale at Fasig-Tipton in 1987, Rutherford sought Lukas' advice.

"I asked him which is the best mare there, and he told me 'that one,' " Rutherford said.

It was Twilight Ridge.

Rutherford had seen her race and noticed her great conformation. "She's built like a tank," he recalled.

And since he bought her?

"She's done nothing but make money," he said. "She's a great mare."

I remembered Twilight Ridge from an earlier sale, the 1984 Fasig-Tipton Kentucky summer yearling sale. She had such a pretty face, with doe eyes and a happy appearance. Her blaze was unusual, narrowing partway down to a mere trickle and then widening again. Her body was solid for a yearling filly, and she seemed to have an exceptional mind. The Cox's Ridge filly readily marched in and out of her stall for prospective buyers.

I clicked one frame and moved on. Klein bought her for $350,000.

Lukas trained her throughout her campaign in which she won four of fifteen races, including the grade I Breeders' Cup Juvenile Fillies and grade III Astoria Stakes. She finished second or third seven times and earned $743,083.

In the mid-1980s Lukas was red-hot, especially with his fillies, and two of Twilight Ridge's losses were to the Lukas trainees Lady's Secret and Life At the Top. When Twilight Ridge won the Breeders' Cup Juvenile Fillies, the Klein-Lukas filly Family Style finished second. (Family Style ended up with the Eclipse Award.)

"It's like finishing first and second in the Super Bowl," crowed Klein, former owner of the San Diego Chargers, a franchise that never won football's ultimate prize.

While photographing Twilight Ridge in the winner's circle, I noticed her face was familiar — the eyes, the blaze. I checked the pedigree, and, sure enough, she was that lovely yearling.

Twilight Ridge went out a winner in March 1987, and later that year she entered the sales ring again. Rutherford bought her for $1,325,000 in foal to Saratoga Six and sent her to his Manchester Farm.

Situated on a road directly behind Keeneland Race Course, Manchester Farm is a stunning showplace often featured in Kentucky tourism promotions. Countless visitors drive past the idyllic farm to view its beauty and in the spring, brilliantly flowering trees frame the driveway in pink and white.

Horses bred at Manchester include multiple grade I winner Lakeway, and 2007 champion three-year-old colt Bernardini's first and second dams, Cara Rafaela and Oil Fable. Oil Fable is a daughter of one of Rutherford's first top race mares, Northern Fable.

Twilight Ridge produced fourteen foals, — eight fillies and six colts. Early on, Game Coin finished second in the grade III Louisiana Derby and earned $117,760. Then came Daylight Ridge, who won six of ten, including three stakes, and earned $177,695. Next was La Rosa, who won four of fourteen

Twilight Ridge as a yearling in 1984; opposite, as a broodmare in 2004

starts, capped by the grade II Demoiselle Stakes. She earned $267,194. Twilight Ridge's 2004 Thunder Gulch filly, Orange Twilight, is her latest foal to win, a maiden victory in May 2007.

By the time Rutherford chose to breed Twilight Ridge to Gone West, a Mill Ridge Farm stallion, she had proven her quality. So had Gone West. Rutherford spoke with Mill Ridge's owner, Alice Chandler. When he mentioned his interest in breeding Twilight Ridge to Gone West, Rutherford remembers her response: "With that mare you can breed to a donkey and get a racehorse."

Mill Ridge approved her date. The resulting foal, Cowhand, won or placed in four of fourteen starts and earned nearly $70,000.

Twilight Ridge's final foal, born in 2006, is an unnamed colt by Victory Gallop. A photo of the proud mother and son appeared in *The Blood-Horse*, along with mention of Twilight Ridge's pensioning. She was twenty-three.

Rutherford retained several of Twilight Ridge's daughters for his broodmare band and, now, her daughter's daughters. A recent addition is La Rosa's multiple stakes-winning daughter Taittinger Rose.

"She probably had one of the best first foals we've ever had, conformation-wise," Rutherford said. "We bred her to Bernardini [in 2007]. You have two strong families [Northern Fable and Twilight Ridge], and we mixed them."

While Twilight Ridge's days are simple, she still enjoys a good spoiling.

"One day last year, Bob [Powell, farm manager] and I took her to the barn. She was all muddy and dirty," Rutherford said. "He took her in the tack room and gave her a good bath, and did her mane up and everything. She pranced all the way back to the paddock like she just came from the beauty parlor."

Twilight Ridge was sparkling when I saw her at Manchester Farm. She was twenty-three and as professional and relaxed as any other horse I'd ever photographed. She even yawned a few times.

When asked to pose in various positions, including an angle to match my yearling photograph from two decades earlier, she obliged. Her face was longer and shaped differently, and she had that powerhouse broodmare body. But her blaze matched, and then there were her eyes. They might have been a little less sparkly, but they were still unusually benevolent.

"You can put her out with anybody," Rutherford said. "She doesn't fight, and she gets along with all the mares, and they don't mess with her."

It's either because she's kind, he said, or "because she's a big, strong mare. Those little horses know. Sometimes we turn her out with the yearling fillies. She's very quiet, and nothing bothers her. So, you have a thunderstorm, the horses run around, but she's real calm. She has a lovely disposition.

"She will stay [at Manchester Farm] until she dies. It's her home."

Urigo

1982 DK. B/BR. H. BY HORATIUS—LADY FROLIC, BY JOHN WILLIAM

The verdict is in: The man is guilty of loving his horse.

And Norris Gelman, a criminal lawyer from Philadelphia, doesn't plan to appeal the verdict or the sentence. He freely admits it: He's a prisoner of Urigo.

Who?

It might be racing's best-kept secret that Urigo, a sweet, twenty-five-year-old dark bay stallion by Horatius, boasts statistics that tower over the continent's best stallions. Urigo's average earnings per starter is an astronomical $179,104. By comparison, Storm Cat's is $124,823. None of 2006's five leading sires in North America come close either.

Granted, Urigo's statistics might require an asterisk: He has sired only five foals to race. But that doesn't detract from Gelman's devotion to the horse, whom he calls Go.

"I represent many celebrity clients and have won many legal battles," Gelman said. "I would rather be known as Urigo's owner than as a lawyer. With most cases you can readily recall something really unflattering about the client, the judge, the prosecutor, or the victim. That cannot be done with Go.

"He never set about hurting anyone, never belittled a person or sought to deprive them of their dignity … He asked little and gave whatever he had to give … He was not cut out to be a great horse — but he wanted to be a great horse, and he never stopped trying to be one."

Named for a Roman general, Urigo won six of forty-nine starts and finished second or third sixteen other times. That includes third-place finishes in three stakes — the Pennsylvania Futurity, Hirsch Jacobs Stakes, and Delaware Valley Handicap.

By the time Gelman entered his life, however, Urigo had slipped into claiming events. In partnership with Lee Vosters and Steve Lovelady, Gelman claimed Urigo for $10,000 in March 1987.

His competitive nature — and unusually endearing personality off the track — won Gelman's heart.

"Go was a fierce competitor on the track, trying every step of the way and coming back time and time again from injuries that would have led a lesser spirit to sour on racing," Gelman said. "When I view the tapes — now converted to DVDs — of the races he won for us, I again see the vitality that pulsed through him and led him to his victories. He would surge from behind and just run down his field."

After Urigo bowed a tendon for the second time, the partners sold him in January 1989, although Gelman was against it, he said. He didn't rest easy until he got him back. That happened three months later at Delaware Park when Urigo, for his new owner, ran for the third time in fourteen days — in the mud in a cheap claiming race. He bowed for the third time.

"Go might have faced a horrible fate if I had not been there," Gelman said. "He could have gone to the killers — but not while there was a breath in my body."

After the race he had a cast placed on Urigo's leg, and Gelman waited for Vosters to come with her van.

"Go would look at me, look at his injured front leg, and then look at me again as if he were saying, 'Look, boss, I can sure use a friend,' " Gelman said. "I vowed he would never again be out of my hands."

Urigo was retired to Lee and Neil Vosters' Randalia Farm in Chesapeake City, Maryland. At first, Gelman planned to keep the horse as a pet. After a

Urigo with Lee Vosters; her daughter, Christina; and assorted friends

delphia Park named a $25,000 starter handicap for him. And Urigo's most recent foal to race, Chords of Fame, born in 1997, won nine of forty-two starts and earned $195,574.

Combined, the five Urigos have earned $895,521. He has two more chances to top the million-dollar mark: a two-year-old colt named Darrow and an unnamed yearling colt.

Although Go was bred to a "record" four mares in 2006, none got in foal and he — very quietly — was pensioned. He lives a life of luxury at Randalia.

Most stallions are aggressive or mouthy — not Urigo. The gentle, compact dark bay, with happy eyes and trusting ways, adores people.

When Lee Vosters has a bad day, she often makes her way to Urigo's paddock and kneels on the ground near him. He inevitably wanders up to say hello, often resting his head on her shoulder.

"He is the best of friends," Vosters said.

For our photo shoot, Lee and her daughter, Christina, dragged the old boy here and there, asking him to stand on loading ramps and visit with their dogs. He cheerily obliged. Lee even put an apple in her mouth, and Urigo, ever so gently, took it with his teeth.

"I've been around thousands and thousands of horses," she said. "And if ever an animal was reincarnated from a saint, this horse would be close to that. I've always said that if he were a guy, he'd be the best date."

few years, however, he decided to give him a chance as a stallion, and Urigo was advertised in stallion rosters. People laughed at Gelman's "backyard stallion," saying he lacked the pedigree and race record to be a successful sire.

The only person who bred Thoroughbred mares to Urigo was Norris Gelman, by himself or in partnership. And by early 2007, astonishingly, all five of Urigo's racing-age foals had won. One is a stakes winner.

The first was Bjoerling, born in 1992. He won five of forty starts and earned $34,492. In 1993, Urigo produced a career-high two foals: Lilacsandlaughter won ten of thirty-four starts and earned $87,400 while Darrow's Legacy won sixteen of 103 races and earned $188,366.

The Maccabee, born in 1996, won twenty-one of sixty — including two stakes — and earned $389,689. He was such a popular performer that Phila-

Why Me Lord

1974–2006 DK. B/BR. M. BY BOLD REASONING— TOMORROWLAND, BY *PAPPA FOURWAY

A flag atop a pole displays Gallagher's Stud racing colors and marks the final resting place of Jerome Brody. He was a world-renowned restaurateur and owner of such landmarks as Gallagher's Steak House, the Grand Central Oyster Bar and Restaurant, the Four Seasons, and the Rainbow Room. Brody, who died in 2001, is buried in a memorial garden at his cherished Gallagher's Stud in Ghent, New York.

He's in good company. Why Me Lord, one of Brody's best broodmares and producer of German champion and grade/group I winner Allez Milord, lies buried in her paddock next to Brody's memorial. It's fitting that the two lie close to one another. She gave the Brodys their champion and was a farm favorite.

Brody and his wife, Marlene, bought three mares in 1978, their entrée into racing. Five years later Mr. Brody, seeking a Bold Reasoning mare, purchased Why Me Lord for $60,000 at the Keeneland January sale. She was in foal to Tom Rolfe. Why Me Lord, a winner once in eleven starts, was nine — the same age as Bold Reasoning's most famous offspring, Seattle Slew.

A handsome, unmarked dark bay, she had already produced a six-race winner, but her resulting Tom Rolfe foal attracted no takers at the 1984 Keeneland July yearling sale when offered with a $40,000 reserve. The Brodys decided to race him, and they named him Allez Milord.

Allez Milord rewarded them richly with a brilliant international racing career, winning four graded/group stakes including the grade I Oak Tree Invitational and Germany's group I Puma Europa Preis. The New York-bred also won two English group III events and placed second in the Japan Cup. Crowned Germany's champion three-year-old in 1987, Allez Milord was eventually sold to Japan for stud duty.

Even though Why Me Lord produced ten winners, Allez Milord was — by far — her shining star. She was pensioned in 1997.

The first time I visited she was a happy, healthy thirty-one-year-old, carefully tended to — and adored — by Gallagher's Stud employees. The farm Web site reflected their love for the old girl: "31-year-old Why Me Lord, who was retired eight years ago, is being treated like a queen. She is fed a special diet, gets routine acupuncture from Dr. Jennifer Jones and masses of carrots."

Her eyes reflected a soulful intelligence, and long ears plopped forward on a kindly face. Winter's chill had made her dark coat unusually thick. Her back dipped just slightly, and while she had always toed in, her knees and legs were strong. Why Me Lord tolerated the photo shoot but seemed quite pleased to be released back into her paddock.

The last time I saw her, in January 2006, farm manager Mallory Mort proudly set up a generational photo in Why Me Lord's paddock. The aged mare had recently lost her right eye due to infection, but she seemed comfortable. She posed with her winning daughter Blond Lady and two of Blond Lady's offspring. One of them, Bestowed, became a stakes winner later that year.

Why Me Lord was again polite, but she became impatient with the time-consuming shoot, and when it was over, she quickly shuffled away with her ears back. Yet when a group of yearlings was led past her to their paddock minutes later, she galloped enthusiastically — with her ears pricked — along the fence line near them.

Several days later Marlene Brody wrote in an e-mail that Why Me Lord "has become totally lovable with age (wasn't always), loves her carrots, loves being outdoors (hates being indoors) and is indispensable as a babysitter for youngsters who need company but not a lot of running around … For me, every added year of her life is a miracle."

The miracles soon ran out, and her age finally caught up with her. On April 21, 2006, Why Me Lord was euthanized.

Two days later Mrs. Brody sent another note: "It saddens me to have to tell you that my lovely, wonderful old friend is no longer with us on earth. Of course, she will always be with me in thoughts and memories. This past Friday — a spectacular spring day — she was put to rest in her paddock near the yellow barn close to Mr. Brody's 'garden.'

"Yesterday … and today … it has, quite fittingly, been raining steadily."

❧

Mrs. Brody has commissioned the renowned sculptor Liza Todd Tivey to create a bronze relief of Why Me Lord to be placed on the mare's longtime stall.

Opposite: Why Me Lord, age 32, with her daughter Blond Lady

Winning Colors

1985 RO. M. BY CARO (IRE)—ALL RAINBOWS, BY BOLD HOUR

The first time D. Wayne Lukas saw Winning Colors, she was simply the Caro—All Rainbows yearling consigned by Echo Valley Horse Farm at the 1986 Keeneland July sale. The future Hall of Fame trainer was so impressed that he snuck back to look at her again. He was impressed with the entire package, from her unusually muscular body to her beautifully feminine face. In typical poker-faced fashion, he feigned disinterest and asked to see another horse.

"But my heart was hammering, and I knew I had seen the one I wanted," Lukas told *The Blood-Horse*. "She scored the highest of any yearling in that particular sales crop at Keeneland for me. I rated her an eight-plus out of ten, and I'd only given two nines in my life."

Lukas got that right.

The tremendously athletic filly, so large and powerful she was called "the Amazon," became Lukas' first Kentucky Derby winner. He bought her for owner Eugene Klein, the one-time principle owner of the San Diego Chargers, for $575,000.

"I was prepared to sit right in there and hammer away till we got her," Lukas said.

Two-year-old Winning Colors won her first start, a Saratoga maiden race, over that year's eventual Breeders' Cup Juvenile Fillies winner Epitome. Sensing he might have a truly special one, Lukas put her away until December 27.

Gary Stevens hopped aboard for that Santa Anita allowance victory. The future Hall of Fame jockey was perhaps even more impressed than Lukas had been.

"I remember walking back in the jocks' room after riding her the first time," Stevens told a *Baltimore Sun* reporter. "Jacinto Vasquez was riding here that winter, and his locker was right next to mine. I told him, 'I'm going to win my first Kentucky Derby on that filly I just rode.' And he looked at me and said, 'You're nuts. You've got a long way to go before you can start predicting Derby wins.' "

Stevens' prediction didn't seem so farfetched after Winning Colors clobbered the boys in the Santa Anita Derby. She romped by 7½ lengths and headed to Churchill Downs as one of the leading three-year-olds, male or female.

Winning Colors was co-favored at 3-1 with Private Terms in the 1988 Kentucky Derby. She was a natural speedster, a high-willed runner winging it on the front end. But history was against her: In more than a hundred Derbies, only two fillies had ever won — Regret in 1915 and Genuine Risk in 1980.

Rather than sacrifice their horses, the trainers all hoped Winning Colors would back up down that long Churchill Downs homestretch.

Stevens recounted the race:

"She was a very uptight filly, and it wouldn't take much to set her off. I got along with her very well. I was able to soothe her and keep her relaxed. That was my main duty warming her up, just keeping her quiet. She didn't want the pony person touching her when she was going to the gate. That's how finicky she was.

"Our game plan was to try and establish an easy lead, which we did, and dictate the pace. She was a real free-running filly. I'd actually have a little slack in my rein early on, and it was almost like she was fishing for the bit to get in her mouth. And she would wait.

"I talked to her, trying to keep her distracted a little bit and paying attention to me. That's what's amazing. You can be going forty miles an hour, and in a very soothing voice maybe say, 'Whoa, momma, whoa, big momma.' And that's as loud as it gets. 'Easy, momma.' At forty miles an hour you'll see her ears flutter, one cocked back, and she'll get a breather for you.

"My cue to her was I would snug her up, and shorten my cross up and just start to move in a rhythm with her. That was her first cue. OK, it's time to pick it up. And then when I came to the stretch I chirped at her.

"Once we entered the turn and hit the three-eighths pole, our plan was just to go for broke. Normally I wouldn't push the button that early, but she was so quick it was almost like an explosion. When we hit the three-eighths pole, it was almost like rebreaking out of the starting gate. She was able to open up an insurmountable lead.

"That was definitely the decisive point. It took everybody out of the race. Forty Niner did come running late. But I felt very, very confident that I was going to win the race."

Stevens got that right.

In the Preakness, Forty Niner pushed Winning Colors early, and the filly settled for third. In the Belmont, she finished sixth.

After the Triple Crown series, Winning Colors' most notable performances were two tough losses at three. The first was the Maskette Stakes, when the older Personal Ensign caught her at the wire. Winning Colors' chart read: "Gamely."

The second was a race considered by many as the most exciting in history: the 1988 Breeders' Cup Distaff at Churchill Downs. The Derby winner, her tongue flapping and ears pinned, seemed a certain winner down the stretch. But again Personal Ensign, seemingly coming from nowhere, nipped Winning Colors in the final stride.

Winning Colors was named the 1988 champion three-year-old filly. She retired at the end of her four-year-old season with eight wins, three seconds, and one third from nineteen starts, and earnings of $1,526,837.

The next year Klein dispersed his bloodstock, and Winning Colors was sold for $4.1 million at the Keeneland November sale. Gainesway Bloodstock Services signed the ticket for Gainesway Farm owner Graham Beck and businessman Peter Brant.

Their partnership eventually dissolved, and Winning Colors went through the auction ring again in 1994. Her Mr. Prospector filly, a beauty, was the top-priced filly at the sale at $1.05 million, and her second foal, Minden Rose, also by Mr. Prospector, had just won at first asking.

By then, however, Winning Colors' face was marred by a large melanoma on her left temple. It apparently caused no discomfort, and veterinarians stated it would probably never bother her. But Japanese buyers, especially, who were very actively bidding at the sale, steered clear of the Derby winner. *The Blood-Horse* noted: "There was a noticeable lack of Japanese bidding on Winning Colors, and the reason might have been as clear as the melanoma on her face." Gainesway Farm brought Winning Colors home for $2 million.

Winning Colors still resides at Gainesway. Some of her ten foals are scattered around the world — France, Japan, South Africa. While she has not yet produced an exceptional racehorse, one of her daughters is a stakes producer.

From 2000 through 2005, Winning Colors did not produce a live foal. In 2006, however, she delivered an attractive Orientate filly, and when I visited early in 2007, she was in foal to Mr. Greeley. A filly was born March 3.

Seeing Winning Colors was a dream come true. I remembered her as an unraced dark gray two-year-old, training at Saratoga under the tutelage of Lukas' son, Jeff. I cheered heartily when Winning Colors won the Kentucky Derby. And I gained even more respect for her when she nearly held off Personal Ensign.

When Gainesway's manager Neil Howard escorted Winning Colors outdoors, I was awestruck. Her coat was nearly white and she was heavy with foal, yet she was still tremendous — oversized, thick legs, bright eyes. She had an air of dignity that only age can provide. The melanoma did not hide her still beautiful face.

Howard worried that Winning Colors might misbehave as she could still, on occasion, show her displeasure. But on this day, she stood with such grace that she could have been posing for a sculptor. And what a sculpture it would have been.

Winning Colors, the "Amazon" filly, finicky speedster, powerfully explosive Kentucky Derby winner … Lukas and Stevens both had it right.

Zaccio

1976 CH. G. BY *LORENZACCIO — DELRAY DANCER, BY CHATEAUGAY

Horses are not aerodynamically designed to fly," Mrs. Lewis C. "Bunny" Murdock said as we shared finger sandwiches at her home in Peapack, New Jersey. Yet her much-adored steeplechaser, Zaccio, did.

Zaccio, a strong-willed competitor, sailed his way to an unprecedented three Eclipse Awards as steeplechase champion — 1980 through 1982 — at the relatively young ages of four through six. He retired in late 1984, and by 1990, he was enshrined in racing's Hall of Fame.

Trainer W. Burling "Burley" Cocks picked Zaccio out for his clients, Mr. and Mrs. Miles Valentine, purchasing the yearling for $25,000. The following year, after Mr. Valentine's death, Zaccio was back in the auction ring. Cocks, who very much wanted to retain the promising gelding, convinced Murdock to purchase Zaccio. The price this time was $22,000.

Cocks, a highly successful trainer, had a keen eye. By the summer of Zaccio's four-year-old season, before Zaccio had taken home any statuettes, Cocks declared him "the best horse I've ever had my hands on." Zaccio proved him correct.

The immensely popular jumper raced forty-two times and won twenty-two races, ran second or third in ten more, and earned $288,124 — a new steeplechase earnings record. He won eighteen of his twenty-nine races over the jumps. Among his wins in the pre-Breeders' Cup era were such historic events as the Lovely Night Handicap, New York Turf Writers Cup (twice), Grand National Handicap, Colonial Cup International (twice), and the Temple Gwathmey Steeplechase Handicap. Zaccio carried up to 163 pounds in victory and went out a winner in October 1984. He retired to Mr. and Mrs. Murdock's farm in Peapack.

There, the thirty-one-year-old still resides in an attractive, tidy barn, the entrance of which is topped by a chestnut horse-head sculpture, complete with Zaccio-shaped blaze. A sign on the barn's front reads "The Barn That Zack Built — 1982," and, in case anyone needs reminding, Zaccio's Hall of Fame plaque hangs on his stall door.

Mr. Murdock soon saddled him up for his second career: foxhunting. Murdock, a former master of the Essex Foxhounds, rode the strong-willed Zaccio for years, and Zaccio took to hunting with the same verve he did steeplechasing. He jumped powerfully and loved the action. One day, however, the action was a bit much even for him — a veritable beehive. Murdock stopped the horse on a nest of ground bees, Mrs. Murdock told *The Thoroughbred Times*.

"Apparently, it was one of the great rodeos of all time, I gather," she said. "The big problem was getting [Zaccio] to move forward to get away from [the nest], which he didn't want to do. He just kept going straight up in the air."

Zaccio was stung about eighty-three times and was treated with adrenaline. Murdock, fortunately, sustained only a few stings.

Lisa Podraza began tending to the Hall of Famer in 1991, and she, too, remembers Zaccio's headstrong ways.

"At a meet he'd be just standing around, and the next thing Mr. Murdock was just flying through the air," Podraza said. "Zaccio was there, laughing at him, [saying] 'You're not going to ride me today.'

"He had a knack for exploding when he thought the time was right. He'd make a little squealing noise, and you knew you were in trouble."

Podraza, an accomplished horsewoman, took over the reins in earnest when Murdock hung up his tack. She remembers her hunts aboard Zaccio

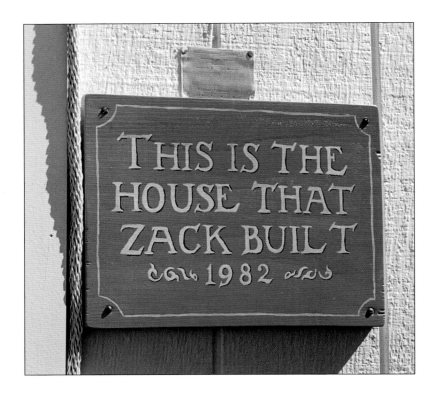

Easter yesterday." She mentioned she had just recently noticed that her old star was aging, but they were providing him "the best spring grass as possible."

When I arrived, Mrs. Murdock was gracious, interesting, and quick, and her manner was comfortable and commonsense. She invited me in for sandwiches, and we sat in her living room. There, she brought out several large, thick albums that contained Zaccio-related articles, photographs, correspondences, and ephemera.

fondly — although it was no ride in the park. "He was strong — you really couldn't rate him — you kind of just had to hold on," she said. "He never refused. But he didn't quite give that rounding feeling that most hunters would over a fence — just a steeplechase leap. Luckily, we didn't have anything that imposing that he couldn't get over.

"I took him to Virginia a few times and hunted him, too. He was a handful. I hunted him until he was nineteen, and that's when you could almost control him," she chuckled.

When I telephoned Mrs. Murdock in April 2004 to inquire about photographing Zaccio, she immediately put me at ease.

"He's turned out and he's a real ham," she said. "I went to wish him happy

Some photos showed Zaccio in full leap, his ears pinned and teeth gritted — as if he were growling. Others showed Mrs. Murdock, beaming, with trophies in various winner's circles. One was a conformation photo of Zaccio at his peak — a grand, long-bodied specimen who fit the mold of an old-fashioned steeplechaser.

We strolled to the barn where Lisa had prepared Zaccio beautifully. While he did not look young, he still looked great. His coat had not yet shed out yet; it was still a bright red. His body was sturdy, his legs were nearly straight, and his mind was obviously alert. He was a bit slimmer, and certainly less toned, than in his competitive days. But I instantly recognized the famous blaze that widened below his large eyes and disappeared into his nostrils.

When he was let loose in a small paddock he stood for a moment, watching us, before jogging its small circumference. It took him a few minutes to realize that his buddy, All Fired, wasn't joining him. When he did, the sunny day suddenly turned dark for him. He circled and circled, neighed, and stopped to stare at us. "Take me back to my paddock" and "where is my friend?" were the clear messages.

Lisa had All Fired waiting in the barn, and she snapped shanks on both of them. She jumped on a small all-terrain vehicle to lead "Zac" and "Alfie" to their regular paddock, and they willingly followed.

Some things just look funny. A Hall of Famer being led by a person on an all-terrain vehicle is one such thing.

Mrs. Murdock died on Christmas Day 2005. She had donated Zaccio's three Eclipse Awards to the National Steeplechase Museum. Her property was sold. Yet Zaccio remains on the land and in his barn, per Mrs. Murdock's wishes.

Lisa has moved on, and she and her fiancé travel the country competing in field trials with their Brittanys, a popular breed of dog. Yet she still regularly visits thirty-one-year-old Zaccio and his buddy.

"I went to see him a couple of weeks ago, and he's just hanging out being Zac," she said in April 2007. "They're two peas in a pod out there."

Zaccio has perhaps lost his wings in his senior years. Yet when he was young, how he could fly.

Acknowledgments

For their help with this project, I am indebted to Jacqueline Duke, Maria Mann, Judy Marchman, Rena Baer, Brian Turner, David Young, Anne Eberhardt, Michele Blanco, Cathy Schenck and Phyllis Rogers of the Keeneland Library, the Lyrical Ballad Bookstore in Saratoga Springs, and Linda McLellan, for allowing the use of her photo of Knightly Spritely in the introduction.

Thank you to my father, James D. Livingston, with whom I watched my first Kentucky Derby (via television) in 1970, my mother, Nancy Thorkildsen, who took me to see Secretariat at Saratoga in 1973, and my sisters Joan and Susan.

A special thanks to Tom Hall, for his tireless research and assistance; Mike Tyner, and Lisa Barnett, for inspiring me; and Tom Keyser, for so many things.

Also, a most heartfelt thank you to everyone who allowed me the honor of photographing their senior Thoroughbreds.

About the Author

Barbara Livingston, who has been photographing horse racing for more than thirty-five years, is widely recognized as one of the sport's top photographers. She has twice been recognized with racing's highest honor, the Eclipse Award for Outstanding Photography.

Barbara's work has graced the covers of countless racing books and magazines, and she is a regular contributor to racing's top weekly, *The Blood-Horse*.

Barbara's work has also appeared in mainstream publications such as *Newsweek*, *People*, *Sports Illustrated* (including their two-page 'Leading Off' spread), *ESPN The Magazine*, *GQ*, and on the cover of *TV Guide*. Her photos have also appeared on MTV, MSNBC, CBS Sunday Morning, ESPN, HBO, and Entertainment Tonight.

Eclipse Press has published three previous books by Barbara: *Four Seasons of Racing* (1998); *Old Friends* (2002); and *Barbara Livingston's Saratoga: Images from the Heart* (2005).

Additionally, she has her own popular Thoroughbred racing Web site, www.barbaralivingston.com, where examples of her equine biographical work and photo journals may be viewed in its archives.

Her extensive photographic record spans approximately seventy years. In addition to her own negatives, Barbara owns the negatives (and their rights) of respected Lexington photographer James W. Sames III. Among them are Kentucky Derby images spanning three decades and the last photograph taken of Man o' War alive.

Barbara graduated with a BFA/Experimental Photography from Syracuse University. She lives in Saratoga Springs, New York.

Anne M. Eberhardt

The author with Tall Glass O'Water